What Your Colleagues Are Saying ...

"One of the most important goals of K–2 math education should be developing a robust understanding of addition and subtraction that can serve as a foundation for later learning. In *Mathematize It!* Morrow-Leong, Moore, and Gojak help teachers transform solving word problems from an activity focused on getting answers to an activity that supports students' understanding of the mathematical principles of the operations. Teaching suggestions are integrated throughout the book in a manner that allows teachers to make adaptations to meet the needs of their students. This book belongs on every primary grade teachers' bookshelf."

Linda Levi
Director
CGI Math Teacher Learning Center, LLC

"Kim Morrow-Leong, Sara Delano Moore, and Linda Gojak have written an essential guide for teachers of grade K–2 mathematics—both those new to the field and those with many years of experience. Read this book and learn how to help students develop a deep understanding of the mathematical principles behind each operation—in other words, effectively help students learn to mathematize problem situations."

Beth Skipper
Elementary Education Consultant
Reston, VA

"Help your students get into the messy fun of true problem solving, where the goal is to make sense of the world—not just arrive at an answer! *Mathematize It!* will engage you in the nuance and power of teaching through context. You'll be surprised and delighted by the student examples, inspired by the teacher commentary, and ready to craft story problems that uncover the big ideas of your grade."

Berkeley Everett
UCLA Mathematics Project (University of California, Los Angeles Mathematics Project)

"*Mathematize It!* is a must-have resource for teachers and teacher leaders. In this comprehensive resource the authors not only introduce a new verb—mathematize—to the primary teacher's vocabulary, they also provide teachers with a 'go-to guide' for teaching problem solving. Features such as the Mathematizing Sandbox as a problem-solving model, the emphasis on the use of multiple representations, and the integration of children's literature provide teachers with instructional tools to help students develop a strong operation sense."

Latrenda Knighten
Elementary Mathematics Instructional Specialist
Baton Rouge, LA

"The list of generational math books to come along and truly synthesize what we know so far and what we need to know is a very short and exclusive list. Well, you can confidently add *Mathematize It!* to this collection. Written by three of the most respected math educators today, the book zeros in on that often poorly traveled journey between the question and answer in problem solving. *Mathematize It!* will be your go-to resource to install the mathematical play revolution in elementary classes everywhere!"

Sunil Singh
Author of *Pi of Life: The Hidden Happiness of Mathematics*
and *Math Recess: Playful Learning in an Age of Disruption*

"*Mathematize It!* is a must-read for anyone who has struggled to teach word problems and is ready to figure out what *really* works. The authors present a plethora of strategies that help students focus on the *thinking* part of the problem-solving process while gently helping the reader understand that so many of our 'tried-and-true' methods, such as key words, really don't work. They help us realize that the real work of solving word problems is in the sense-making phase—once students have made sense of a problem, calculating the solution is the simpler part of the process."

Kimberly Rimbey
National Board Certified Teacher
Co-Founder & CEO, KP Mathematics

"*Mathematize It!* addresses the complexity of problem solving more completely than any other individual resource. It is easy to say that we must teach students to 'mathematize situations' but this book helps us to actually help students learn to do it. The challenge and reflection pieces at the end of each chapter are a game changer for unveiling teaching opportunities, prompting discussion in your PLC, and moving this from a book on the professional shelf to a powerful tool to impact instruction."

Gina Kilday
Math Interventionist and MTSS Coordinator
Metcalf Elementary School, Exeter, RI
Presidential Award for Excellence in Mathematics and Science Teaching Awardee
Former Member of the NCTM Board of Directors

"*Mathematize It!* is a book that should be on the shelf of every classroom teacher and division leader who supports mathematics teaching and leading. This valuable resource helps educators to think about the what, why, and the how to make sense of word problems. It gives a framework and visuals on how to support teachers' understanding around problem types and solving problems and excels in assisting teachers in how to make a commitment to teaching for greater understanding."

Spencer Jamieson
Past President, Virginia Council for Mathematics Supervision (VCMS)
Mathematics Specialist for Virginia Council of Teacher of Mathematics (VCTM)

"This is a game changer . . . even after 20 years of supporting students and their sensemaking of word problems, I am thrilled to learn even more from this trio of authors. They offer practical suggestions, opportunities for practice, and relevant research in order to increase awareness of best practices surrounding word problems. The only key word in this case is MATHEMATIZE! To have this resource in your hands is to have an invitation to the 'mathematizing sandbox'."

Beth Terry
Mathematics Coach
2004 Presidential Award for Excellence in Mathematics and Science Teaching Awardee
Riffa Views International School, Bahrain

"This dynamic author trio brings years of classroom experiences to one of the central problems of teaching and learning mathematics: making sense of word problems. Focusing on the construct of 'mathematizing'—drawing, constructing, describing, representing, and making sense of situations—this clear and practical guide needs to be required reading and discussion fodder for every elementary teacher of mathematics. It's just that clear, informative, and insightful!"

Steve Leinwand
Principal Researcher
American Institutes for Research, Washington, DC

"As our students begin to mathematize the world around them, it becomes extremely important that we listen to their thinking so that we can continue to move their understanding forward. What makes *Mathematize It!* such a useful tool for teachers is that it thoughtfully unpacks student strategies, which helps inform and guide our next move as a classroom teacher."

Graham Fletcher
Math Specialist
Atlanta, GA

"*Mathematize It!* engages readers deeply in the mathematics content through an easy-to-use visual analogy: playing in a sandbox. The authors have found a way to make problem-solving seem like a fun task—one that is akin to something we've all been doing forever: playing. Their clever and applicable problem-solving model of thinking provides a structure teachers can use to support students in tackling word problems and actually enjoying the process. It's time for you to play in the sandbox and more importantly, *Mathematize It!*"

Hilary Kreisberg
Director, Center for Mathematics Achievement
Lesley University, Cambridge, MA
Author of *Adding Parents to the Equation*

"The authors provide a detailed and practical guide on how to take a word problem, uncover the mathematics embedded in it, carefully consider representations, and use it all to solve the problem. The reader begins to realize that all models are not created equal. The authors' careful attention to the nuances within mathematical relationships illustrates how mathematizing differs from answer getting, yet shows us that ideas like operation sense and computation are related. The authors' plain-language explanations empower us to leverage those relationships in order to help students become better mathematicians."

Paul Gray
Chief Curriculum Officer, Cosenza & Associates, LLC
Past President, Texas Council of Teachers of Mathematics
NCTM Representative for NCSM: Leadership in Mathematics Education

"I can't wait to use *Mathematize It!* in my work with teachers and students! The excellent examples, including actual student work and teacher commentaries, highlight the complexity of the problem situations in a way that is clear and usable for classroom teachers and for those of us who support them. The focus on operation sense, understanding the role that each quantity plays, and connecting representations to problems makes this a must read for anyone helping students become successful problem solvers. I especially appreciate the inclusion of non-whole-number examples!"

Julie McNamara
Associate Professor
Author of *Beyond Pizzas & Pies* (With Meghan Shaughnessy) and *Beyond Invert & Multiply*
California State University, East Bay, Hayward, CA

"This book is a must-have for anyone who has faced the challenge of teaching problem solving. The ideas to be learned are supported with a noticeably rich collection of classroom-ready problems, examples of student thinking, and videos. Problem solving is at the center of learning and doing mathematics. And so, *Mathematize It!* should be at the center of every teacher's collection of instructional resources."

John SanGiovanni
Coordinator, Elementary Mathematics
Howard County Public School System, Ellicott City, MD

"Finally! An answer for equipping students in making sense of word problems. *Mathematize It!* clarifies the challenges in problem solving and gives concrete steps and advice on understanding problem contexts and the mathematics involved. The examples, student work, and videos throughout the book bring ideas to life, and make their implementation doable. This is a must-read for every math teacher who desires their students to truly understand the role of mathematics in the world."

Nanci N. Smith
Associate Professor, Mathematics and Education
Arizona Christian University, Glendale, AZ
Author of *Every Math Learner*

"Leaving behind the procedures and the gimmicks, *Mathematize It!* will effectively help develop teachers' understanding of problem types and the pedagogical techniques necessary to teach students how to solve problems through understanding. Using comprehension strategies and varied representations are key to student success with contextualized computation. The sandbox notes, structured techniques, and videos make this book very teacher friendly. The ideas are easily transferable to the mathematics classroom."

Natalie Crist
Coordinator of Elementary Mathematics
Baltimore County Public Schools

Mathematize It!
The Book at a Glance

Every chapter allows you to play and practice in the **mathematizing sandbox** and do some problem solving yourself!

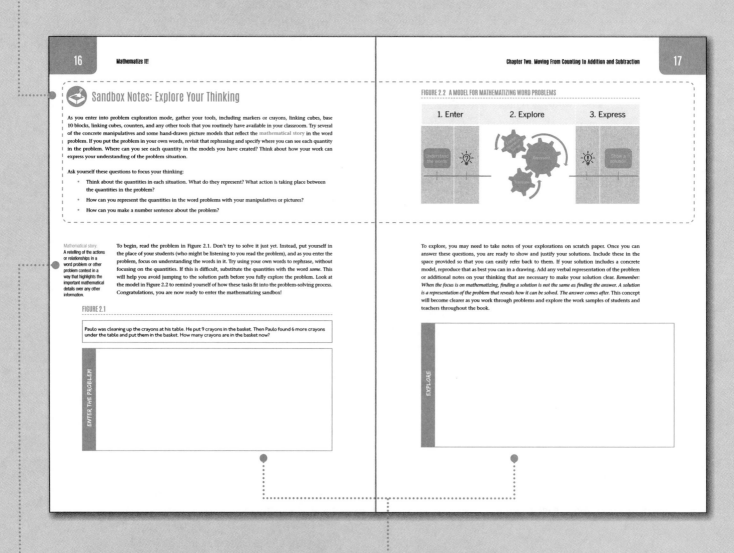

Marginal definitions throughout for easy reference.

Practice the same problem-solving process your students will in these spaces as you **enter** and **explore** the word problem.

Explore how students use various representations to mathematize and describe their problem-solving process.

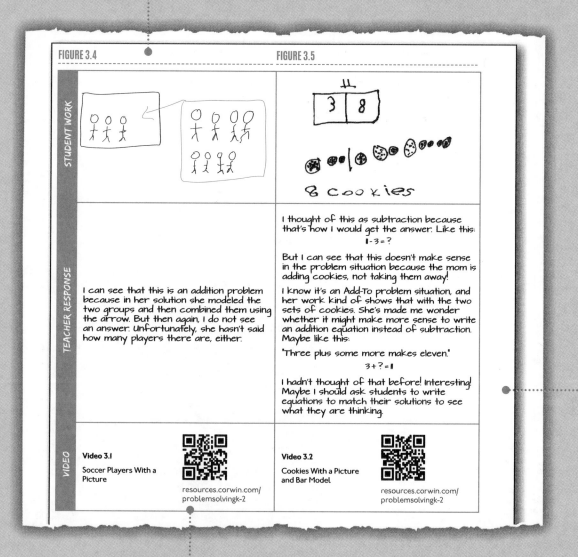

FIGURE 3.4   FIGURE 3.5

STUDENT WORK

8 cookies

TEACHER RESPONSE

I can see that this is an addition problem because in her solution she modeled the two groups and then combined them using the arrow. But then again, I do not see an answer. Unfortunately, she hasn't said how many players there are, either.

I thought of this as subtraction because that's how I would get the answer. Like this:
11 - 3 = ?

But I can see that this doesn't make sense in the problem situation because the mom is adding cookies, not taking them away!

I know it's an Add-To problem situation, and her work kind of shows that with the two sets of cookies. She's made me wonder whether it might make more sense to write an addition equation instead of subtraction. Maybe like this:

"Three plus some more makes eleven."
3 + ? = 11

I hadn't thought of that before! Interesting! Maybe I should ask students to write equations to match their solutions to see what they are thinking.

VIDEO

Video 3.1

Soccer Players With a Picture

resources.corwin.com/
problemsolvingk-2

Video 3.2

Cookies With a Picture and Bar Model

resources.corwin.com/
problemsolvingk-2

QR codes link to **videos** that actively demonstrate problem-solving thinking with manipulatives and drawings.

Learn from teachers' reflections on student work.

Easy-reference charts launch each chapter to help you make sense of and navigate different problem types.

Addition and Subtraction Problem Situations

	Result Unknown	Change Addend Unknown	Start Addend Unknown	
Add-To	Paulo counted 9 crayons. He put them in the basket. Paulo found 6 more crayons under the table. He put them in the basket. How many crayons are in the basket? $9 + 6 = x$ $6 = x - 9$	Paulo counted 9 crayons. He found more and put them in the basket. Now Paulo has 15 crayons. How many crayons did he put in the basket? $9 + x = 15$ $9 = 15 - x$	Paulo had some crayons. He found 6 more crayons under the table. Now he has 15 crayons. How many crayons did Paulo have in the beginning? $x + 6 = 15$ $15 - 6 = x$	

ACTIVE SITUATIONS

	Result Unknown	Change Addend Unknown	Start Addend Unknown	
Add-To	Paulo counted 9 crayons. He put them in the basket. Paulo found 6 more crayons under the table. He put them in the basket. How many crayons are in the basket? $9 + 6 = x$ $6 = x - 9$	Paulo counted 9 crayons. He found more and put them in the basket. Now Paulo has 15 crayons. How many crayons did he put in the basket? $9 + x = 15$ $9 = 15 - x$	Paulo had some crayons. He found 6 more crayons under the table. Now he has 15 crayons. How many crayons did Paulo have in the beginning? $x + 6 = 15$ $15 - 6 = x$	
Take-From	There are 19 students in Mrs. Amadi's class. 4 students went to the office to say the Pledge. How many students are in the class now? $19 - 4 = x$ $4 + x = 19$	There are 19 students in Mrs. Amadi's class. Some students went to class to read the Pledge. There were still 15 students in the classroom. How many students went to the office? $19 - x = 15$ $x + 15 = 19$	4 students went to the office. 15 students were still in the classroom. How many students are there in Mrs. Amadi's class? $x - 4 = 15$ $15 + 4 = x$	

RELATIONSHIP (NONACTIVE) SITUATIONS

	Total Unknown	One Part Unknown		Both Parts Unknown
Part-Part-Whole	The first grade voted on a game for recess. 11 students voted to play four square. 8 voted to go to the playground. How many students are in the class? $8 + 11 = x$ $x - 11 = 8$	The 19 first graders voted on a recess activity. 8 students voted to go to the playground. How many wanted to play four square? $8 + x = 19$ $x = 19 - 8$		The 19 first graders voted on a recess activity. Some wanted to play four square. Some wanted to go to the playground. What are some ways the first graders could have voted? $x + y = 19$ $19 - x = y$
	Difference Unknown	Greater Quantity Unknown	Lesser Quantity Unknown	
Additive Comparison	Jessie's paper airplane flew 14 feet. Jo's paper airplane flew 9 feet. How much less did Jo's paper airplane fly than Jessie's? $14 - 9 = x$ $9 + x = 14$	Jo's paper airplane flew 9 feet. Jessie's paper airplane flew 5 feet more than Jo's. How far did Jessie's paper airplane fly? $9 + 5 = x$ $x - 5 = 9$	Jessie's paper airplane flew 14 feet. Jo's paper airplane flew 5 feet less than Jessie's paper airplane. How far did Jo's paper airplane fly? $14 - 5 = x$ $14 = x + 5$	

Note: The representations for the problem situations in this table reflect our understanding based on a number of resources. These include the tables in the Common Core State Standards for Mathematics (CCSS-M; National Governors Association Center for Best Practices and Council of Chief State School Officers, 2010), the problem situations as described in the Cognitively Guided Instruction research (Carpenter, Hiebert, & Moser, 1981), and other tools. See the Appendix and the book's companion website for a more detailed summary of the documents that informed our development of this table.

KEY IDEAS

1. Five key principles describe counting proficiency: one-to-one correspondence, stable order, cardinality, abstraction, and order irrelevance.

2. If students are not yet proficient counters, assessing their understanding of addition and subtraction problem situations may be complicated, because counting errors could easily be mistaken as calculation errors.

3. Ideally students should grasp the principles of counting before they move into addition and subtraction. However, even if their counting is not yet in place, they may still learn about joining sets.

4. Some aspects of counting collections are conceptual and some are procedural.

5. Counting a collection and adding (joining) two numbers do not involve exactly the same skills.

6. Add-To and Take-From problem situations reflect actions.

7. Add-To and Take-From problem situations follow a common structure where there is a starting value (the beginning of the story), a change, and a result (the end of the story). Any one of the three parts of the problem may be the missing value.

8. An action problem situation can and should be retold in the student's own words. This mathematical story simplifies the details of the problem and focuses on the action.

9. During problem-solving lessons, the focus of learning should be on accurately reflecting the actions or relationships in the problem rather than on computation strategies.

10. When focusing on the meaning of word problems, students should focus on creating concrete or visual (often pictorial), verbal, and symbolic representations that closely match the action (or story) in the problem situation.

11. Diagrams are an abstracted version of a pictorial representation.

Reflect sections give you an opportunity to
bring some of your knowledge and resources to
implementation. Share your answers with a partner
or group.

REFLECT

1. As a team, discuss strategies you use to strengthen students' counting skills while they are learning about addition and subtraction.

2. Now that you have had a chance to think about the difference between counting a set (counting) and joining two sets (addition), talk about what you can do to help students better understand this big idea of addition: How do you find a balance between efficiency in computation and a deep understanding of the meaning of addition?

3. With your team, share one thing that has changed about your understanding of young children's mathematical thinking. How will that influence your instruction?

Try It Out! to implement, practice, and
review the key ideas of the chapter.
Practice with a partner or group!

TRY IT OUT!

IDENTIFY THE PRINCIPLE

Decide for one week (or even just a day) to listen to your students, or other young children,
count. As you watch students, listen for evidence of each principle, or evidence that the principle
is not yet in place. With parents' permission, video-record the counting action and later share
it with your team. For each of the five principles of counting, talk about what evidence you
saw (or didn't see):

1. One-to-one correspondence principle
2. Stable order principle
3. Cardinality principle
4. Abstraction principle
5. Order irrelevance principle

WRITE THE PROBLEM

Read the word problem, and then for each student work sample, discuss whether it is an example
of counting or of joining two sets. Explain why.

1. 5 penguins were catching fish. 9 more penguins joined them. How many penguins
   are catching fish now?

   a. It's 14 c.ze i conted forwdword,
   and stopd at 14 and
   that's how i got 10

Opportunities to stop and think about and
create new problems within each problem type.

FIGURE 4.12 TAKE-FROM ACTIVE SITUATIONS

CONTEXT	START (Beginning Value)	CHANGE (Action in the Story)	RESULT (Ending Value)
Video game	Points on the board	Points are lost	Final score
Party food	Cookies on the plate	Cookies are eaten	Cookies on the plate
Making a donation	Books on the bookshelf	Books are given away	Books on the bookshelf
Spending money	Money in account	Money spent	Money in account
Trading cards			
			Dirty pots in the sink
	Movies you want to see		

A Guide to the Fonts in This Book

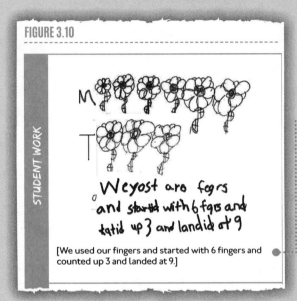

FIGURE 3.10

STUDENT WORK

We yost aro fegrs and startd with 6 fgrs and tatid up 3 and landid ot 9

[We used our fingers and started with 6 fingers and counted up 3 and landed at 9.]

Bracketed text under student work transcribes students' unclear writing.

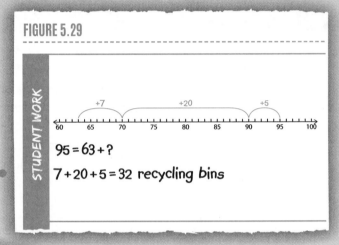

FIGURE 5.29

STUDENT WORK

$95 = 63 + ?$

$7 + 20 + 5 = 32$ recycling bins

The handwriting font used under student work approximates student handwriting.

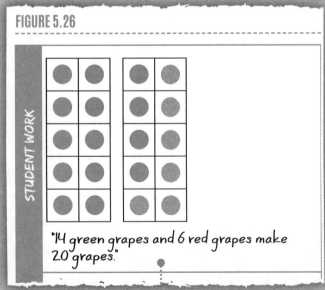

FIGURE 5.26

STUDENT WORK

"14 green grapes and 6 red grapes make 20 grapes."

An adult's handwriting font in quotations is used to translate students' spoken words under their work.

Teachers' responses to student work uses another adult handwriting font.

FIGURE 6.8 ADDITIVE COMPARISON SITUATIONS

CONTEXT	LESSER QUANTITY	DIFFEREN
Weight of pets	Weight of kitten	
Score of the game	Points for the loser	
Snowfall	Dusting of snow	
Number of people in the classroom	2 adults	

Mathematize It!
Grades K-2

Mathematize It!

Going Beyond Key Words to Make Sense of Word Problems

Grades K-2

Kimberly Morrow-Leong
Sara Delano Moore
Linda M. Gojak

CORWIN Mathematics

For information:

Corwin
A SAGE Company
2455 Teller Road
Thousand Oaks, California 91320
(800) 233–9936
www.corwin.com

SAGE Publications Ltd.
1 Oliver's Yard
55 City Road
London, EC1Y 1SP
United Kingdom

SAGE Publications India Pvt. Ltd.
B 1/I 1 Mohan Cooperative
    Industrial Area
Mathura Road, New Delhi 110 044
India

SAGE Publications Asia-Pacific Pte. Ltd.
18 Cross Street #10–10/11/12
China Square Central
Singapore 048423

Publisher, Mathematics: Erin Null

Associate Content
    Development Editor: Jessica Vidal

Production Editor: Tori Mirsadjadi

Copy Editor: Amy Marks

Typesetter: Integra

Proofreader: Talia Greenberg

Indexer: Integra

Cover and Interior Designer: Scott Van Atta

Marketing Manager: Margaret O'Connor

Printed in the United States of America.

Library of Congress Cataloging-in-Publication Data

Names: Morrow-Leong, Kimberly, author. | Moore, Sara Delano, 1966- author. | Gojak, Linda, author.
Title: Mathematize it! : going beyond key words to make sense of word problems, grades K-2 / Kimberly Morrow-Leong, Sara Delano Moore, and Linda M. Gojak.
Description: Thousand Oaks, California : Corwin Press, Inc., [2020] | Includes bibliographical references and index.
Identifiers: LCCN 2019051972 | ISBN 9781544389851 (paperback) | ISBN 9781071811320 (adobe pdf) | ISBN 9781071811375 (ebook) | ISBN 9781071811313 (ebook)
Subjects: LCSH: Word problems (Mathematics) | Mathematics—Study and teaching (Elementary)
Classification: LCC QA63 .M653 2020 | DDC 372.7—dc23
LC record available at https://lccn.loc.gov/2019051972

This book is printed on acid-free paper.

SUSTAINABLE FORESTRY INITIATIVE
Certified Chain of Custody
Promoting Sustainable Forestry
www.sfiprogram.org
SFI-01268

20 21 22 23 24 10 9 8 7 6 5 4 3 2 1

Contents

Visit the companion website at
http://resources.corwin.com/problemsolvingK-2
for downloadable resources.

List of Videos

Preface

The three of us (Kim, Sara, and Linda) spend a lot of time with teachers, talking about how students are successful and what challenges they face. Over and over, we hear that students struggle with problem solving, especially with word problems. We see challenges expressed in teacher comments on Twitter, on Facebook, on community sites like MyNCTM, in conference sessions, even in the news and on other social media. We hear this frustration from parents, from principals, and from math coaches across the country and internationally. We've written this book for classroom teachers and coaches who want to help their students have a more successful and meaningful approach to problem solving. If the approaches you have tried, such as using key words, or even using reading strategies to help students comprehend the problem, have yielded only spotty or unsatisfying results, this book is for you. If your students compute naked numbers efficiently, but when faced with a word problem they seem to pull numbers at random from problems and end up successfully calculating the wrong equations, this book is for you. If your students have ever drawn a picture about a word problem that told you more about, say, squirrels than about the problem itself, this book is for you. We've written this book for all of the teachers whose students look at a word problem and say, "I just don't get what they want me to do!"

How This Book Can Help You

Would you be surprised to know that every addition word problem you can think of can be classified into one of four categories? It's true! The same is true for every subtraction problem. Multiplication and division are a bit more complicated, but not as much as you might think. The hard part about a word problem isn't in using the operations (+ − × ÷) to compute an answer but, rather, it's in figuring out which operation to use in a problem and why. Once you understand the four kinds of addition problem types and can recognize them in a problem's story, the puzzle pieces can start to come together. We don't mean to oversimplify the learning that needs to take place, because it isn't simple, but we want you to know that there is something you can do to help students learn to tackle word problems productively. More important, we want students to tackle real problems that interest them and learn more mathematics as they do so.

> *Solving problems is not only a goal of learning mathematics but also a major means of doing so. Students should have frequent opportunities to formulate, grapple with and solve complex problems that require a significant amount of effort and should then be encouraged to reflect on their thinking.*

> —*Principles and Standards for School Mathematics*
> (National Council of Teachers of Mathematics, 2000, p. 52)

There is no magic elixir to solve the problem of word problems. This book shares our approach, which focuses on helping children mine the problem to uncover the underlying mathematics. Much needs to happen between the reading comprehension and computation stages of the problem-solving process. Yes, students need support to read and comprehend the words, context, and language of the problem. Yes, they need to know how to compute the answer. But there is a whole middle ground of exploration and understanding that students often rush through, where they could instead turn what they read into a solvable mathematical story and apply their operation sense to solve the puzzle. This is where we so often see a gap. We've written this book to fill that gap. We want students to see their world mathematically and to know that mathematics can help them solve real problems. This is bigger (and more important) than passing a test.

To that end, this book is about problem solving. It's about deciphering the kinds of word problems you see in normal, everyday lessons in classrooms like yours. It's about the kinds of problems that are placed at the end of the lessons in your textbooks, the ones that your kids skip because they don't know what to do. It's about word problems. Story problems. Make-sense-of-the-math, practice-a-skill problems. Sometimes these problems can seem artificial or contrived, but their straightforward simplicity is also a strength because they target the mathematical thinking we want students to develop. Wrestling productively with word problems can lay a foundation for the more complex and open-ended problems students will also encounter. These problems also have the potential to *do* and *be* more in their own right.

> *Solutions to these (routine word) problems, particularly the solutions of younger children, do in fact involve real problem-solving behavior. . . . Word problems can provide insights into the development of more complex problem-solving abilities.*

> (Carpenter, 1985, p. 17)

How to Use This Book

As a reader, you'll get the most out of this book if you dig in and do the mathematics along the way. We've given you space to restate problems and draw pictures of your thinking with a focus on the mathematics. You'll also find a collection of manipulatives helpful as you work through the book. Gather some counters, some base 10 blocks, and any other manipulatives you use regularly to use as aids while you solve problems. Think about how your students can use them too. Pictures and manipulatives can hold an idea in place right in front of you so that you can think about it more deeply. With manipulatives, you can do even more. You can make a change more quickly and easily: Manipulatives allow students to act out what happens in a problem, and to use attributes like color and size to highlight features of a problem. As you'll see, the best tool for the job depends on the problem. There will be plenty of examples for you to explore.

There are places in the book where we've suggested you stop and talk with your colleagues. If you're reading the book as part of a professional learning community, plan your discussions around these stopping points. You'll find that there are plenty of opportunities for conversations about student thinking and the operations. But you're never truly reading alone! Throughout each chapter you'll find student work samples. Several times in each chapter you'll also find teacher commentary on the work samples. These comments are honest. Sometimes the teachers are bewildered, and sometimes the teachers are excited by what they see. Let these teacher voices be your companions as you tackle the new ideas. Use the teacher comments and the thinking breaks as reminders to take a pause and extend your own ideas a little further. The end of each chapter also has exercises and reflection questions that will help you and your colleagues connect what you've learned to your own classrooms.

After each chapter we also suggest that you look at the problems in your textbook and categorize them—not just for practice recognizing the structures you'll soon learn about, but also to evaluate how much exposure your students are getting to the full range of problem types. Many experts recommend that primary students have exposure to a wide variety of problem situations even if they will struggle with some versions in the beginning. We encourage you to keep this recommendation in mind as you make instructional decisions. If you discover that your textbook does not present enough variety, this book will give you the tools needed to make adjustments.

We recognize that many of the problems shared in this book will be unfamiliar contexts for your students. If you find yourself thinking that your students will not understand a problem context, we invite you to change the problem! Make sense of the problem situation yourself so that you know what mathematical features are important and then change the details. Even better, invite your students to craft and pose their own meaningful word problems to solve. Your students have many life experiences already, and you share many of those experiences in school with them. With your new understanding of the problem situations, you will have all the tools you need to guide your students.

We have to be honest. The ideas in this book may challenge your current understandings of some mathematical ideas. At times, we will ask you to look at something you have been doing since you were 3 or 4 years old and revisit it with new eyes. This may cause some disequilibrium, and it may be uncomfortable at first. It's as if we are asking you to walk, but by switching the foot you lead with. (Try it! It's not easy!) When the familiar becomes unfamiliar, we encourage you to take a deep breath, trust us, and lead with the other foot. We'll get you there. Here's to lifelong learning!

Acknowledgments

You can't write a book like this in a vacuum. We have met and worked with countless educators over the years and have discussed the ideas in this book with them. You know who you are and we hope you hear your voice in these pages. Thank you for your contribution to these thoughts and ideas. We credit you and appreciate you deeply.

We would also like to thank Erin Null, who started with one vision of this book, received a draft of another interpretation, and worked with us to land on the third—and we think best—vision. Your patience, support, and diligence pushed us continually forward. We also extend a profound debt of gratitude to Paula Stacey, who asked us the questions we needed to answer in a way that made the first manuscript better. Thank you also to Kimberly Rimbey, Julie McNamara, Jeff Shih, and Linda Levi, whose thoughtful comments challenged us to know better and do better. We are indebted to you for your positive feedback, but even more so for your constructive criticism. Any flaws that remain are ours alone.

I would first like to thank Linda and Sara for trusting me enough to invite me to join this project. I appreciate your confidence, but more than anything, I appreciate your friendship. I also want to thank Dr. Megan Murray of the University of Hull, who introduced me to the idea that addition and subtraction problems weren't all the same. Thank you to Juanita Copley. I learned more about young students and counting from assisting you in a professional development session than I have from any other source. To the staff of GBW, Julie R., Pat S., Kim R., and Michelle S. and her friend the second-grade teacher: Thank you for sharing your time and brilliant students who have helped us collect and interpret their thinking from many different angles. Finally, thank you to my husband, Greg, who watched me take the big leap of writing a book and never questioned my sanity.

—Kim

Thanks to Kim and Linda for coming on this journey with me. I appreciate your knowledge, your experience, your care, and your friendship. Thanks to Margie Mason, who first brought me into the world of mathematics education, and to all my friends and colleagues in this community, including those at ETA hand2mind and ORIGO Education, who have encouraged and supported me along the way. Thank you to the teachers who came before me, particularly my mother and grandmother, for showing me that learning is important and good teaching is invaluable. And thanks to Bill, for loving and supporting me always.

—Sara

Writing a book is always a challenge! While it seems that writing on a topic you feel passionate about should be easier, it is actually a bigger challenge because you want to get it right. I thank Kim and Sara for their vision and our many long conversations. I learned so much from both of you. I want to thank the elementary teachers and coaches with whom I work who challenge my thinking and force me to make ideas clearer. I thank my colleagues Ruth Harbin Miles, Annemarie Newhouse, and Jerry Moreno, whose friendship I value and who make this career a joy.

—Linda

Publisher's Acknowledgments

Corwin gratefully acknowledges the contributions of the following reviewers:

Kevin Dykema
Middle School Math Teacher
Mattawan Middle School
Mattawan, MI

Julie McNamara
Assistant Professor of Mathematics Education
California State University, East Bay
Hayward, CA

Kimberly Rimbey
Executive Director of Curriculum, Instruction, and Assessment
Buckeye Elementary School District
Buckeye, AZ

About the Authors

Kimberly Morrow-Leong is an adjunct instructor at George Mason University in Fairfax, Virginia, and a consultant for Math Solutions. She is a former grade 5–9 classroom teacher, K–8 mathematics coach, researcher at American Institutes for Research, and coordinator of elementary professional development for the National Council of Teachers of Mathematics (NCTM). She recently completed an elected term as vice president and 2018 program chair for NCSM, Leadership in Mathematics Education. She has written for a textbook company, the journal *Teaching Children Mathematics*, and is coauthor of the *Mathematize It!* series. She holds a BA in French language and a masters in linguistics (TESOL), as well as an MEd and PhD in mathematics education leadership from George Mason University. Kim is the 2009 recipient of the Presidential Award for Excellence in Mathematics and Science Teaching (PAEMST) from Virginia. She is happiest when working with teachers and students, putting pencils down and getting messy with manipulatives!

Sara Delano Moore currently serves as director of professional learning at ORIGO Education. A fourth-generation educator, Sara's work emphasizes the power of deep understanding and multiple representations for learning mathematics. Her interests include building conceptual understanding to support procedural fluency and applications, incorporating engaging and high-quality literature into mathematics and science instruction, and connecting mathematics with engineering design in meaningful ways. Prior to joining ORIGO Education, Sara served as a classroom teacher of mathematics and science in the elementary and middle grades, a mathematics teacher educator at the University of Kentucky, director of the Kentucky Center for Middle School Academic Achievement, and director of mathematics and science at ETA hand2mind. She presents regularly to school districts, at conferences, and on EdWeb.net and has authored numerous articles in professional journals. Sara is a coauthor for several Corwin Mathematics titles, including V*isible Learning for Mathematics, Teaching Mathematics in the Visible Learning Classroom* (grades 3–5 and grades 6–8), and the *Mathematize It!* series. She lives in Kent, Ohio.

Linda M. Gojak worked as an elementary mathematics specialist and classroom teacher for 28 years. She directed the Center for Mathematics and Science Education, Teaching, and Technology at John Carroll University for 16 years, providing support for districts and more than 10,000 teachers. Linda continues to work with K–8 mathematics teachers and coaches nationally and internationally. She is a recipient of the PAEMST from Ohio. She served as the president of NCTM, NCSM, and the Ohio Council of Teachers of Mathematics. Linda is the coauthor of other books for Corwin Mathematics—*The Common Core Math Companion, K–2; The Common Core Math Companion, 6–8; Visible Learning for Mathematics, Grades K–12*; and the *Mathematize It!* series. Linda also wrote *Path to Problem Solving for Grades 3–6* (ETA Hand to Mind, 2008) and *What's Your Math Problem?* (Teacher Created Materials, 2011).

CHAPTER ONE

Introduction
Why You Need to Teach Students to Mathematize

Imagine you are a new teacher. You are teaching second grade at a new school and are eager to get to know your students—their interests, skills, and how prepared they are to meet the challenges of second grade. You have just emerged from your teacher education program knowing various approaches you have seen modeled in classrooms and described in the literature, some of which you have tried with varying degrees of success. You aren't sure what approaches you want to use but are excited about challenging your students, introducing the rigor you have read so much about. But first, you need to know what your students can and can't do.

You decide to start with a couple of word problems, ones that involve friendly numbers and relatively simple mathematical operations:

> *Daphne has 35 shells in her collection, 4 more than Nathan. How many shells does Nathan have?*

> *Raphine had 18 books. He bought 13 more at the library book sale. How many books does Raphine have now?*

You circulate around the room, noting who draws pictures, who writes equations, and who uses the manipulatives you have put at the center of the table groups. While some students take their time, quite a few move quickly. Their hands go up eagerly, indicating they have solved the problems. As you check their work, one by one, you notice most of them got the first problem wrong, writing the equation $35+4=39$. Some even include a sentence saying, "Nathan has 39 shells." Only one student in this group draws a picture. It looks like this:

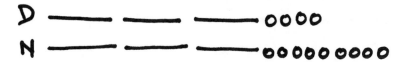

Even though the second problem includes regrouping, a potentially complicating feature, most of these same students solve it correctly. They wrote the equation $18+13=31$ and were generally able to find the correct solution of 31 books in Raphine's collection. You notice a few students

Mathematize It!

used the base 10 blocks available at tables to help them solve these problems. A number of the students used a number track that looked something like this:

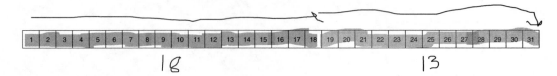

18　　　　　　　　　　　13

To learn more about how students went wrong with the first problem, you call them to your desk one by one and ask about their thinking. A pattern emerges quickly. All of the students you talk to quickly zeroed in on two key elements of the problem: (1) the total quantity of shells Daphne has and (2) how many more Nathan has. One student tells you, "*More* always means to add. I learned that a long time ago." Clearly, she wasn't the only student who read the word *more* and assumed she had to add. This assumption, which led students astray in the first problem, luckily worked for these students in the second problem, where simple addition yielded a correct answer.

Problem-Solving Strategies Gone Wrong

In our work with teachers, we often see students being taught a list of "key words" that are linked to specific operations. Students are told, "Find the key word and you will know whether to add, subtract, multiply, or divide." Charts of key words often hang on classroom walls. Focusing on key words is a strategy that works often enough that teachers continue to rely on it. As we have seen in the shell problem, though, not only are key words not enough to solve a problem, but they can easily lead students to the wrong operation or to a single operation when other operations need to come into play (Karp, Bush, & Dougherty, 2014). As the shell problem reveals, students can call upon different strategies and operations depending on how they approach the problem—that is, counting on from an estimated value, or subtraction. The simple one-step addition operation we saw in the student's solution to the first problem, the one the student associated with the key word *more*, does not lead to a correct answer.

Let's return to your imaginary classroom. Having seen firsthand the limitations of key words—a strategy you had considered using—where to begin? What approach to use? A new colleague has a suggestion. She agrees that relying on only key words can be too limiting. Instead, she is an enthusiastic proponent of a procedure called CUBES, which stands for teaching students these steps:

Circle the numbers

Underline important information

Box the question

Eliminate unnecessary information

Solve and check

She tells you that whenever she introduces a new kind of word problem, she walks students through the CUBES protocol using a "think-aloud," sharing how she is using the process to take the problem apart to find what to focus on. That evening, as you settle down to plan, you decide to walk through some problems like the shell problem using CUBES. Circling the numbers is easy enough. You circle 35 (shells) and 4 (the difference between Daphne and Nathan).

Then you tackle "important information." What is important here in this problem? Daphne has 35 shells is important. Certainly the fact that this is 4 more than Nathan is important, but unfortunately that phrase includes the problematic word *more*. You box the question and realize there's not an action verb in this problem. Based on the student work and thinking you see, this will be challenging for many students to act out.

If you think this procedure has promise as a way to guide students through an initial reading of the problem, but leaves out how to help students develop a genuine understanding of the problem, you would be correct.

What is missing from procedural strategies such as CUBES and strategies such as key words, is—in a word—*mathematics*, and the understanding of where it lives within the situation the problem is presenting. Rather than helping students to learn and practice quick ways to enter a problem, we need to focus our instruction on helping them develop a deep understanding of the mathematical principles behind the operations and how they are expressed in the problem. They need to learn to *mathematize*.

What Is Mathematizing? Why Is It Important?

Mathematizing is the uniquely human process of constructing meaning in mathematics (from Freudenthal, as cited in Fosnot & Dolk, 2001). Meaning is constructed and expressed by a process of noticing, exploring, explaining, modeling, and convincing others of a mathematical argument. When we teach students to mathematize, we are essentially teaching them to take their initial focus off specific numbers and computations and put their focus squarely on the actions and relationships expressed in the problem, what we will refer to throughout this book as the **problem situation**. At the same time, we are helping students see how these various actions and relationships can be expressed and the different operations that can be used to express them. If students understand, for example, that comparison problems, like the shell problem, involve two quantities and the size of the gap between them, then they can learn where and how to use the values in the problem to create a number sentence. If we look at problems this way, then finding a **solution** involves connecting the problem's context to its general kind of problem situation and to the operations that go with it. The rest is simple computation.

Making accurate and meaningful connections between different problem situations and the operations that can fully express them requires **operation sense**. Students with a strong operation sense

- Understand and use a wide variety of models of operations beyond the basic and **intuitive model of an operation** (Fischbein, Deri, Nello, & Marino, 1985)

- Use appropriate representations of actions or relationships strategically

- Apply their understanding of operations to any quantity, regardless of the class of number

- Can mathematize a situation, translating a contextual understanding into a variety of other mathematical representations

Mathematizing: The uniquely human act of modeling reality with the use of mathematical tools and representations.

Problem situation: The underlying mathematical action or relationship found in a variety of contexts. These are often called "problem type" for short.

Solution: A description of the underlying problem situation along with the computational approach (or approaches) to finding an answer to the question.

Operation sense: Knowing and applying the full range of work for mathematical operations (for example, addition and subtraction).

Intuitive model of an operation: An intuitive model is "primitive," meaning that it is the earliest and strongest interpretation of what an operation, such as multiplication, can do. An intuitive model may not include all the ways that an operation can be used mathematically.

FOCUSING ON OPERATION SENSE

Many of us may assume that we have a strong operation sense. After all, the four operations are the backbone of the mathematics we were taught from day one in elementary school. We know how to add, subtract, multiply, and divide, don't we? Of course we do. But a closer look at current standards reveals nuances and relationships within these operations that many of us may not be aware of, may not fully understand, or may have internalized so well that we don't recognize we are applying an understanding of them every day when we ourselves mathematize problems both in real life and in the context of solving word problems. For example, current standards ask that students develop conceptual understanding and build procedural fluency in four kinds of addition and subtraction problems, including Add-To, Take-From, Compare, and what some call Put Together/Take Apart (we will refer to this category throughout the book as Part-Part-Whole). On the surface, the differences between such categories may not seem critical. But we argue that they are. Only by exploring these differences and the relationships they represent can students develop the solid operation sense that will allow them to understand and mathematize word problems and any other problems they are solving, whatever their grade level or complexity of the problem. But just as important, word problems offer the unique opportunity to engage in such exploration. Operation sense is not simply a means to an end. It has value in helping students naturally come to see the world through a mathematical lens.

USING MATHEMATICAL REPRESENTATIONS

What would such instruction—instruction aimed at developing operation sense and learning how to mathematize word problems—look like? It would have a number of features. First, it would require that we give students time to focus and explore by doing fewer problems, making the ones they do count. Next, it would facilitate students becoming familiar with various ways to represent actions and relationships presented in a problem context. We tend to think of solving word problems as beginning with words and moving toward number sentences and equations in a neat linear progression. But this isn't how problem solving works. It is an iterative and circular process, where students might try out different representations, including going back and rewording the problem, a process we call telling "the story" of the problem. The model that we offer in this book is based on this kind of active and expanded exploration using a full range of mathematical representations. Scholars who study mathematical modeling and problem solving identify five modes of representation: verbal, contextual, concrete, pictorial, and symbolic (Lesh, Post, & Behr, 1987).

VERBAL A problem may start with any mode of representation, but a word problem is first presented verbally, often in written form, and may be read aloud for young learners. After that, verbal representations can serve many uses as students work to understand the actions and relationships in the problem situation. Some examples are restating the problem; thinking aloud; describing the math operations in words rather than symbols; and augmenting and explaining visual and physical representations such as graphs, drawings, counters, base 10 blocks, or other concrete items. Verbal representations do not have to be written.

CONTEXTUAL The contextual representation is simply the real-life situation that the problem describes. Prepackaged word problems are based on real life, as are the shell and book problems

Problem context: The specific setting for a word problem.

Mathematical representations: Depictions of a mathematical situation using one or more of these modes or tools: concrete objects, pictures, mathematical symbols, context, or language.

described earlier in this chapter, but alone they are not contextual. Asking students to create their own problems based on real-life contexts will bring more meaning to the process and will reflect the purposes of mathematics in real life, such as when scientists, business analysts, and meteorologists mathematize contextual information in order to make predictions that benefit us all. This is a process called **mathematical modeling** (Garfunkel & Montgomery, 2016).

CONCRETE Using physical representations such as blocks, concrete objects, and real-world items (for example, money, measuring tools, or items to be measured such as beans, sand, or water), or acting out the problem in various ways, is called **modeling**. Such concrete models often offer the closest and truest representation of the actions and relationships in a problem situation.

PICTORIAL Pictures and diagrams can illustrate and clarify the details of the actions and relationships in ways that words and even physical representations cannot. Using dots and sticks, bar models, arrows to show action, number lines, boxes to show regrouping, and various graphic organizers helps students see and conceptualize the nature of the actions and relationships.

SYMBOLIC Symbols can be operation signs (+, −, ×, ÷), relational signs (=, <, >), variables or unknowns (typically expressed first with a box, space, or question mark and later as x, y, a, or b), or a wide variety of symbols used in later mathematics (k, ∞, ϕ, π, etc.). Even though numerals are familiar, they are also symbols representing a value (2, 0.9, $\frac{1}{2}$, 1000).

There are two things to know about representations that may be surprising. First, mathematics can be shared *only* through representations. As a matter of fact, it is impossible to share a mathematical idea with someone else without sharing it through a representation! If you write an equation, you have produced a *symbolic* representation. If you describe the idea, orally or in writing, you have shared a *verbal* representation. Representations are not solely the manipulatives, pictures, and drawings of a mathematical idea: They are any mode that communicates a mathematical idea between people.

Second, the strength and value of learning to manipulate representations to explore and solve problems is rooted in their relationship to one another. In other words, the more students can learn to move deftly from one representation to another, translating and/or combining them to fully illustrate their understanding of a problem, the deeper will be their understanding of the operations. Figure 1.1 reveals this interdependence. The five modes of representation are all equally important and deeply interconnected, and they work synergistically. In the chapters that follow, you will see how bringing multiple and synergistic representations to the task of problem solving deepens understanding.

Mathematical modeling: A process that uses mathematics to represent, analyze, make predictions, or otherwise provide insight into real-world phenomena.

Modeling: Creating a physical representation of a problem situation.

FIGURE 1.1 FIVE REPRESENTATIONS: A TRANSLATION MODEL

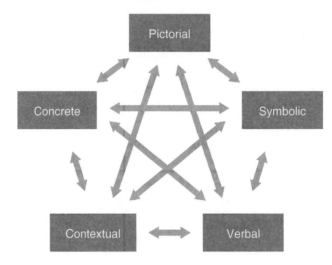

Source: Adapted from Lesh, Post, and Behr (1987).

Teaching Students to Mathematize

As we discussed earlier, learning to mathematize word problems to arrive at solutions requires time devoted to exploration of different representations with a focus on developing and drawing on a deep understanding of the operations. We recognize that this isn't always easy to achieve in a busy classroom; hence, the appeal of the strategies we mentioned at the beginning of the chapter. But what we know from our work with teachers and our review of the research is that, although there are no shortcuts, structuring exploration to focus on actions and relationships is both essential and possible. Doing so requires three things:

1. Teachers draw on their own deep understanding of the operations and their relationship to different word problem situations to plan instruction.

2. Teachers use a model of problem solving that allows for deep exploration.

3. Teachers use a variety of word problems throughout their units and lessons, to introduce a topic and to give examples during instruction, not just as the "challenge" at the end of the chapter.

In this book we address all three.

BUILDING YOUR UNDERSTANDING OF THE OPERATIONS AND RELATED PROBLEM SITUATIONS

The chapters that follow explore the different operations and the various kinds of word problems—or problem situations—that arise within each. To be sure that all of the problems and situational contexts your students encounter are addressed, we drew on a number of sources, including the Common Core State Standards for Mathematics (National Governors Association Center for Best Practices and Council of Chief State School Officers, 2010); the work done by the Cognitively Guided Instruction projects (Carpenter, Fennema, & Franke, 1996; Carpenter, Fennema, Franke, Levi, & Empson, 2014); earlier research; and our own work with teachers to create tables, one for addition and subtraction situations (Figure 1.2) and another for multiplication and division situations (Figure 1.3). Our versions of the problem situation tables represent the language we have found to resonate the most with teachers and students as they make sense of the various problem types, while still accommodating the most comprehensive list of categories. These tables also appear in the Appendix at the end of the book.

NOTES

_____

_____

_____

_____

_____

_____

_____

_____

_____

_____

_____

_____

_____

FIGURE 1.2 ADDITION AND SUBTRACTION PROBLEM SITUATIONS

ACTIVE SITUATIONS

	Result Unknown	Change Addend Unknown	Start Addend Unknown	
Add-To	Paulo counted 9 crayons. He put them in the basket. Paulo found 6 more crayons under the table. He put them in the basket. How many crayons are in the basket? $9+6=x$ $6=x-9$	Paulo counted 9 crayons. He found more and put them in the basket. Now Paulo has 15 crayons. How many crayons did he put in the basket? $9+x=15$ $9=15-x$	Paulo had some crayons. He found 6 more crayons under the table. Now he has 15 crayons. How many crayons did Paulo have in the beginning? $x+6=15$ $15-6=x$	
Take-From	There are 19 students in Mrs. Amadi's class. 4 students went to the office to say the Pledge. How many students are in the class now? $19-4=x$ $4+x=19$	There are 19 students in Mrs. Amadi's class. Some students went to class to read the Pledge. There were still 15 students in the classroom. How many students went to the office? $19-x=15$ $x+15=19$	4 students went to the office. 15 students were still in the classroom. How many students are there in Mrs. Amadi's class? $x-4=15$ $15+4=x$	

RELATIONSHIP (NONACTIVE) SITUATIONS

	Total Unknown	One Part Unknown	Both Parts Unknown
Part-Part-Whole	The first grade voted on a game for recess. 11 students voted to play four square. 8 voted to go to the playground. How many students are in the class? $8+11=x$ $x-11=8$	The 19 first graders voted on a recess activity. 8 students voted to go to the playground. How many wanted to play four square? $8+x=19$ $x=19-8$	The 19 first graders voted on a recess activity. Some wanted to play four square. Some wanted to go to the playground. What are some ways the first graders could have voted? $x+y=19$ $19-x=y$

	Difference Unknown	Greater Quantity Unknown	Lesser Quantity Unknown	
Additive Comparison	Jessie's paper airplane flew 14 feet. Jo's paper airplane flew 9 feet. How much less did Jo's paper airplane fly than Jessie's? $14-9=x$ $9+x=14$	Jo's paper airplane flew 9 feet. Jessie's paper airplane flew 5 feet more than Jo's. How far did Jessie's paper airplane fly? $9+5=x$ $x-5=9$	Jessie's paper airplane flew 14 feet. Jo's paper airplane flew 5 feet less than Jessie's paper airplane. How far did Jo's paper airplane fly? $14-5=x$ $14=x+5$	

Note: The representations for the problem situations in these tables reflect our understanding based on a number of resources. These include the tables in the Common Core State Standards for Mathematics (CCSS-M; National Governors Association Center for Best Practices and Council of Chief State School Officers, 2010), the problem situations as described in the Cognitively Guided Instruction research (Carpenter, Hiebert, & Moser, 1981), and other tools. See the Appendix and the book's companion website (resources.corwin.com/problemsolvingk-2) for a more detailed summary of the documents that informed our development of these tables.

FIGURE 1.3 MULTIPLICATION AND DIVISION PROBLEM SITUATIONS

ASYMMETRICAL (NONMATCHING) FACTORS

	Product Unknown	Multiplier (Number of Groups) Unknown	Measure (Group Size) Unknown	
Equal Groups	Mayim has 8 vases to decorate the tables at her party. She places 2 flowers in each vase. How many flowers does she need? $8 \times 2 = x$ $x \div 8 = 2$	Mayim has some vases to decorate the tables at her party. She places 2 flowers in each vase. If she uses 16 flowers, how many vases does she have? $x \times 2 = 16$ $x = 16 \div 2$	Mayim places 16 flowers in vases to decorate the tables at her party. There are 8 vases and each vase has the same number of flowers. How many flowers will be in each vase? $8 \times x = 16$ $16 \div 8 = x$	
	Resulting Value Unknown	**Scale Factor (Times as Many) Unknown**	**Original Value Unknown**	
Multiplicative Comparison	Amelia's dog is 5 times older than Wanda's 3-year-old dog. How old is Amelia's dog? $5 \times 3 = x$ $x \div 5 = 3$	Sydney has $15 to spend at the movies. Her sister has $5. How many times more money does Sydney have than her sister has? $x \times 5 = 15$ $5 = 15 \div x$	Mrs. Smith has 15 puzzles in her classroom. That is 3 times as many puzzles as are in Mr. Jackson's room. How many puzzles are in Mr. Jackson's room? $3 \times x = 15$ $15 \div 3 = x$	

SYMMETRICAL (MATCHING) FACTORS

	Product Unknown	One Dimension Unknown	Both Dimensions Unknown
Area/Array	Bradley bought a new rug for the hallway in his house. One side measured 5 feet and the other side measured 3 feet. How many square feet does the rug cover? $5 \times 3 = x$ $3 + 3 + 3 + 3 + 3 = x$ $3 \times 5 = x$ $5 + 5 + 5 = x$	The 12 members of the student council lined up on the stage to take yearbook pictures. The first row started with 6 students and the rest of the rows did the same. How many rows were there? $6 \times x = 12$ $x = 12 \div 6$	Daniella was building a house foundation using her building blocks. She started with 20 blocks. How many blocks long and wide could the foundation be? $x \times y = 20$ $20 \div x = y$
	Sample Space (Total Outcomes) Unknown	**One Factor Unknown**	**Both Factors Unknown**
Combinations (Fundamental Counting Principle)	Karen has 3 shirts and 7 pairs of pants. How many unique outfits can she make? $3 \times 7 = x$ $3 = x \div 7$	Evelyn says that she can make 21 unique and different ice cream sundaes using just ice cream flavors and toppings. If she has 3 flavors of ice cream, how many kinds of toppings does Evelyn have? $3 \times x = 21$ $21 \div 3 = x$	Audrey can make 21 different fruit sodas using the machine at the restaurant. How many different flavorings and sodas could there be? $x \times y = 21$ $x = 21 \div y$

Note: In the upper elementary grades, students begin the long journey of learning to think multiplicatively and proportionally. Part of this process involves moving away from counting and repeated addition to represent ideas that are better expressed with multiplication, but the primary years are still focused mostly on counting and adding. Some standards leverage that strength to introduce early ideas of multiplication: Counting squares in an array is one of them, and skip counting is another. We have included multiplication and division equations for our adult readers. K–2 students are not typically expected to represent these operations in equation form.

In the chapters—each of which corresponds to a particular problem situation and a row on one of the tables—we walk you through a problem-solving process that enhances your understanding of the operation and its relationship to the problem situation while modeling the kinds of questions and explorations that can be adapted to your instruction and used with your students. Because this volume emphasizes the work of grades K–2, we begin with a discussion about counting and then look deeply at each situation addressed by addition and subtraction. We end with a chapter introducing the early ideas of multiplication and division that have their roots in primary mathematics.

In each chapter, you will have opportunities to stop and engage in your own problem solving in the workspace provided. We end each chapter with a summary of the key ideas for that problem situation and some additional practice that can also be translated to your instruction.

PLAYING IN THE MATHEMATIZING SANDBOX: A PROBLEM-SOLVING MODEL

To guide your instruction and even enhance your own capacities for problem solving, we have developed a model for solving word problems that puts the emphasis squarely on learning to mathematize (Figure 1.4). The centerpiece of this model is what we call the "mathematizing sandbox," and we call it this for a reason. The sandbox is where children explore and learn through play. Exploring, experiencing, and experimenting by using different representations is vital not only to developing a strong operation sense but also to building comfort with the problem-solving process. Sometimes it is messy and slow, and we as teachers need to make room for it. We hope that the model illustrated in the figure will be your guide.

FIGURE 1.4 A MODEL FOR MATHEMATIZING WORD PROBLEMS

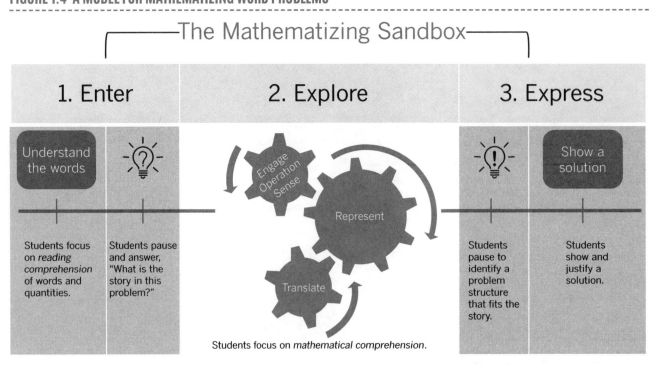

The Mathematizing Sandbox

1. Enter	2. Explore	3. Express

Understand the words — Students focus on *reading comprehension* of words and quantities.

Students pause and answer, "What is the story in this problem?"

Engage Operation Sense · Represent · Translate

Students focus on *mathematical comprehension.*

Students pause to identify a problem structure that fits the story.

Show a solution — Students show and justify a solution.

The mathematizing sandbox involves three steps and two pauses:

Step 1 (Enter): Students' first step is one of reading comprehension. Students must understand the words and context involved in the problem before they can really dive into mathematical understanding of the situation, context, quantities, or relationship between quantities in the problem.

Pause 1: This is a crucial moment when, rather than diving into an approach strategy, students make a conscious choice to look at the problem a different way, with a mind toward reasoning and sense-making about the *mathematical story* told by the problem or context. You will notice that we often suggest putting the problem in your own words as a way of making sense. This stage is critical to moving beyond the "plucking and plugging" of numbers with no attention to meaning that we so often see (SanGiovanni, 2020).

Step 2 (Explore): We call this phase of problem solving "stepping into the mathematizing sandbox." This is the space in which students engage their operation sense and play with some of the different representations mentioned earlier, making translations between them to truly understand what is going on in the problem situation. What story is being told? What are we comparing, or what action is happening? What information do we have, and what are we trying to find out? This step is sometimes reflected in mnemonics-based strategies such as STAR (stop, think, act, review) or KWS (What do you know? What do you want to know? Solve it.) or Pólya's (1945) four steps to problem solving (understand, devise a plan, carry out a plan, look back) or even CUBES. But it can't be rushed or treated too superficially. Giving adequate space to the explore phase is essential to the understanding part of any strategic approach. This is where the cognitive sweet spot can be found, and this step is what the bulk of this book is about.

Pause 2: The exploration done in the mathematizing sandbox leads students to the "a-ha moment" when they can match what they see happening in the problem to a problem situation (see Figures 1.2 and 1.3). Understanding the most appropriate problem situation informs which operation(s) to use, but it also does so much more. It builds a solid foundation of operation sense.

Step 3 (Express): Here students leave the sandbox and are ready to express the story either symbolically or in words or pictures, having found a solution they are prepared to discuss and justify.

LEVERAGING THE POWER OF CHILDREN'S LITERATURE

We just shared with you a problem-solving model for children to understand the context, or brief "story," as it is presented in a word problem. The model also offers guidance to work through what the problem means and how the numbers in it relate. Because children are naturally drawn to stories in order to make sense of their world, there are some additional, even broader ways to integrate the power of stories into helping students mathematize their world and build operation sense—using the kinds of literary stories found in children's books you already have in your classroom or school library. Throughout this book we will share examples, explaining how the following four strategies might work for you as you use children's literature to engage students in problem posing. You will come away with ideas for a few specific books, but, more important, you will consider how to use these strategies to explore books in your own school or classroom library to engage students in problem posing and problem solving.

STRATEGY #1: MAKE PREDICTIONS Many book-length stories rely on repetitive patterns or suspense in the story arc, and students learn to anticipate or predict what might happen. The Make Predictions strategy for problem posing pauses the action in a story, represents what's happening using a mathematical equation or representation, and gives students the opportunity to consider different ways the story might unfold. This strategy supports students' growing awareness of the structure of a story, using clues in the text to decide appropriate pivots in the story for predicting the outcomes.

STRATEGY #2: CREATE ANOTHER OUTCOME The events in some longer or more complex stories encourage readers to imagine a different way that the story might have unfolded. Maybe the main character makes a single decision that changes the whole story. Maybe an unfortunate event happens that might have been avoided. Or perhaps so much happens in the story that changing the story can be a great puzzle. Start with an initial reading, then mathematize the action in the story (identify quantities), and finally experiment with different changes to the story. This strategy supports literature standards that ask students to describe how characters in a story respond to major events and challenges.

STRATEGY #3: FIND THE UNKNOWN QUANTITY Some stories are told using quantities that are important to the story but are never given to the reader. In these stories, students have the opportunity to imagine quantities that make sense and write their own mathematical interpretations. Fairy tales, tall tales, and fables often rely on narratives of this kind, but rarely are actual numbers used. This strategy loans numbers to the story, or it invites students to consider different outcomes for the story using different quantities. This strategy, perhaps more than the others, relies on students to mathematize the details of a story. The strategy encourages them to use illustrations or other details in the story to gather information about the magnitude of the measurable or countable details of the story.

STRATEGY #4: TRANSCRIBE THE ACTION OR RELATIONSHIP Some stories give explicit quantities and the reader follows along as a quantity increases or decreases because of the action in the story (Monroe & Young, 2018). Many nursery rhymes, like *Ten Little Monkeys*, for example, rely on this narrative strategy. The mathematics lesson is designed to translate those changes into mathematical language. The students have the job of recording what happens to the quantities in the story using manipulatives, pictures, or equations in a way that is appropriate for their grade level. This strategy focuses student attention on the rhythm or structure of a story, using the details to quantify it or to translate it into a mathematical representation.

Final Words Before You Dive In

We understand that your real life in a school and in your classroom puts innumerable demands on your time and energy as you work to address ambitious mathematics standards. Who has time to use manipulatives, draw pictures, and spend time writing about mathematics? Your students do! This is what meeting the new ambitious standards actually requires. It may feel like pressure to speed up and do more, but paradoxically, the way to build the knowledge and concepts that are currently described in the standards is by slowing down. Evidence gathered over the past 30 years indicates that an integrated and connected understanding of a wide variety of representations of mathematical ideas is one of the best tools in a student's toolbox (or sandbox!) for a deep and lasting understanding of mathematics (Leinwand, Brahier, & Huinker, 2014). We hope that this book will be a valuable tool as you make or renew your commitment to teaching for greater understanding.

CHAPTER TWO

Moving From Counting to Addition and Subtraction

Thinking About Counting, Addition, and Subtraction

In this chapter we introduce the principles of early counting and make connections to the work students first do with the operations of addition and subtraction. You might think of addition and subtraction as being fairly straightforward operations, but as you'll see in this book, there is some nuance in the way children make sense of these operations that is important to keep in mind. In this chapter we will talk about two kinds of *active situations*—meaning that something is moving within the problem, that is, something is being added to or taken away. We refer to these as Add-To and Take-From situations. We will focus on the Result Unknown variation of these problems in order to compare the action with counting. We'll get into other kinds of situations in later chapters. Let's get started.

Pretend you are walking into a workshop. This is the first of six workshops exploring problem situations that all students will encounter in grades K through 2. In this workshop, as in the other five, you will be exploring in detail aspects of these problems and the operations associated with them that you may not have considered before. Doing so requires that you take on the role of student, see the problems with new eyes, and let yourself try out representations and models for yourself.

Addition and Subtraction Problem Situations

	Result Unknown
Add-To	Paulo counted 9 crayons. He put them in the basket. Paulo found 6 more crayons under the table. He put them in the basket. How many crayons are in the basket? $9 + 6 = x$ $6 = x - 9$
Take-From	There are 19 students in Mrs. Amadi's class. 4 students went to the office to say the Pledge. How many students are in the class now? $19 - 4 = x$ $4 + x = 19$

Note: The representations for the problem situations in this table reflect our understanding based on a number of resources. These include the tables in the Common Core State Standards for Mathematics (CCSS-M; National Governors Association Center for Best Practices and Council of Chief State School Officers, 2010), the problem situations as described in the Cognitively Guided Instruction research (Carpenter, Hiebert, & Moser, 1981), and other tools. See the Appendix and the book's companion website for a more detailed summary of the documents that informed our development of this table.

ACTIVE SITUATIONS

	Result Unknown	Change Addend Unknown	Start Addend Unknown
Add-To	Paulo counted 9 crayons. He put them in the basket. Paulo found 6 more crayons under the table. He put them in the basket. How many crayons are in the basket? $9 + 6 = x$ $6 = x - 9$	Paulo counted 9 crayons. He found more and put them in the basket. Now Paulo has 15 crayons. How many crayons did he put in the basket? $9 + x = 15$ $9 = 15 - x$	Paulo had some crayons. He found 6 more crayons under the table. Now he has 15 crayons. How many crayons did Paulo have in the beginning? $x + 6 = 15$ $15 - 6 = x$
Take-From	There are 19 students in Mrs. Amadi's class. 4 students went to the office to say the Pledge. How many students are in the class now? $19 - 4 = x$ $4 + x = 19$	There are 19 students in Mrs. Amadi's class. Some students went to class to read the Pledge. There were still 15 students in the classroom. How many students went to the office? $19 - x = 15$ $x + 15 = 19$	4 students went to the office. 15 students were still in the classroom. How many students are there in Mrs. Amadi's class? $x - 4 = 15$ $15 + 4 = x$

RELATIONSHIP (NONACTIVE) SITUATIONS

	Total Unknown	One Part Unknown	Both Parts Unknown
Part-Part-Whole	The first grade voted on a game for recess. 11 students voted to play four square. 8 voted to go to the playground. How many students are in the class? $8 + 11 = x$ $x - 11 = 8$	The 19 first graders voted on a recess activity. 8 students voted to go to the playground. How many wanted to play four square? $8 + x = 19$ $x = 19 - 8$	The 19 first graders voted on a recess activity. Some wanted to play four square. Some wanted to go to the playground. What are some ways the first graders could have voted? $x + y = 19$ $19 - x = y$
	Difference Unknown	Greater Quantity Unknown	Lesser Quantity Unknown	
Additive Comparison	Jessie's paper airplane flew 14 feet. Jo's paper airplane flew 9 feet. How much less did Jo's paper airplane fly than Jessie's? $14 - 9 = x$ $9 + x = 14$	Jo's paper airplane flew 9 feet. Jessie's paper airplane flew 5 feet more than Jo's. How far did Jessie's paper airplane fly? $9 + 5 = x$ $x - 5 = 9$	Jessie's paper airplane flew 14 feet. Jo's paper airplane flew 5 feet less than Jessie's paper airplane. How far did Jo's paper airplane fly? $14 - 5 = x$ $14 = x + 5$

online resources ↘ Visit **http://resources.corwin.com/problemsolvingk-2** to download a copy of the full Addition and Subtraction Problem Situations Table.

Sandbox Notes: Explore Your Thinking

As you enter into problem exploration mode, gather your tools, including markers or crayons, linking cubes, base 10 blocks, linking cubes, counters, and any other tools that you routinely have available in your classroom. Try several of the concrete manipulatives and some hand-drawn picture models that reflect the mathematical story in the word problem. If you put the problem in your own words, revisit that rephrasing and specify where you can see each quantity in the problem. Where can you see each quantity in the models you have created? Think about how your work can express your understanding of the problem situation.

Ask yourself these questions to focus your thinking:

- Think about the quantities in each situation. What do they represent? What action is taking place between the quantities in the problem?

- How can you represent the quantities in the word problems with your manipulatives or pictures?

- How can you make a number sentence about the problem?

Mathematical story:
A retelling of the actions or relationships in a word problem or other problem context in a way that highlights the important mathematical details over any other information.

To begin, read the problem in Figure 2.1. Don't try to solve it just yet. Instead, put yourself in the place of your students (who might be listening to you read the problem), and as you enter the problem, focus on understanding the words in it. Try using your own words to rephrase, without focusing on the quantities. If this is difficult, substitute the quantities with the word *some*. This will help you avoid jumping to the solution path before you fully explore the problem. Look at the model in Figure 2.2 to remind yourself of how these tasks fit into the problem-solving process. Congratulations, you are now ready to enter the mathematizing sandbox!

FIGURE 2.1

> Paulo was cleaning up the crayons at his table. He put 9 crayons in the basket. Then Paulo found 6 more crayons under the table and put them in the basket. How many crayons are in the basket now?

ENTER THE PROBLEM

FIGURE 2.2 A MODEL FOR MATHEMATIZING WORD PROBLEMS

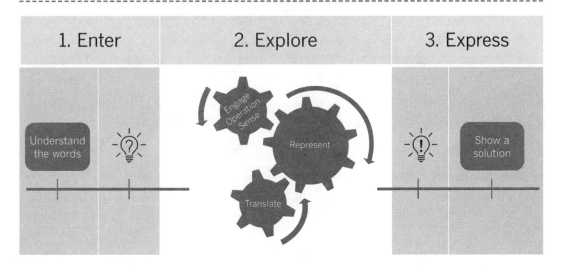

To explore, you may need to take notes of your explorations on scratch paper. Once you can answer these questions, you are ready to show and justify your solutions. Include these in the space provided so that you can easily refer back to them. If your solution includes a concrete model, reproduce that as best you can in a drawing. Add any verbal representation of the problem or additional notes on your thinking that are necessary to make your solution clear. *Remember: When the focus is on mathematizing, finding a solution is not the same as finding the answer. A solution is a representation of the problem that reveals how it can be solved. The answer comes after.* This concept will become clearer as you work through problems and explore the work samples of students and teachers throughout the book.

You have taken your first trip to the mathematizing sandbox. You've translated the story of the problem into your own words and explored several different concrete, pictorial, and symbolic representations of the problem situations. You likely have translated your representations into a number sentence that you can then solve, or the answer may have come out of another representation. You have used your operation sense to approach this word problem in a way that reflects deep understanding of the situation rather than simply using computational knowledge.

STUDENTS AND TEACHERS THINK ABOUT THE PROBLEM

Look at the student work in Figures 2.3 and 2.4 and consider how these students describe or draw what is happening in the same word problem.

FIGURE 2.3

FIGURE 2.4

STUDENT WORK	"I counted 15 crayons."	 "First I counted 6 and then I counted 9 more."
TEACHER RESPONSE	I can see the number 15, and 15 crayons in a basket, but I'm not sure if this drawing represents just her answer or her understanding of what happened in the problem. There is no way to know where the 6 is or where the 9 is.	I see that she has drawn a set of 6 crayons and a set of 9 crayons. Both addends are here. I think I will ask her why she drew 6 crayons first rather than 9 crayons, mostly because the story discusses 9 crayons to start with, and 6 added on. Maybe she made a group of 6 crayons first because it was the last number she heard.
VIDEO	**Video 2.1** Cleaning Up Crayons With an Answer To read a QR code, you must have a smartphone or tablet with a camera. We recommend that you download a QR code reader app that is made specifically for your phone or tablet brand. You can also view videos at resources.corwin.com/ problemsolvingk-2	**Video 2.2** Cleaning Up Crayons With a Counting-On Strategy resources.corwin.com/ problemsolvingk-2

Look at the teacher commentary that follows the student work and consider what the teachers noticed about it. There is also a video available showing each student's solution to the problem, which you may want to watch once you have read through the student work and teacher comments.

What do you notice? Both students give 15 as an answer to the problem and show 15 crayons. In Figure 2.3, the crayons in the basket are presented in a line, but that is the only indication that the student understands this problem as an **Add-To** situation. By contrast, the work in Figure 2.4 appears to be showing both addends, separated by a line, as well as a sum of 15. We want to highlight the distinction between the skill of counting and the skill of adding. In both of these cases, the students likely know how to count to 15 effectively and may even recognize the sum of 9 and 6 as a known fact, but the pictorial representations they each create are different in important ways. As we explore the difference between adding and counting, we will explore how problem solving can differ from computation.

Add-To: A problem situation that includes action happening in the problem. Some quantity is being added to the original quantity.

THE DEVELOPMENT OF COUNTING

Counting a collection of objects is a process of matching words to objects and, after tagging the last object, arriving at a value that represents the whole set. Often, pre-K and kindergarten students will demonstrate some components of the skill of counting but not always the whole coordinated procedure. Because counting is a precursor to addition, it's important to first understand the underlying principles. There are five principles to effective counting (Gelman & Gallistel, 1978): one-to-one correspondence, stable order, cardinality, abstraction, and order irrelevance. Let's look at each one in turn.

ONE-TO-ONE CORRESPONDENCE PRINCIPLE When counting, the child who has the coordinated skills of one-to-one correspondence matches one number word to one object in the collection at a time and tags it. Matching a number word to an object is called *tagging*. Children who have proficiency counting may move each object to one side to show that they have counted it or they may turn it over. If they're counting on a page, they may mark it or cross it out. Distinguishing this way, between counted and uncounted objects, is called *partitioning*. Children who are still developing one-to-one correspondence may point to empty spaces between objects or wave their hands indiscriminately over the collection while saying number words. These actions show neither accurate tagging nor partitioning. Providing students a structure like a counting mat with designated areas for both tagged and not-yet-tagged objects may help them organize their counting. You can also guide their practice by helping them touch, name, and move each object one at a time. In the following example, Maria does not yet demonstrate one-to-one correspondence:

> *A set of nine blocks sits in front of Maria, arranged in a 3 × 3 array. Maria begins to count. She taps one block with her right hand and says, "One." She taps another and says, "Two." Her left hand comes up and points to a different block, and she says, "Three." She then begins to wave her hands over the collection of blocks while racing through the number sequence, "Four, five, six, seven!"*

STABLE ORDER PRINCIPLE When children tag the objects they are counting, the words they say have to come out in the same order each time. Perhaps this is obvious, but children cannot effectively count higher than their stable order of counting sequence. This is the reason why most kindergarten standards include a standard for counting out loud up to a certain number—for example, 100—but the standard for counting concrete objects may only go up to 20. The counting sequence must be stable before it can be used to actively count. Children can also have a stable order in multiple languages. In the following example, Raul is counting cookies:

> *Six cookies sit on the table in front of Raul. He begins to count, saying, "One, two, three, six, seven, eight!" The teacher responds with, "Could you count them again, Raul?" He responds, "One, two, three, five, six, . . . eight!" The teacher then responds with, "¿Raul, puedes contar esto?" [Can you count this?] He counts, "¡Uno, dos, tres, quatro, cinco, seis!" [One, two, three, four, five, six!] Raul repeats his count accurately. Based on this vignette, Raul may have a stable order of numbers in Spanish but not yet in English.*

CARDINALITY PRINCIPLE The principles described so far are about matching one object to one number word. The cardinal number of a set instead does two things. First, it matches the last object to a counting word. Second, it describes a property of the whole collection of objects by answering the question, "How many are there?" Students who don't yet understand the cardinality of the set don't know the answer to this question, even after they have finished counting. They return to the collection and do the count again, or they keep on counting. It takes experience for children to recognize that the last tag refers to a property of the whole set as well as to the count of the last tagged item. Consider the following example:

> *Four plastic dinosaurs sit on a table in front of Brian. The teacher asks him to count the dinosaurs. He taps one and says, "One." He taps the next three, one at a time, and says, "Two, three, four." The teacher asks, "How many dinosaurs are there, Brian?" Brian responds, "Five, four, three, two, one!" while counting on his fingers. Brian may have accurately counted four dinosaurs, but we aren't sure that he knows that "Four" also represents the quantity of dinosaurs.*

These first three counting principles describe *how* to count efficiently. In some ways these skills are similar to other procedural skills students learn. The last two principles of counting extend the *hows* of counting to the *whats*.

ABSTRACTION PRINCIPLE What is countable? People are countable, but are imaginations or dreams countable? Does a collection of four elephants have the same numerosity (or cardinality) as four pennies? It takes children some time to recognize categories that are countable and to recognize that "4" can represent four large objects or four small objects, four concrete or four abstract objects, and still have the same numerosity of "4." For this reason, we emphasize the importance of naming the unit we are counting. The word *quantity* is chosen intentionally in this book because it represents both ideas—numerosity and the unit being counted. For example, the student whose work is featured in Figure 2.3 identifies 15 "crans" (crayons), but the student whose work is shown in Figure 2.4 does not mention the word at all. The teacher

Quantity: A number, including its unit of measure (Kelemanik, Lucenta, & Creighton, 2016).

made the assumption that the child is discussing crayons (likely based on the drawing), but it is just an assumption that should be regularly confirmed with a question: "You have 15 what?" An interesting answer might be "15 students." How does this change your interpretation of the student's understanding of the problem? As students count sets of objects, continue to ask what they are counting.

ORDER IRRELEVANCE PRINCIPLE The most important idea about the order irrelevance principle is that objects in a collection can be counted in any order, as long as each is counted exactly once. In some ways, order irrelevance is like the commutative property of addition, an idea that students will learn to understand in grades K–2 but may not name until later. Challenge students to change which object is the first to be counted. Another, more challenging task is to ask students to count a collection of objects and tell them which one should be the last one counted. For example, "Count these bears any way you want, but I want you to count the red one last."

> Commutative property of addition: **The property of addition that states that two quantities can be added in either order without changing the sum.**

Understanding the basic principles of the counting procedure highlights the conceptual ideas that students must make sense of and also the skills they must acquire to count efficiently. These are skills that generally precede learning the action of addition. It's important to recognize these early ideas about counting as you listen to students working. Observe their counting, even as they enter second grade; and when students make errors in their addition and subtraction, consider assessing whether or not their counting skills are responsible for those errors. As you explore addition with your students, you may realize they are missing one or more of these counting principles. Look for opportunities to pause and address the counting skills that may still be developing when you encounter a concern. The focus of this book is on understanding the problem contexts that underlie most word problems and the operations that represent them. In this chapter we will identify important counting skills and then begin to apply them to word problems that can be represented with addition or subtraction.

COUNTING OR ADD-TO?

Earlier in this chapter we briefly introduced the Add-To problem situation with the student work in Figure 2.4. This book is focused on developing students' operation sense and strengthening their ideas of what an operator like addition or subtraction can do within the context of a problem situation. Because of this focus, we highlight the difference between the context of the problem and the computation that it takes to solve it. Counting is an algorithm or procedure, in some ways like adding double-digit numbers. There are concepts to understand, and the goal is also for students to count efficiently.

Try focusing on the problem situation in Figure 2.1 and read it like a story. Paulo has some crayons (start). Paulo finds more crayons (change). Paulo now has a new quantity of crayons (result). Any one of these quantities could be missing in a word problem, but in this case we have to find the result, or how many crayons Paulo has at the end of the story.

When problem solving, we want students to act out what happens in a story. Fortunately, young children naturally focus on the narrative when they solve word problems (Kilpatrick, Swafford, & Findell, 2001), but as students get older they tend to do this less because our efforts to teach them to do calculations may turn their attention away from what is happening in the problem. When working with young children, this is a great opportunity to capitalize on what they naturally want to do—act it out! This will help them build good problem-solving habits early.

Return to the student work in Figure 2.4. One might say that it shows a true representation of an Add-To problem because it starts with 6 crayons and adds 9 more. But we would argue that this may not be the case. In the problem situation, Paulo starts with a set of 9 crayons and adds an additional set of 6 crayons to the basket. The student work in Figure 2.4 appears to begin with a set of 6 crayons and then adds 9 crayons. The sum is the same, so you might say it doesn't matter. But it might. Perhaps the student started drawing crayons from the right side, in which case she started with 9 crayons, as the story requires, but the scrunched-up crayon drawings on the right make that unlikely. Maybe she has a robust sense of the order irrelevance principle or of the commutative property and knows that the answer will be the same no matter in what order the addends are put together. The teacher has an entirely different theory about the student's choice to start with 6. Without the opportunity to ask or observe, it is unclear why the student started with 6 crayons, and without learning more from the student, we don't know if she sees this situation accurately (as written), even though her answer is correct.

The straight line of 15 crayons in Figure 2.3 shares a different picture. It is possible that the student counted to find 15, rather than actively joining two sets of crayons. Maybe the student already knew the fact $9 + 6 = 15$ and therefore did not act out the problem but instead represented only the sum of 15. It is also possible that the student drew 9 crayons and then drew 6 more crayons before going back to show the cardinality of the set of 15; however, nothing in the drawing indicates a separation between the addends. We would need more information to know what the student was thinking, but there is little evidence that she is modeling two different addends in this representation. In a lesson focused on problem solving, this difference matters greatly because we are interested in how students are making sense of the problem situation.

The student work shown in Figure 2.5 better shows the action of the story. The problem situation starts with 9 crayons, and 6 more are added (the computation shows a counting-on strategy, sometimes also called adding on or counting up). The quantity 9 is the start, adding 6 is the change, and the result is shown as 15 crayons. Maybe you acted this out using counters when you solved the problem at the beginning of the chapter, which is appropriate because Add-To problem situations are easily represented with action.

FIGURE 2.5

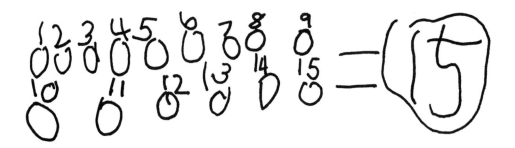

If we want students to understand what is happening in a problem situation and to use their tools to accurately act out, draw, or otherwise model that situation, we have to pay the most attention to this process. Sometimes students show us efficient calculation strategies and can get to correct answers—which are also important accomplishments—but does that always show they understand the situation? As we focus our attention here on the actions and relationships in word problems, we might look differently at a student sample like the one in Figure 2.6. Does this student understand the problem situation? Or not? How could we know? There is evidence that the student understands this fact family, but this work sample does not reveal information about how the student made sense of the word problem itself.

FIGURE 2.6

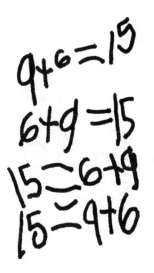

REPRESENTING PROBLEM SITUATIONS OR REPRESENTING ANSWERS?

As you look at the problem in Figure 2.7, think about the many ways it could be represented. Translate it into your own words and think about the drawings or manipulatives you might use to represent the story in the problem. What representations might your students choose?

FIGURE 2.7

There were 9 eggs in the carton. Emily ate 2 eggs for her breakfast. How many eggs are left in the carton?

Look at the four samples of student work in Figures 2.8–2.11 and how the students described or drew what is happening in the given word problem. What do you notice? What do you wonder?

STUDENT WORK

FIGURE 2.8	FIGURE 2.9
 $4+3=7$ $5+2=7$ $8-1=7$ $9-2=7$ $10-3=7$ Daniel	$2+5=7$ Brandon

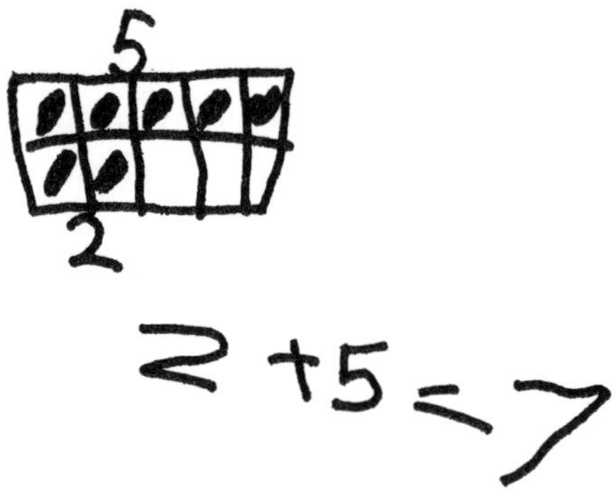

FIGURE 2.10	FIGURE 2.11
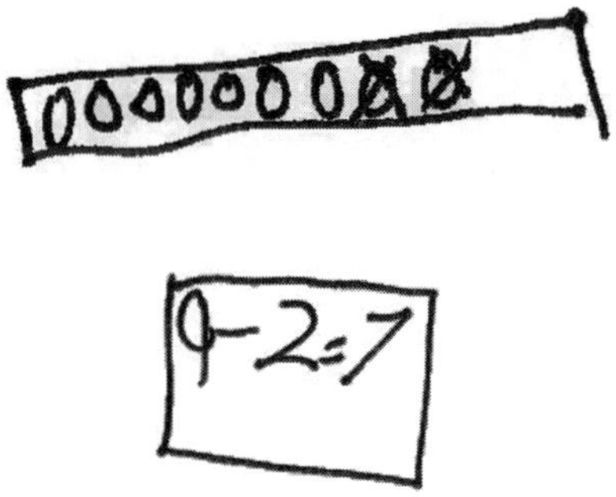 $9-2=7$ Heather	$0+0+0$ are left Bradley

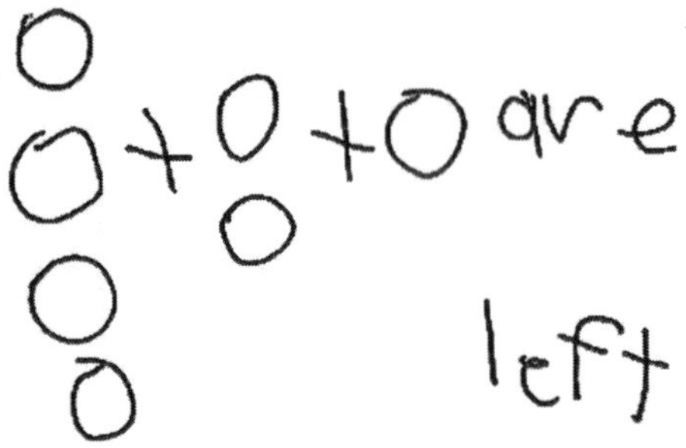

TEACHER RESPONSE

I approached this table because I heard all of the students say, in unison, "Seven!" They were quite excited to have found a common answer.

I stayed at the table to study their various representations for a few minutes but didn't quite know what to say to them. I was happy that they all had the correct response, but something wasn't quite right about their work. I needed some time to think!

Of the four student work samples, only one is an appropriate representation of what is happening in the problem situation. Read the teacher commentary that follows the student work and take a moment to discuss these work samples with your partner teachers. Which sample do you think is the only appropriate representation of the problem situation? Why are the other three not representations of the problem situation?

The egg problem is an example of a Take-From problem situation. Similar to an Add-To problem situation, the context involves noticeable action taking place in the story: Eggs are eaten, money

Take-From: A problem situation that includes an action and a quantity being removed from the original quantity.

is spent, etc. This active problem situation reads like a story in that there is a start to the problem, a change, and a result, just as we saw in the Add-To problems earlier in the chapter. In Chapters 3 and 4 we will explore the different variations in the problem structure with the start and change unknown in the problem, but in all of the examples in this chapter, the result is unknown. For example, in the egg problem we are given the start (9 eggs) and the change (eating 2 eggs), but the result (the eggs that remain) is unknown.

The egg problem is not a complicated one, even for the youngest primary student. However, the September second graders who answered this problem in Figures 2.8 through 2.11 tell a different story! While agreeing on an answer of 7, only Heather has represented the problem situation in her solution (see Figure 2.10). Heather's drawing starts with a carton holding 9 circles, which we assume are representing eggs. Two of the eggs are crossed out, as if they were taken away to be eaten. Seven eggs remain in the carton. The *solution* accurately represents the context of the problem. Heather was part of the chorus of voices that said, "Seven!" So we also know that her *answer* was accurate as well, even if she does not explicitly note that in her work.

At the same time, despite an accurate answer of 7, the remaining students' solutions are not accurate representations of the problem situation. Daniel's work is a celebration of number facts that make a sum or difference of 7 (see Figure 2.8). Brandon shows a sum of 7 rather than a difference of 7, and although we see a 2, we do not see 9 represented (see Figure 2.9). Bradley's work is a demonstration of a way to make 7 from three different addends; however, there is nothing in the action of the problem that would be represented by $4+2+1$ (see Figure 2.11). None of the remaining three solutions tells the mathematical version of the story that is presented in the original problem. We might choose to celebrate the students' flexibility with numbers but still recognize that we have no information about how these three students arrived at an answer of 7 in the first place.

When you decide to focus students' attention on problem solving, it is important to keep the context of the problem at the forefront. The answer becomes less important, and we focus more attention on students' understandings about the actions and relationships in the problem situation, whether it is a routine word problem or a problem that students themselves posed. Recognizing that an important emphasis of the primary grades is making sense of the base 10 number system, learning basic facts, and learning to compute, it is challenging to turn our attention away from efficient calculations because these are important skills and understandings. However, as we saw in the incorrect solutions to the egg problem, a correct answer can still easily mislead both students and teachers into believing that a correct answer means that students understand what is happening in a word problem. That is not always the case.

To preempt this challenge, be sure to balance your computational lessons with lessons focused on making sense of problem situations in which students create and draw representations that reflect the actions and relationships in a problem. Also, throughout the year, continue to practice all problem situations. We often see students assume that the word problems they're solving will involve the operation they focused on that day and simply plug numbers in without really thinking about the situation itself. They have good reason to expect the connection between their daily work and the problems on that page, but if we do this every day, we may deny them the opportunity to decide for themselves which operation is needed. Challenge their sense-making by changing it up regularly. You might also invite students to pose their own problems and use those as a springboard to sense-making lessons. You'll find some starting points for lessons like these at the end of this chapter and the rest of the chapters in this book.

Using Children's Literature to Explore Add-To and Take-From Situations

When we look for the mathematics in the kind of story told in a book, sometimes it appears in counting rhymes, in repetitive patterns, or in the use of, for example, geometric shapes as characters. There is a place for these mathematics-focused books. But the mathematics doesn't need to be explicit (Columba, Kim, & Moe, 2017)—with experience and practice it can come from the fertile imagination of the students in your class. The "Using Children's Literature" section in each chapter of this book is not meant to provide an absolute list. Our goal is to suggest books through which students can explore the problem situation featured in each chapter using one or more of the four strategies described in Chapter 1. We encourage you to find such opportunities in other books on your library shelves.

In this chapter we start with Strategy #4, Transcribe the Action or Relationship. We invite you to think about other stories you know and love that might also be revealed in a mathematical sense. As you begin, remember to address the literary value of each book that you choose. Many books provide counting practice on pages, or they might show bundles of 10, or they might show familiar objects broken into fractional pieces. That isn't the genre of book we are addressing here. You might use the suggested books for story time or to introduce a writing or social studies lesson. Finding the mathematics in these books encourages students to mathematize the world around them.

TRANSCRIBE THE ACTION OR RELATIONSHIP

Last Stop on Market Street (de la Peña, 2015) is an award-winning picture book that captures a world many children know well. Once a week, CJ and his nana take the #5 bus to the end of Market Street. As the bus continues on its route, CJ's nana warmly greets the people they meet on the bus. CJ grumbles that he could be doing other things on this wet afternoon, but his nana is persistent, calling attention to the colorful individuals and scenery they encounter on their way.

Think of the many opportunities to find and pose problems about the quantities in this book. Here are some general examples of what your students could count or measure: How long could Market Street be? How many people are on the bus? How much might the bus driver collect from the passengers? How much money could the guitar man make? For how many people could CJ and his nana serve lunch?

Recall from Chapter 1 that transcribing the action is a strategy in which the class records what happens to the quantities in the story using manipulatives, pictures, or equations in a way that is appropriate for their grade level. Let's look at an example of how you might do this.

In the story we learn that before CJ and his nana board the bus, there are five people on the bus. This is the start of the mathematical story. We might represent this with five counters in a row—the people already on the bus.

CJ and his nana boarding the bus represents a change in the story: Two more people are added to the bus, which we see represented not only with counters but also with the arrow indicating the action that changes the problem. Now think about how your students can read and understand the verbal statement of the problem. Say and write the verbal statements as they move physical counters. Show the same action using a drawing, making the connection to the verbal number sentences using sentence strips or by writing it on the board. Of course, students can count the people on the bus, but we can also use this opportunity to move from counting to joining sets.

5 people and CJ and his nana make how many people on the bus?

$$5+1+1=?$$

Once students are comfortable with the verbal number statements, you can begin to introduce the symbolic equation, depending on the students' age and the grade-level standards.

Is the number of people on the bus critically important to the story? No, of course not. And we would never choose to reduce the literary value of this book to this one mathematical activity. However, for every book you read to your students, there will be opportunities to invite students to pose and represent their own word problems. When students make up the problems themselves, they begin to mathematize the narrative, and that's the goal.

Now that you have had an introduction to how you might use any favorite book to generate a mathematical lesson, select a book and try it yourself. To try another book with similar mathematical action to *Last Stop on Market Street*, and one that can be used to generate Add-To problem situations, try to generate a problem situation from *Stellaluna* (Cannon, 1993).

Moving Beyond 20

In the second part of each chapter, we expand our set of numbers to include whole numbers beyond 20, to more closely align with the grade-level content that students in second grade should learn. The numbers in the problems should not affect students' understanding of problem situations. But in our experience, when the computation itself poses challenges, students can't rely as much on good estimates and known facts to propose an answer. If they don't have experience modeling quantities or problem situations, or if they don't have experience modeling with greater quantities using grouped counters, they have little else to fall back on. That's when we are likely to hear a student say, "I don't get what they want me to do!"

As you pause before again entering the mathematizing sandbox, think about how you might use manipulatives to focus student attention on the actions taking place in the problems in Figures 2.12 and 2.13. Act out the problems and think about the many ways they could be represented. Anticipate challenges students might encounter. For example, it is tempting to go straight to an

Warning: The next pages include student examples of the problem situations you will be practicing. If you find it difficult to resist looking forward while practicing in the sandbox on page 28, consider covering the facing page (page 29) with a sheet of paper.

Grouped counters: Objects that represent units that are grouped together, such as a base 10 rod.

algorithmic approach because that is something we do when computing an answer. Instead, focus first on the context of the problems and how the manipulative model chosen supports students' understanding of what happens in the problem.

FIGURE 2.12

FIGURE 2.13

Thuy counted 38 seeds in the first scoop of her pumpkin's insides. The next scoop had 14 pumpkin seeds. How many pumpkin seeds has Thuy taken out of her pumpkin?	Shruti bought 52 Valentines for her classmates. There are 38 kids in her class and she gave one to each. She wondered how many she would have left.

ENTER THE PROBLEM

EXPLORE

STUDENTS AND TEACHERS THINK ABOUT THE PROBLEMS

Examining the student work produced during the explore phase of the mathematizing sandbox can tell us a great deal of information about how students think about the problems. The student solution in Figure 2.14 is a representation of the pumpkin seed problem (Figure 2.12), and Figure 2.15 represents the Valentines problem (Figure 2.13). Note the comments and questions the teacher asked as she monitored their work. Think about what other kinds of representations might also support these explorations.

FIGURE 2.14   **FIGURE 2.15**

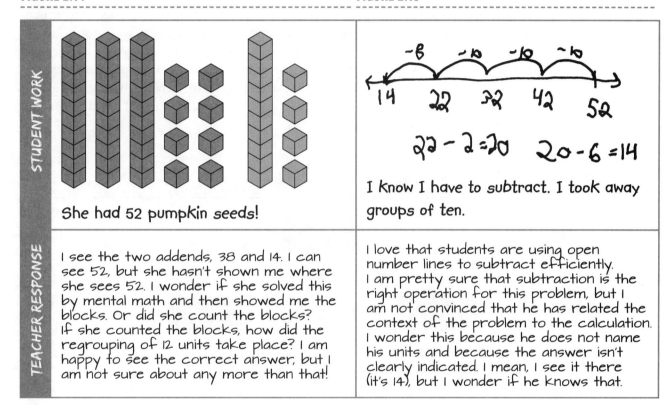

STUDENT WORK

She had 52 pumpkin seeds!

I know I have to subtract. I took away groups of ten.

TEACHER RESPONSE

I see the two addends, 38 and 14. I can see 52, but she hasn't shown me where she sees 52. I wonder if she solved this by mental math and then showed me the blocks. Or did she count the blocks? If she counted the blocks, how did the regrouping of 12 units take place? I am happy to see the correct answer, but I am not sure about any more than that!

I love that students are using open number lines to subtract efficiently. I am pretty sure that subtraction is the right operation for this problem, but I am not convinced that he has related the context of the problem to the calculation. I wonder this because he does not name his units and because the answer isn't clearly indicated. I mean, I see it there (it's 14), but I wonder if he knows that.

REPRESENTING PROBLEM SITUATIONS MULTIPLE WAYS

When students use concrete models to show their mathematical thinking, they might stop with the model and not explain their thinking or write an equation to go with it. Sometimes they might even just show the parts of the problem but not use the tools to actually solve the problem. For example, the teacher comment in Figure 2.14 points out that the student showed two addends and then shared an answer that is not at all connected to the base 10 blocks. Of course, her answer shows 52 pumpkin seeds, but where did that quantity come from? Often, we are so pleased to see a correct answer that we may overlook where it came from. Sometimes we make assumptions that are expedient, but they may not be accurate. If you are not sure how a student arrived at an answer, ask for more information. Perhaps asking the student to write an equation or number sentence would give more information. We know teachers are sometimes tempted to provide the equation to students while correcting work or providing feedback, in an effort to model the connection between the representation and an equation. But would it be perhaps more helpful to ask, "Where do you see 52? Show me." If you are reading this book with teammates, discuss the difference between asking students to write an equation and providing the written equation yourself. How does that change the learning experience for the students?

The student whose work is represented in Figure 2.15 shows a detailed solution process, but as the teacher noted, he doesn't actually tell us his answer. As a teacher you may be quite happy to see the efficient calculation strategy from this student. Now compare the subtraction demonstrated to the action in the problem situation. Do they match? Do you think the student makes a connection between taking away three 10s and eight more, and giving away 38 Valentines? Again, if you are reading this book with teammates, discuss whether we can assume that the student makes this connection. You may think so, or perhaps not, but the important lesson for us is to make a point to ask students to make these connections more explicit. This can be done verbally, with pictures, or even with diagrams making the connections. The more we ask, the more we know.

Recall that in Chapter 1 we described five different ways to represent mathematical ideas. Figure 2.16 gives us a model for exploring challenging word problems by making repeated connections among the five modes of representation. This is often called the translation model. We'll explore the reasons for that as we dig into the model.

FIGURE 2.16 FIVE REPRESENTATIONS: A TRANSLATION MODEL

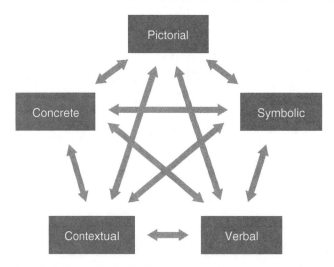

Source: Adapted from Lesh, Post, and Behr (1987).

Figure 2.17 shows how the Valentines problem can be represented using all five of the representations we introduced in Chapter 1. Drawing and creating multiple representations can foster a deeper understanding of problem situations. For example, there are two versions of pictorial representations, one resembling the concrete manipulative and the other an open number line, a more abstract mathematical representation we call a **diagram**. This area might also have included drawings of 52 cards, with 38 of them in the process of being given away.

Diagram: **An abstract representation of a situation, rather than a literal one.**

FIGURE 2.17 FIVE WAYS TO REPRESENT THE VALENTINES PROBLEM

REPRESENTATION	EXAMPLE
Contextual	Shruti bought 52 Valentines for her classmates. There are 38 kids in her class and she gave one to each. She wondered how many she would have left.
Pictorial	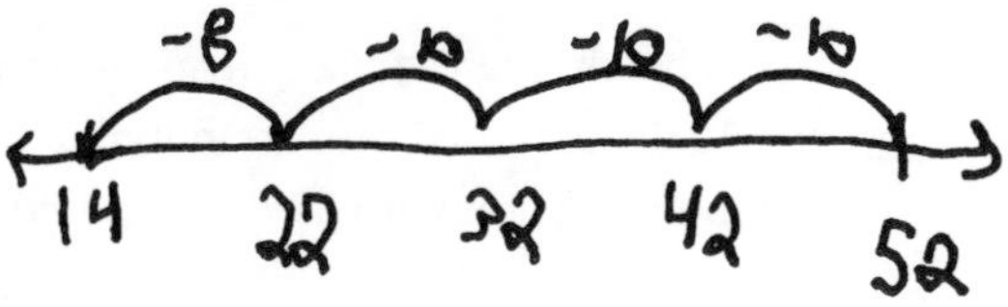
Concrete	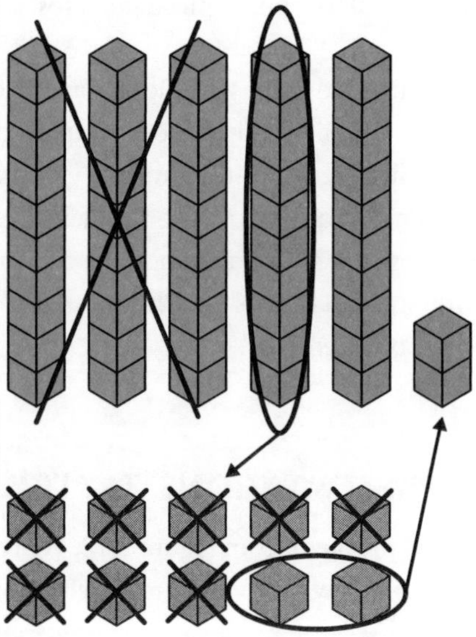 **Video 2.3** Valentine's Cards With Base 10 Blocks resources.corwin.com/problemsolvingk-2
Verbal	Shroti had 52 and she gave away 38. She gave away 10 at a time I think
Symbolic (Equation)	$52 - 38$ $52 \rightarrow 40,\ 12$ $40 - 30 = 10$ $\quad$ $12 - 8 = 4$ 14

Making connections between the representations (often called translations) is key to unlocking the full understanding of the relationships within a problem context. Here are just a few of the many translations that can be made around this problem context:

Pictorial → Verbal: The verbal explanation makes a direct connection to the open number line because it mentions subtracting 10 at a time, which is an obvious feature of the open number line representation.

Concrete → Symbolic: The base 10 blocks are the likely inspiration here. The base 10 blocks show one 10 decomposed into 10 individual units. This is also shown in the symbolic version with 52 decomposed into 40 and 12.

Contextual → Concrete: In this problem, Shruti is giving away Valentines. In the concrete representation, 38 of the 52 pieces are crossed out.

Taken together, the networked and connected representations have been shown to support all learners in making sense of mathematical ideas. Furthermore, multiple, connected representations contribute to mathematical comprehension because students can visualize the problem situation and represent the relationships between the objects in the problem in multiple ways. Students who can make sense of the relationships in a situation can make a connection between what is happening in the problem and a mathematical operation. They see the important elements of the problem and the relationship among those elements.

TRANSLATING THE FIVE REPRESENTATIONS: TRY IT OUT

Now let's turn back to the pumpkin seed problem from Figure 2.12. We can create a mathematical story for the problem and enter it by starting with a verbal representation, distilling the problem to the following:

> *Thuy took some seeds out and then she took more seeds out.*

Before diving into the work of moving through multiple representations on your own, we would like to say more about verbal representations and writing stories. Verbal representations can come in many shapes and forms and be used at various points to clarify and define. Sometimes they are used to explain and add meaning to other representations. As we will suggest throughout this book, a story that distills the problem into its essentials or an effort to restate the problem in your own words provides a verbal representation and serves as a useful beginning. Translating it to other representations (e.g., pictorial, concrete) moves students down the path of exploration. By later translating those representations into a different verbal representation, students clarify and hone their understanding even further. For young students, much of this work may be done in class, during class discussions. But students should continue to have opportunities to explore a variety of ways to express the meaning of problems using language, both written and verbal.

Now dive deeply into this problem context, using Figure 2.18 to create and connect five different representations of the pumpkin seed problem from Figure 2.12. The opening problem and one of the student's representations are included to give you a start. The student who created this concrete representation, however, did not include a description of the strategy used, nor did the student include any symbols, like an equation or labels of the units. Complete the student's response by providing a representation for all five categories, including two pictorial representations (that is, a picture and an abstract diagram). Be sure to make translations among the five representations. How are the particular elements in one representation expressed in the others?

FIGURE 2.18 FIVE WAYS TO REPRESENT THE PUMPKIN SEED PROBLEM

REPRESENTATION	EXAMPLE
Contextual	Thuy counted 38 seeds in the first scoop of her pumpkin's insides. The next scoop had 14 pumpkin seeds. How many pumpkin seeds has Thuy taken out of her pumpkin?
Pictorial	*Picture* *Diagram*
Concrete	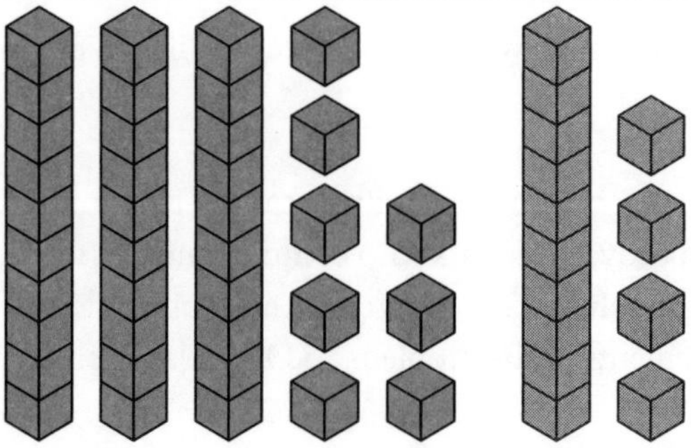
Verbal	
Symbolic (Equation)	

Both the Valentines problem and the pumpkin seed problem show why it is important to help students make connections between the representations they choose and the actions or relationships in the problem. The goal of problem solving is not to focus on finding an answer but, instead, to identify useful strategies and ways to use them to solve future problems. One strategy that students should learn is to distill problem situations down to only the actions or relationships that hold the quantities in the problem together. You may know a problem-solving strategy often called "eliminate unnecessary information." Rather than focus on what should *not* be in the problem, instead put the focus on what *should* be included in order for the story to make sense.

Another important strategy for students to work on is explicitly connecting their different representations. Here are some sample questions that you can adapt to different problem situations. You can even ask your youngest students these questions to draw their attention to the details of their mathematical representations:

> I see two yellow counters. How did you know you needed two yellow counters?
>
> There is a five in your number sentence. Can you tell me where the five is in the problem?
>
> There are five bears on your paper. Where are the five bears in your drawing?
>
> You wrote a four here. Could you tell me what that four means?
>
> Where else do you see a quantity of eight on your paper?
>
> If I drew a picture of your thinking, how many apples would I start with?
>
> I saw you add three to that pile. Could you tell me why you added three?
>
> If the rabbit ate two carrots, what would that look like in a number sentence? In a picture?

Mathematical comprehension occurs when students can see and understand the problem situation from a mathematical perspective. Students who comprehend the mathematics of a situation can make a connection between what is happening in the problem and a mathematical operation. They see the important elements of the problem and the relationship among those elements. We call this *operation sense*.

TEACHING STUDENTS TO USE CONCRETE AND PICTORIAL MODELS

In the previous section we shared two pictorial representations, one object based and the other a number line diagram. These are representations that one can reasonably expect students in grades 1 and 2 to start learning to use meaningfully. Moving from more literal pictures (portraits of family members or detailed sketches of base 10 blocks, for example) to using diagrams like rods and dots that represent base 10 blocks or number lines is a process, and exposure to this process and experience with it are the best strategies for building student competence using these models of problem situations (Gutstein & Romberg, 1995).

Why are diagrams necessary? First, diagrams help students record what they understand about the elements of a problem and the relationships between the quantities in it. Students may already understand the relationship, but putting it down on paper or capturing it in a set of objects reflects their own thinking back at them. Think of these visuals as placeholders for their thinking.

They can stop to think and look back at their visuals as a reminder of where their thought process started. Second, using a diagram may help students start to sort out the different relationships and actions inherent in the problem situations. Perhaps they might not otherwise recognize that an Add-To or Take-From problem situation implies that action takes place. Finally, deep mathematical understanding comes when students are comfortable using all five forms of representations we explored here: concrete, pictorial, verbal, contextual, and symbolic. This is the thinking behind the problem-solving model we offer here and, in particular, the role of the mathematizing sandbox. Learning to create diagrams is an important component of generating visual representations of the elements and relationships in a problem. Translating among all five forms of representations defines deeper understanding.

How many forms of visual representation should students know how to create? Some teachers may think that limiting the variety of models we ask students to learn is the best strategy. Others would prefer to offer students an open smorgasbord of models and allow students to make their own choices. Still others believe that we should offer no guidance on selecting models but instead make materials available. The strongest evidence supports offering students a variety of tools and allowing them to make their own choices, but with some guidance (Leinwand et al., 2014). In general, we recommend the approach illustrated in Figure 2.19 when supporting students as they express their mathematical thinking using multiple representations, particularly concrete and pictorial representations.

FIGURE 2.19 ENCOURAGING MULTIPLE MODELS IN PROBLEM SOLVING

1. **Choose:** Encourage individual choice of pictorial representations.

2. **Explain:** Ask students to explain what the parts of their pictorial representation mean and to explain the relationships between those parts.

3. **Justify:** Challenge students to defend their choices. Challenge students' correct representations just as much as you would ask them to justify incorrect representations.

4. **Model:** Explicitly model new forms of diagrams or manipulatives that you choose to use, explaining your decisions as you demonstrate how you are using the tool. Note that we are *not* suggesting you explicitly teach students to use the tool. Simply, model your own thinking process as you employ a visual, but reinforce to students that you are held to the same standard for justifying your decisions as they are.

5. **Connect:** Ask students to describe how two representations or models relate to each other. Encourage them to identify how each element of the problem appears in each model. Ask them to explain when they might prefer one model or representation over another.

6. **Share:** Ask students to explain a novel visual approach to their peers and discuss how they model their thinking process.

7. **Expect:** Communicate that you expect to see visual diagrams or manipulatives used to explain mathematical ideas.

8. **Crash:** No representation works in every context or situation. Expect any model to fail at some point, and encourage students to change their representation when the model crashes.

We recognize that students in grade 2 start to work with whole-number values up to, and perhaps beyond, 100, but we recommend following our example in this chapter and using smaller, easier-to-manipulate numbers when introducing students to exploration of the connectedness among mathematical representations. Evidence indicates that when faced with more challenging numbers, students resort to "number plucking and plugging," grabbing numbers and applying randomly chosen operations to them (SanGiovanni, 2020). Expect this and start with numbers and calculations that are just beyond students' known facts and work your way into the grade-appropriate quantities.

KEY IDEAS

1. Five key principles describe counting proficiency: one-to-one correspondence, stable order, cardinality, abstraction, and order irrelevance.

2. If students are not yet proficient counters, assessing their understanding of addition and subtraction problem situations may be complicated, because counting errors could easily be mistaken as calculation errors.

3. Ideally students should grasp the principles of counting before they move into addition and subtraction. However, even if their counting is not yet in place, they may still learn about joining sets.

4. Some aspects of counting collections are conceptual and some are procedural.

5. Counting a collection and adding (joining) two numbers do not involve exactly the same skills.

6. Add-To and Take-From problem situations reflect actions.

7. Add-To and Take-From problem situations follow a common structure where there is a starting value (the beginning of the story), a change, and a result (the end of the story). Any one of the three parts of the problem may be the missing value.

8. An action problem situation can and should be retold in the student's own words. This mathematical story simplifies the details of the problem and focuses on the action.

9. During problem-solving lessons, the focus of learning should be on accurately reflecting the actions or relationships in the problem rather than on computation strategies.

10. When focusing on the meaning of word problems, students should focus on creating concrete or visual (often pictorial), verbal, and symbolic representations that closely match the action (or story) in the problem situation.

11. Diagrams are an abstracted version of a pictorial representation.

TRY IT OUT!

IDENTIFY THE PRINCIPLE

Decide for one week (or even just a day) to listen to your students, or other young children, count. As you watch students, listen for evidence of each principle, or evidence that the principle is not yet in place. With parents' permission, video-record the counting action and later share it with your team. For each of the five principles of counting, talk about what evidence you saw (or didn't see):

1. One-to-one correspondence principle
2. Stable order principle
3. Cardinality principle
4. Abstraction principle
5. Order irrelevance principle

WRITE THE PROBLEM

Read the word problem, and then for each student work sample, discuss whether it is an example of counting or of joining two sets. Explain why.

1. 5 penguins were catching fish. 9 more penguins joined them. How many penguins are catching fish now?

   a.

   It's 14 coze i conted forwdword, and stopd at 14 and that's how i got 19.

   [It's 14 because I counted forward by 1s and stopped at 14. That's how I got 14.]

   b.

(continued)

(continued)

2. Megan drew pictures of 11 friends. Sarah drew pictures of 7 more friends. How many friends did they draw together?

a.

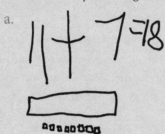

b.

For each student work sample (in problems 1 and 2), discuss whether it represents a solution for the problem, an answer to the problem, or both. Remember, a solution is a completed shared approach or strategy for the problem. It may or may not include an answer. The answer includes only the answer to the question asked in the problem and alone does not explain the student's thinking. Explain why you think one response is a solution and why one is an answer.

CHANGE IT UP

Use the table below to explore representations of the word problem that appears in the "Contextual" row.

REPRESENTATION	EXAMPLE
Contextual	Rosa collected 73 pine cones at the park. She gave 28 of them to her sister. How many pine cones does she have now?
Pictorial	
Concrete	

REPRESENTATION	EXAMPLE
Verbal	
Symbolic (Equation)	

When you have at least one representation in each row, connect one representation to another. For example, a translation might be to show 73 two-color counters, which is the same 73 we can see in the word problem. Make at least three translations:

1.

2.

3.

1. As a team, discuss strategies you use to strengthen students' counting skills while they are learning about addition and subtraction.

2. Now that you have had a chance to think about the difference between counting a set (counting) and joining two sets (addition), talk about what you can do to help students better understand this big idea of addition: How do you find a balance between efficiency in computation and a deep understanding of the meaning of addition?

3. With your team, share one thing that has changed about your understanding of young children's mathematical thinking. How will that influence your instruction?

CHAPTER THREE

Add-To Problems
Locating the Change

Thinking About Active Addition Situations

In this chapter we explore more deeply the active Add-To problem situations introduced in Chapter 2. As we saw in Chapter 2, the Add-To problem situation is one of two active situations, a designation that will become more meaningful to you in the next few chapters and then when we contrast active problem types with those that show relationships. Each of the active problem situations has one of three elements unknown: Result Unknown, Change Addend Unknown, or Start Addend Unknown. In this chapter we will turn our focus to understanding problems with either the change or the start unknown. Let's get started!

Addition and Subtraction Problem Situations

	Result Unknown	Change Addend Unknown	Start Addend Unknown	
Add-To	Paulo counted 9 crayons. He put them in the basket. Paulo found 6 more crayons under the table. He put them in the basket. How many crayons are in the basket? $9 + 6 = x$ $6 = x - 9$	Paulo counted 9 crayons. He found more and put them in the basket. Now Paulo has 15 crayons. How many crayons did he put in the basket? $9 + x = 15$ $9 = 15 - x$	Paulo had some crayons. He found 6 more crayons under the table. Now he has 15 crayons. How many crayons did Paulo have in the beginning? $x + 6 = 15$ $15 - 6 = x$	

ACTIVE SITUATIONS

	Result Unknown	Change Addend Unknown	Start Addend Unknown	
Add-To	Paulo counted 9 crayons. He put them in the basket. Paulo found 6 more crayons under the table. He put them in the basket. How many crayons are in the basket? $9 + 6 = x$ $6 = x - 9$	Paulo counted 9 crayons. He found more and put them in the basket. Now Paulo has 15 crayons. How many crayons did he put in the basket? $9 + x = 15$ $9 = 15 - x$	Paulo had some crayons. He found 6 more crayons under the table. Now he has 15 crayons. How many crayons did Paulo have in the beginning? $x + 6 = 15$ $15 - 6 = x$	
Take-From	There are 19 students in Mrs. Amadi's class. 4 students went to the office to say the Pledge. How many students are in the class now? $19 - 4 = x$ $4 + x = 19$	There are 19 students in Mrs. Amadi's class. Some students went to class to read the Pledge. There were still 15 students in the classroom. How many students went to the office? $19 - x = 15$ $x + 15 = 19$	4 students went to the office. 15 students were still in the classroom. How many students are there in Mrs. Amadi's class? $x - 4 = 15$ $15 + 4 = x$	

RELATIONSHIP (NONACTIVE) SITUATIONS

	Total Unknown	One Part Unknown	Both Parts Unknown
Part-Part-Whole	The first grade voted on a game for recess. 11 students voted to play four square. 8 voted to go to the playground. How many students are in the class? $8 + 11 = x$ $x - 11 = 8$	The 19 first graders voted on a recess activity. 8 students voted to go to the playground. How many wanted to play four square? $8 + x = 19$ $x = 19 - 8$	The 19 first graders voted on a recess activity. Some wanted to play four square. Some wanted to go to the playground. What are some ways the first graders could have voted? $x + y = 19$ $19 - x = y$
	Difference Unknown	Greater Quantity Unknown	Lesser Quantity Unknown
Additive Comparison	Jessie's paper airplane flew 14 feet. Jo's paper airplane flew 9 feet. How much less did Jo's paper airplane fly than Jessie's? $14 - 9 = x$ $9 + x = 14$	Jo's paper airplane flew 9 feet. Jessie's paper airplane flew 5 feet more than Jo's. How far did Jessie's paper airplane fly? $9 + 5 = x$ $x - 5 = 9$	Jessie's paper airplane flew 14 feet. Jo's paper airplane flew 5 feet less than Jessie's paper airplane. How far did Jo's paper airplane fly? $14 - 5 = x$ $14 = x + 5$

Note: The representations for the problem situations in this table reflect our understanding based on a number of resources. These include the tables in the Common Core State Standards for Mathematics (CCSS-M; National Governors Association Center for Best Practices and Council of Chief State School Officers, 2010), the problem situations as described in the Cognitively Guided Instruction research (Carpenter, Hiebert, & Moser, 1981), and other tools. See the Appendix and the book's companion website for a more detailed summary of the documents that informed our development of this table.

online resources — Visit **http://resources.corwin.com/problemsolvingk-2** to download a copy of the full Addition and Subtraction Problem Situations Table.

Sandbox Notes: Explore Your Thinking

As you enter into problem exploration mode, gather your tools, including markers or crayons, base 10 blocks, linking cubes, counters, and any other tools that you routinely have available in your classroom. Try several of the concrete manipulatives and some hand-drawn picture models that reflect the mathematical story in the word problem. If you put the problem in your own words, revisit that rephrasing and specify where you can see each quantity in the problem. Where can you see each quantity in the models you have created? Think about how your work can express your understanding of the problem situation.

Ask yourself these questions to focus your thinking:

- Think about the quantities in each situation. What do they represent? What action is taking place between the quantities in the problem?

- How can you represent the quantities in the word problems with your manipulatives or pictures?

- How can you make a number sentence about the problem?

To begin, read the problems in Figures 3.1 and 3.2. Don't try to solve them just yet. Instead, put yourself in the place of your students, and as you enter each problem, focus on understanding the words in each one. Try using your own words to rephrase, without focusing on the quantities. If this is difficult, substitute the quantities with the word *some*. This will help you avoid jumping to the answer using known facts before you fully explore the problem.

FIGURE 3.1

FIGURE 3.2

There were 3 soccer players at practice. 8 more came. How many players practiced soccer?	Maria had 3 cookies on her plate. Her mother gave her more cookies. Then she had 11 cookies. How many cookies did her mother give her?

ENTER THE PROBLEM

FIGURE 3.3 A MODEL FOR MATHEMATIZING WORD PROBLEMS

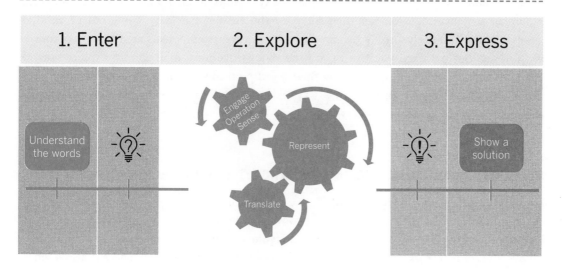

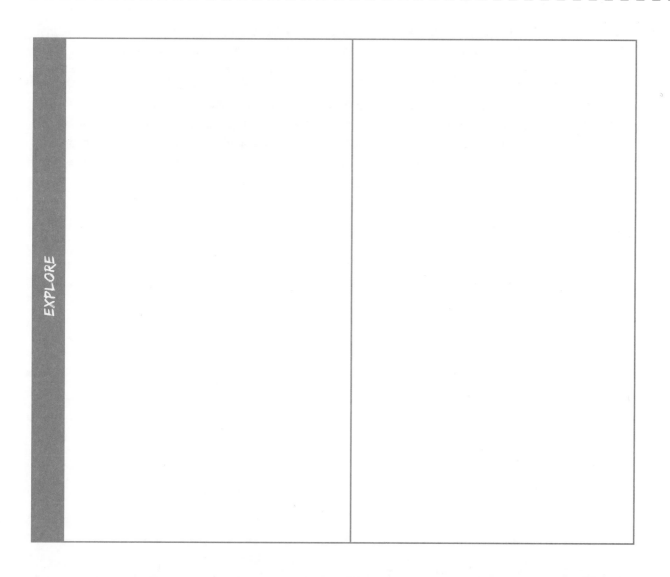

EXPLORE

You have taken another trip to the mathematizing sandbox. You've translated the story of each problem into your own words and explored several different concrete, pictorial, and symbolic representations of the problem situations. You may have translated your representations into a number sentence that you can then solve, or the answer may have come out of another representation. You likely already had an answer because these problems are based on a known fact for you, but we asked you to suspend that knowledge for a moment. To explore how to build operation sense while approaching these word problems, we have to consider them from the young student's point of view, in a way that reflects deep understanding rather than an overreliance on computation or known facts.

STUDENTS AND TEACHERS THINK ABOUT THE PROBLEMS

Look at the student work in Figures 3.4 and 3.5 on the facing page and consider how these students describe or draw what is happening in the two word problems. The soccer problem is shown in Figure 3.4, and the cookie problem is shown in Figure 3.5. Look at the teacher commentary that follows the student work and consider what the teacher noticed about it. There is also a video available showing each student's solution to the problem, which you may want to watch once you have read through the student work and teacher comments.

What do you notice? Did you notice that there is action in both of these problems? The first problem started with some soccer players and then more came to practice. In the second, Maria has cookies on her plate and her mom gives her more. These actions of *adding* more players to the team or *giving* cookies signal joining two sets into one set. Both of these problems are examples of an Add-To situation, introduced in Chapter 2. In the soccer problem, we know that 3 players were there at first and that 8 players joined, but we don't know how many were there afterward. In the cookie problem, we know the start and the result, but we do not know the change that happened in the story. The story starts with 3 cookies, some are added, and the result is a total of 11 cookies.

FIGURE 3.4	FIGURE 3.5

| | STUDENT WORK | |

8 cookies |
|---|---|---|

| TEACHER RESPONSE | I can see that this is an addition problem because in her solution she modeled the two groups and then combined them using the arrow. But then again, I do not see an answer. Unfortunately, she hasn't said how many players there are, either. | I thought of this as subtraction because that's how I would get the answer. Like this:

$11 - 3 = ?$

But I can see that this doesn't make sense in the problem situation because the mom is adding cookies, not taking them away!

I know it's an Add-To problem situation, and her work kind of shows that with the two sets of cookies. She's made me wonder whether it might make more sense to write an addition equation instead of subtraction. Maybe like this:

"Three plus some more makes eleven."

$3 + ? = 11$

I hadn't thought of that before! Interesting! Maybe I should ask students to write equations to match their solutions to see what they are thinking. |
|---|---|---|

| VIDEO | **Video 3.1**

Soccer Players With a Picture

resources.corwin.com/ problemsolvingk-2 | **Video 3.2**

Cookies With a Picture and Bar Model

resources.corwin.com/ problemsolvingk-2 |
|---|---|---|

The soccer problem solution shown in Figure 3.4 is like those we saw in Chapter 2. It is an Add-To problem situation, with the Result Unknown. Result Unknown problem situations are the most common variety, so they are often the first variation of a problem type that students can understand and model. In this case, the student has drawn the correct number of players for the problem situation and she has distinguished one addend from the other $(3+8)$ using stick figures. You might notice, though, as the teacher did, that even though the student's solution as seen in her representation is correct and clear, there is no answer given! We can say that the solution is a model or a demonstration of the student's thinking to arrive at an answer. Sometimes we see students' thinking and recognize their solution strategies but then note that they don't follow up with an answer. Sometimes we see the opposite. Students may share an answer but not indicate in any way how they approached the problem or how they modeled it. In other words, they shared an answer but not a solution. Both the answer and the solution are important indicators of students' current understanding.

The student work in Figure 3.5 shows a line separating 3 cookies and 8 cookies in the drawing, which means the student recognizes that two sets of cookies make up the total of 11 cookies. She has also created a bar model to show the full quantity of 11 cookies. However, the student's representation does not tell us how she found the quantity of 8. Recall that the change was the missing part of this problem situation, and at no point in her solution do we see how she figured that out. She may have counted on from 3, up to 11. She may have known the number fact $3+8=11$ and used that knowledge to find 8. She may have drawn cookies through trial and error, adding one more cookie at a time, counting them all, and finally getting the answer of 8 after many trials. Consider the different thinking processes that lie beneath each of these very different solution strategies! Having the same correct answer of 8 does not necessarily mean that students have the same depth of understanding. What would you ask this student so that you can understand how she arrived at an answer of 8? How does her answer change your assessment of her current understanding of solving a problem like this one?

The teacher, by contrast, definitely expected a subtraction equation for the cookie problem and had to think hard about how to represent the situation with an addition equation. So why would she choose subtraction if it doesn't match the Add-To problem situation? The teacher adopted an efficient calculation strategy to solve the Change Unknown problem, one she is likely familiar with because of her own school math experiences. Your students will learn to do that as well, but in the meantime they should try to find solutions in different ways.

Remember that the focus of this book is on understanding operations when they are directly tied to the problem situation. Some students will notice right away that it takes less time to subtract than it does to count up, and we should certainly share that strategy with the class, but recognize that it is a computation strategy. Recall that a computation strategy is an important mathematical topic and focus for instruction, but it isn't the focus here. Computation is concerned with finding an answer, but in the mathematizing sandbox we are exploring many solutions that help us understand the actions in the problem. We are asking how the addition or subtraction operations can best represent those actions, and that turns our attention to *how* the student figured out that the change was 8 cookies.

If students do not have a lot of experience with Change Unknown problems, both students and their teachers may consider them to be "tricky" problems. A common mistake is one that we see in Figure 3.6, in response to the cookie problem.

FIGURE 3.6 A CONTEXT-RELATED ERROR

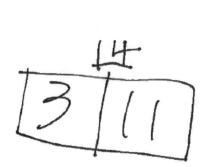

I cawtid
on the Mhradr
grid I Stoid
at 3 I Cawtid
u9 11

[I counted on the number grid.
I started at 3. I counted up 11.]

The student started at 3 and counted up on the number grid, but instead of *counting on until* 11, she *counts on* 11 squares on the number grid, arriving at 14. She did $3+11=?$ instead of $3+?=11$. Rather than considering this to be a calculation error, we can more correctly interpret it as a context-related error. One study of students' problem solving found that 47 percent of word problem errors occurred before any sort of calculation process had taken place (Newman, 1977, as cited in Watson, 1980). This tells us that 14 is wrong not because the student cannot compute a correct answer (she did). Instead, the answer 14 was the right answer to the wrong question. It was a question about a different problem situation.

What questions about the story in the problem could we ask this student? How might we use her understanding of a number grid to help her make sense of the situation? Perhaps you could pair this student with another student who is interpreting the problem situation correctly but still has an incorrect answer. The student whose work is represented in Figure 3.7 might be a good partner. Look at his work and make sense of his thinking.

FIGURE 3.7 A COUNTING OR CALCULATION ERROR

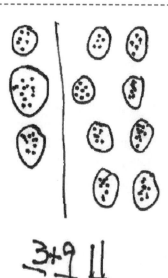

9 cookies

The student has recognized the cookie problem as an addition problem, has accurately represented 3 cookies to start, and has ended with 11 cookies, just as the problem situation describes. Unfortunately, he has a counting or calculation error, even though he drew the correct number of cookies. By pairing these two students to discuss their solutions, the two might arrive at a working strategy as well as a correct answer.

As we continue to explore the nature of Add-To and Take-From problem situations in this chapter, we will continue to pay attention to the distinction we introduced in Chapter 2, between the computation used to get an answer and the operation that matches the problem situation. Along the way, you may find that you look differently at student work.

FINDING THE UNKNOWN: THREE STORY STRUCTURES

As we alluded to in Chapter 2, active mathematical stories, like the Add-To situations we just saw, have a narrative structure—a beginning, a middle, and an end, just like a story does. In the beginning there is a starting value. How many crayons does Paulo have to start with? How many cookies were on the plate? How much money was in the bank account? The middle of the story brings a change in quantity: More crayons are acquired. More cookies are baked. The child earns money. And the end of the story is the result of the change: the final number of crayons in the basket, cookies on the plate, money in the bank. In most word problems, only one of these three quantities is unknown. Thus, as the table at the beginning of the chapter indicates, the unknown in an active problem situation could be the start, the change, or the result, reflecting the arc of your storyline. Identifying the unknown—in other words, finding the information we need to know—is the first step in problem solving.

RESULT UNKNOWN The Result Unknown variation of the active problem situation is likely the first one students will master (McCallum, Daro, & Zimba, n.d.). Because the starting value and the change value are known, this is the most straightforward version for young learners to act out. For example, if the action shows a quantity being added, the operation is going to be addition. The soccer problem from Figure 3.1 is an example of an Add-To, Result Unknown problem situation. Below you can see that the first line is the mathematical story, the words that distill the action into its simplest form, and the second line is an equation that represents the problem situation, as it is described in the problem itself:

3 players plus 8 more players makes *how many* players?

$$3 + 8 = ?$$

CHANGE UNKNOWN The next variation that students explore is Change Unknown, which students are often expected to become fluent with by the end of first grade. In this case, we know the beginning and the end of the story (the starting and resulting values) and have to figure out what happened in the middle—what change led from the start to the result? The cookie problem that opened this chapter (Figure 3.2) is typical of what we might expect first graders to be able to make sense of, with modeling and with practice. We can write a mathematical story and a matching equation for the cookie problem situation:

3 cookies plus *how many more* cookies makes 11 cookies?

$$3 + ? = 11$$

START UNKNOWN The Start Unknown variation is the most challenging for students. In this case, the action works backward from the end of the story, through the change, to figure out the starting value. This requires a different kind of reasoning, and students are not expected to be fluent with this final variation (with grade-appropriate values) before the end of second grade. Here is the problem about Maria and the cookies rewritten as a Start Unknown problem situation:

Maria had some cookies on her plate. Her mother gave her 8 more cookies.
Now there are 11 cookies. How many cookies were on the plate at the beginning?

How many cookies plus 8 more cookies make 11 cookies?

$$? + 8 = 11$$

Consider how you might create a model of this variation of the problem. How is it different from the original?

It might be tempting to present the variations of problem types in the order in which they were just described—for example, avoiding the Start Unknown variation in the early primary years—but that is not the best strategy. Students should see a variety of all of the problem types and keep their focus on understanding and mathematizing problem situations. The grade-level timeline is suggested in the Common Core progressions documents (McCallum et al., n.d.), but it refers to the year in which students might become fluent recognizing and understanding each problem structure, not when they should start learning them. Start early, but recognize that some variations pose more challenges than others.

STORY STRUCTURES: IMPLICATIONS FOR TEACHING

When we ask teachers to compose Add-To word problems, we find that almost 75 percent of the ones they create are of the Result Unknown variation. No wonder Change Unknown or Start Unknown problems sometimes feel like trick questions to teachers and students! Without being aware of it, we may be ignoring these kinds of problems, to students' detriment. Skipping these variations limits students' ability not only to grasp the dynamics of these stories but also to transfer their thinking to other problem situations. As you'll see in the examples that follow, it is easy to adjust a problem from one variation to another, and it is critically important to make sure that students have experience with all three variations. Then they will be better prepared to recognize Add-To situations in any form. People who work with these problem types in many settings with children recommend that all students see examples of all of the variations of the problem types, even those that are more challenging (Franke, 2018).

To help with your planning, use the chart in Figure 3.8 to list some Add-To action situations that will be familiar to your students. As you read the list, visualize the story and focus less on the quantities and more on the setting and the action. Imagine yourself in that setting and consider what story you or your students could craft that matches each prompt in the table. The first few have been done for you.

Asking students to come up with their own word problems while leaving the quantities blank can be an effective strategy for helping them consider the structure of the story within the problem without the added complication of coming up with an answer. Posing their own problems helps students realize that math isn't just about numbers and values. It is about solving problems, whether they are problems in textbooks, or on tests, or real-life problems that matter to them.

One way to start is by introducing students to a context or setting that interests them or, better yet, to let the events in your classroom, school, or community serve as the setting for the story, but keep the emphasis on quantities they can count or measure. Students this age love to create stories. Our job is to help them mathematize what they create. Once students are comfortable with creating stories, you can move to developing stories that are built around quantities. One strategy for encouraging this is to ask students to add quantities to a story one at a time. Observe a starting quantity (a value and unit) in your classroom and ask students to tell a number story beginning with that quantity in its context. Your students are mathematizing here; they are seeing the world around them in mathematical terms. As students become more comfortable with this process, they will probably become more inventive.

FIGURE 3.8 ADD-TO ACTION SITUATIONS

CONTEXT	START (Beginning Value)	CHANGE (Action in the Story)	RESULT (Ending Value)
Soccer game	Points on the board	Points are earned	Final score
Party food	Sandwiches on the plate	More sandwiches are made	Sandwiches on the plate
Shopping	Books on the bookshelf	Books are bought	Books on the bookshelf
Winning a contest	Pets in the house	Some goldfish are won	Pets in the house
Trading cards			
		A baby is born	
			Dirty cups in the sink
	Movies you've seen		

MODELING THE ACTIVE PROBLEM SITUATION

Ungrouped counters: Objects that represent an individual or single unit with a quantity of one.

Grouped counters: Objects that represent units that are grouped together, such as a base 10 rod.

One of the things we know about mathematics is that there is always more than one way to approach a problem. Students can benefit from using concrete and pictorial models where they can show the action unfold in an active problem situation. The model they use can involve ungrouped or grouped counters used to act out a problem situation, or it can be a number line that uses arrows or other marks to show action.

Reread the problem in Figure 3.9 carefully. Use the space below to put the story into your own words and show your representation of the action in the problem. Then continue reading to see how students modeled the problem.

FIGURE 3.9

Tarun grows flowers in his yard. On Monday he picked 6 flowers. He put them in a vase. On Tuesday he picked 3 more flowers and put them in the vase. How many flowers did he put in the vase altogether?

Because the stories in Add-To problem situations are active, the most effective way to represent them is to act them out with counters or other manipulatives. Despite this, students sometimes need to represent their thinking only with pictures. Since these are Add-To action problems, there is still a need to show the joining of two sets: How can this be done?

YOUR WORKSPACE

We saw a student use an arrow in the soccer problem in Figure 3.4. As you look at the student work in Figures 3.10 and 3.11, consider how each student showed the quantities, and how they showed the action in their solutions.

FIGURE 3.10   **FIGURE 3.11**

STUDENT WORK

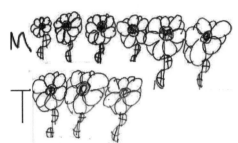

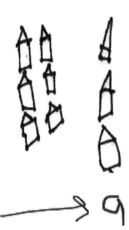

Weyost aro fegrs
and stortid with 6 fgrs and
tatid up 3 and landid ot 9

[We used our fingers and started with 6 fingers and
counted up 3 and landed at 9.]

TEACHER RESPONSE

Marianna had been working for a long time on this problem, even after her group had discussed a solution, so I went over to check on her progress. It didn't surprise me to see that she had made such elaborate drawings–it's her favorite thing to do, after all. But I did wonder how I could I encourage her to take less time on the creativity because it seems to distract her from the mathematical thinking.

Then, I wondered if that was the right thing to do because her verbal response was perfectly appropriate. I would hate to stifle her creativity!

I think I need some guidance on this.

Luis and Marianna were in the same group, but you'd never know it by looking at their drawings! Luis's flowers are not recognizable as flowers, but I appreciate the mathematical information he communicated with his other markings. The line between the 6 flowers and the 3 flowers leads me to believe that he is joining sets. I have never seen an arrow show the joining, but why not?

In the end I think it is good that he has started to abstract his quantities and represent them visually rather than as literal pictures.

VIDEO

Video 3.3

Flowers With Literal Sketches

resources.corwin.com/
problemsolvingk-2

Video 3.4

Flowers With Abstract Sketches

resources.corwin.com/
problemsolvingk-2

One of the things we know about mathematics is that there is always more than one way to approach a problem, but it isn't possible to watch every student produce a solution to every problem as they work. Teaching students strategies to represent the actions in their pictorial representations gives you a better view of their thinking process. The following sections offer some ideas to think about as you help students make more productive visual representations.

MODEL ACTIONS Students can use a variety of concrete models where they can show the action unfold in an active problem situation. It is more challenging to show the same joining action with a pictorial model, but students can learn to communicate their understanding using marks on the page. Marianna's work on the flower problem, shown in Figure 3.10, describes how she used her fingers to represent the first set of flowers, and then counted on the quantity in the second set. The solution not only shows two separate sets, but it also shows that she joined two sets to find the result. Luis, whose work is shown in Figure 3.11, drew a line that separated the 6 flowers picked on Monday from the 3 flowers picked on Tuesday. The arrow may be a way to show action, moving toward the result of 9, as the teacher noted.

One way to make students' thinking more visible in their written work, particularly with problems that represent action happening, is to point out when they apply useful marks themselves. Here we saw an arrow being used to show action. Another student made a reference to counting on her fingers, taking us into her own model of the solution. There are many more techniques, like looping a set of counters, showing a stick figure running, and more. Keep your eye out for strategies your students use and feature them in class discussions to encourage other students.

DISTINGUISH PICTURES FROM PICTORIAL REPRESENTATIONS To ask young students to tell a story or to represent their work pictorially invites potential complications. Children are intensely creative and they have many thoughts on their mind. They can easily become distracted by the creative or artistic potential of representing a problem situation. Even a question as simple as "Do you have flowers in the yard at your house?" can unleash a delightful, but unfocused circle-time discussion. The same is true when students are invited to share their interpretations of problem situations. Marianna's work, shown in Figure 3.10, involves intricate and detailed drawings to describe Tarun's flowers. All of this artistic detail, while interesting, does not contribute to the mathematical understanding of the problem situation. As a matter of fact, drawings this elaborate can take attention away from the mathematical action in the problem. By contrast, Luis's work, shown in Figure 3.11, depicts shapes that are not like flowers at all.

We suggest that you recognize literal representations of the quantities in a problem situation as a highly appropriate step in children's problem-solving learning. After all, it means they are visualizing details of the problem, and they may be more likely to share their interpretation of the mathematical story being told. That doesn't mean that students should be just as literal and detailed in their drawings every time. Devote a math class meeting to discussing what parts of a drawing are necessary. Display an example of a detailed drawing, a simpler drawing, and another representation made with a simple mark like a circle, and ask students to identify the important information that connects all three representations. For example, in the flower problem, they should identify 6 objects, 3 objects, and an action that joins them to make 9 objects. Are the stems important? No. Are the petals of the flower important? No. Is it important that there are 9 flowers? Yes. You can acknowledge and honor student creativity but still focus attention on the critically important mathematical structure of their representations by featuring it in discussions.

IDENTIFY IMPORTANT FEATURES As you've seen in some of the examples so far, another way you might encourage students to focus on the mathematical features of their representations is with manipulatives or other physical objects. Recall that students achieve the abstraction principle of counting when they can recognize numerosity as an attribute of a set. In this problem, we might ask students to share the many ways the class showed the quantities of 6 flowers, 3 flowers, and 9 flowers, so that they can recognize the attribute that ties each solution together. Figure 3.12 shows some examples that might lead to productive discourse in your classroom.

FIGURE 3.12   REPRESENTING NUMEROSITY WITH MANIPULATIVES

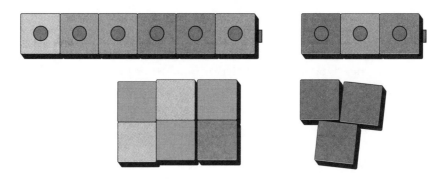

CREATIVELY MEET STUDENTS' NEEDS Some students—especially those still developing fine motor skills—may be reluctant to write or draw their responses. Give those students an opportunity to use manipulatives to show their problem and use a camera or video to record their actions. If you need to capture this work for student portfolios or to send it home to parents, there are apps that can translate video footage into single images, which can be printed. Technology changes rapidly, so we will not recommend a specific product, but search "video create a stop motion clip" for the most current options for an app that you can use. If students simply do not want to draw a representation, be aware that their resistance may reflect the fact that they are uncertain about how to do it. If this is the case, return to the most basic and primitive problem-solving strategy: Act it out.

The benefit of these strategies relates to our discussion of translation in Chapter 2. Helping students translate fluently among the different representations of acting out, building, drawing, or writing as part of their problem-solving process is not only a way to record and reflect back their thinking, but it also sharpens their understanding of what might otherwise seem like disconnected pieces of knowledge. This is what students do in a playground sandbox: They experiment and refine their skills as they play. Learning to solve problems is what happens in the mathematizing sandbox.

Using Children's Literature to Explore Add-To Situations

One way to engage students with the actions in problem situations is to find them in the books they love. One beloved book is *So Many Cats* (De Regniers, 1985). In this book, a family has a single, lonely cat but somehow ends up with a dozen cats by the end of the book. Based on just this synopsis, what mathematical ideas come to you right away?

In this chapter we are addressing Start Unknown and Change Unknown problem situations: The narrative of *So Many Cats* is a real-life example of the Change Unknown variety because at the beginning of the book the family starts with 1 cat and it is a mystery how they finish the book with 12 cats. In the sections that follow, we suggest two ways that you might use this story to introduce a mathematics lesson on problem situations.

MAKE PREDICTIONS

Examine the front cover of the book and ask students how many cats there are (12 cats). Surely some students will share how many cats they have, and you can use this information to ask how many is too many cats? Would one cat be happy living alone? Open to the first page to read:

"We have sister cats
and brother cats,
father cats
and mother cats.
How come we have a dozen cats?
Here's how:"

We want to encourage students to think about relating what happens in this story to the problem situations, in this case, an Add-To, Change Unknown problem situation. First, we can establish that the family didn't always have 12 cats. Students may not recognize that this stanza implies that the family has not always had a dozen cats. Establish that this fact is the result, or the end, of the story. You may choose to use chart paper or the board to record 12 as the end of the story. Read the next page.

"We had a cat—
An Only Cat.
She was a sad and lonely cat."

Again, it is important to use discussion to help students describe the sequence of this story. At the start, or the beginning, the family had only one cat. Now you are free to highlight what unknown change took place that led to the family having 12 cats. Ask students to predict ways that a family might come to take in more cats. Transcribe their numerical predictions into a verbal number story or an equation depending on your students' comfort with equations. Afterward, read the rest of the story first for pleasure and for its literary value. Then read the story again to transcribe what happened in the story into a mathematical story.

TRANSCRIBE THE ACTION OR RELATIONSHIP

After you read the book for the pleasure of reading the story, discuss the sequence of the story—when did the family have one cat? When did they have a dozen cats? How did they get more cats? Ask any other questions that you normally pose at the end of a story.

Ask students how many more cats the family adopted. Did the cats come all at once? Record "Only Cat" at the top of a piece of chart paper or on the board and then record "A Dozen Cats" at the bottom as a result. You may use words, maybe equations, or even felt cutout cats, but emphasize the empty space where the class will record how the cats are adopted (the change). Begin the second read, asking students to tell you how to add more cats. At the end, the students could have an equation that looks something like this:

Image source: Marina Piskunova/iStock.com

Or you may choose to write the equations this way:

I	Poke
I+I=2	Tammy
2+3=5	Fluffy, Muffy, Smoke
5+I=6	Kitty
6+I=7	Pretty
7+3=I0	Jenny, Penny, Bloke
I0+2=I2	Dawn, Night

Read the book again so that students can check their equations with the story. At certain points in the book, the author counts the cats and reports the current status. This is an opportunity for students to pause and check their own equations and then perhaps ask how many more cats will they adopt.

After reading the book, offer individual practice for students, writing a different sequence of events in the change part of the arc of the story. What other ways could the family have acquired more cats and ended with a dozen cats? After students write the equations, they can share their stories. You may even make separate cards for each event in the sequence of the story and ask students to retell the story in a different order, making a number sentence as they go.

Take some time with your team to share books that you love to read to your students each year. Think about those stories again with a mathematical lens and discuss how you might bring the mathematics out in those books while still enjoying the stories.

Digging Deeper Into Start Unknown Situations

We want to shift gears and explore the Start Unknown variation of Add-To problems more deeply and expand our set of numbers to include values up to 120, to reflect the range within which many second-grade students are expected to work. The numbers in the problems should not affect students' understanding of problem situations, which is our focus in this book. But in our experience, when the computation itself poses challenges, students cannot rely as much on good or quick calculation estimates to get an answer. If they don't have experience modeling quantities or problem situations, in particular, they have little else to fall back on. That's when we are likely to hear, "I don't get what they want me to do!"

The book problem featured in Figure 3.13 is still an Add-To problem situation. When you solve it, pull out a set of manipulatives that are available to you and think about other types of drawings, diagrams, and pictorial images you might use to capture the action in these problem situations. We will share different manipulative models, some of which you may not currently have access to. You may find that you have good substitutes, or you may find a "must-have" tool for next year's supply list.

Warning: The next pages include student examples of some new problem situations. If you find it difficult to resist looking forward while practicing in the sandbox on page 58, consider covering the facing page with a sheet of paper.

As you pause before entering the mathematizing sandbox, think about how you can use the manipulatives to focus student attention on the actions taking place in the problem. Act out the problems. Anticipate challenges students might encounter. For example, it's tempting to worry right away about whether regrouping is involved, which is something we do when *computing* an answer to this problem. Instead, focus first on the *context* of the problems and how the manipulative model chosen supports students' understanding of what happens in the problem.

If you aren't sure, revisit the Sandbox Notes at the beginning of the chapter for guiding questions and other suggestions.

Before we look closely at how the students modeled this problem, read through it carefully, putting the story in your own words. Note which quantity is missing: the start, the change, or the result.

FIGURE 3.13

There were some books on our class bookshelf. Then our class won a set of 63 books in the reading contest. Now there are 114 books on the bookshelf. How many books did our class have before the contest?

YOUR WORKSPACE

$$? + 63 = 114$$

COMPLICATING THINGS: THE START UNKNOWN VARIATION

Before we consider the work of two students, let's take a moment to identify the problem situation and problem structure. As we noted early on, the Start Unknown variation of an active problem type is the last variation with which students are expected to develop fluency. Now that you have read and worked on the problem yourself, think about the challenges that Start Unknown problems present, but also think about how retelling the stories in our own words, creating matching models, and acting out the problems can contribute to student sense-making. Because the Start Unknown variation can be challenging, we will present several strategies that can help students to find working strategies for this problem situation:

- Model the action
- Try a simpler case
- Don't start at the beginning

The student work in Figures 3.14 and 3.15, and the accompanying teacher responses, explore a variety of models students might produce to reflect the action in an Add-To problem situation.

FIGURE 3.14

FIGURE 3.15

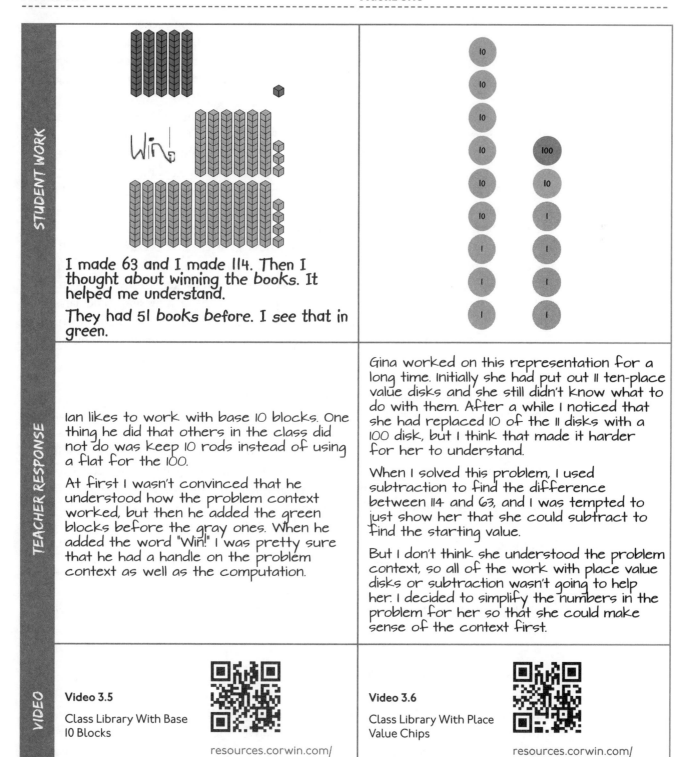

STUDENT WORK

Figure 3.14:

I made 63 and I made 114. Then I thought about winning the books. It helped me understand.

They had 51 books before. I see that in green.

TEACHER RESPONSE

Figure 3.14:

Ian likes to work with base 10 blocks. One thing he did that others in the class did not do was keep 10 rods instead of using a flat for the 100.

At first I wasn't convinced that he understood how the problem context worked, but then he added the green blocks before the gray ones. When he added the word "Win!" I was pretty sure that he had a handle on the problem context as well as the computation.

Figure 3.15:

Gina worked on this representation for a long time. Initially she had put out 11 ten-place value disks and she still didn't know what to do with them. After a while I noticed that she had replaced 10 of the 11 disks with a 100 disk, but I think that made it harder for her to understand.

When I solved this problem, I used subtraction to find the difference between 114 and 63, and I was tempted to just show her that she could subtract to find the starting value.

But I don't think she understood the problem context, so all of the work with place value disks or subtraction wasn't going to help her. I decided to simplify the numbers in the problem for her so that she could make sense of the context first.

VIDEO

Video 3.5

Class Library With Base 10 Blocks

resources.corwin.com/ problemsolvingk-2

Video 3.6

Class Library With Place Value Chips

resources.corwin.com/ problemsolvingk-2

STRATEGIES FOR MAKING SENSE OF START UNKNOWN PROBLEM SITUATIONS

The fact that the quantities in the problem are greater than 100 has no effect on the underlying pattern or structure in the problem situation. We can assure students that these are the same problem situations they have already learned, but we can also use models and manipulatives to make the action more visible. Encourage students to build models and act out the story. It can be difficult to model a Start Unknown story, however, because the beginning quantity is unknown: It's challenging to tell a story when you don't know the beginning of it! That's why students are not expected to be fluent in this particular problem variation until the end of second grade.

MODEL THE ACTION Although the missing start of the story within the problem complicates the process, modeling the action is still a productive strategy for finding the unknown start of a problem. In Figure 3.14, Ian's strategy follows the narrative of the story in the word problem. We know this because he began the problem by modeling the beginning of the story with no blocks present, before counting out the change with 63 green blocks. Modeling the result of 114 books, he was able to visualize the difference between 63 and 114 to figure out that the start value had to be 51 blocks. The teacher's notes tell us that he added the green blocks to the start position at the end of his modeling of the problem. Ian's strategy is effective because he directly acted out what happened in the story. He was fortunate that the quantities involved did not require any regrouping, but it would be interesting to see how that would impact his solution strategy. Although modeling the problem's action is complicated by the missing start value, Ian's work shows us that modeling can still reveal useful information. In challenging problem structures like this one, it is even more important to enter the mathematizing sandbox with tools in hand. Creating models can help students see the mathematical story in the problem.

TRY A SIMPLER CASE Another strategy the teacher considered was to simplify the word problem for Gina (Figure 3.15), who may have been struggling with both the problem situation and the quantities in the problem. As a teacher, she has two choices—she can simplify the quantities or she can simplify the problem structure. Since our goal in this book is to work on understanding the problem situations, we will explore the option of simplifying the quantities instead. Figure 3.16 has the same word problem, rewritten with quantities that are more manageable, but still retaining the Add-To/Start Unknown problem structure.

FIGURE 3.16

There were some books on our class bookshelf. Then our class won a set of 4 books in the reading contest. Now there are 16 books on the bookshelf. How many books did our class have before the contest?

Using the modified problem, Gina and another student, Hannah, worked with the teacher to make sense of this problem with simpler quantities that gave them the opportunity to model the problem. The teacher asked the students to act out the problem situation and offered them a set of snap cubes as a concrete manipulative. She also provided access to premade number lines. In Figures 3.17 and 3.18 you can see the work that students did on the modified word problem.

FIGURE 3.17

FIGURE 3.18

STUDENT WORK

BOOKS 12

I put 4 blocks. I counted more until I made 16.

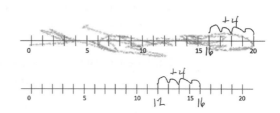

I started with 16 and imagined winning 4 more. Except I didn't start with 16. That was hard. Then I thought about it some more and knew I had to go back 4 but I can't explain.

TEACHER RESPONSE

Hannah had been working hard on translating word problems into bar models, and I was surprised she didn't use a bar model in the original problem! Here, I see that she created a bar model with cubes first, starting with 4 cubes and counting up to 16 before drawing a picture of those cubes. Only after directly representing the cubes did she draw the more abstract bar model. I realize that she still needs time with the physical models, particularly with the Start Unknown variations.

My students have a hard time making number lines. There's a lot involved-lines, intervals, numbering-all before working on the problems. Finally, I decided to make a set of premade number lines for students to use. I cut them into strips and placed them in a basket on the math table. I was happy to see that Gina chose to use one of the number lines to make sense of this problem.

I actually pulled Gina's first try at this modified problem out of the recycling bin. She had started with 16 and had made a set of 4 jumps up to 20. I think watching Hannah act out the problem with snap cubes made a big difference.

VIDEO

Video 3.7

Simpler Class Library With Counters and a Bar Model

resources.corwin.com/ problemsolvingk-2

Video 3.8

Simpler Class Library With a Number Line

resources.corwin.com/ problemsolvingk-2

In Figure 3.18 the number line solution helped Gina recognize the change of 4 books, and we see evidence in her first draft that she struggled with deciding how to use that information. It's clear that the Start Unknown is still challenging for her, but the simplified version of the problem gave her an opportunity for sense-making. The action can be more difficult to show on a number line, but you will see in Gina's work that there are still strategies for making action visible. In Video 3.8, the +4 shows the action or movement from a starting value to an ending value. She recognized that the distance covered is the amount of change and was able to use it to identify the start value. The video narrates approaches to solving the problem using this number line model and identifies how the three elements of the story—start, change, and result—can be seen on the number line.

DON'T START AT THE BEGINNING When there is no starting quantity in the story, students have to adapt and use different strategies. One way to solve a Start Unknown problem is the way Hannah did it: She started with the change (4 cubes representing the books) in the story, essentially reversing the roles of the start and the change to get to the known result (16 cubes). She counted out more cubes until she arrived at a total of 16 cubes and then went back to count what she had added. As you watch Video 3.7, note how this strategy is similar to counting-on strategies that students use for counting collections. In this case, Hannah started with the change and, while making sense of the problem situation, she was able to use the change of the problem to figure out the starting point of the action.

SEPARATING COMPUTATIONS FROM OPERATIONS

Building a model and trying a simpler case are two strategies that helped students understand the underlying problem situation. We also saw that solving the Start Unknown variation of the Add-To problem situation isn't always done with addition. As you read the problem in Figure 3.19, think about how you would solve it and how you might model it before reading the student work and teacher comments that follow.

FIGURE 3.19

> Some students in second grade signed up for the school's fun run on the first day. On the second day 21 more students signed up. Now there are a total of 35 students signed up to run. How many students signed up on the first day?

As you explore the student work in Figures 3.20 and 3.21, remember that the goal is to explore how the Add-To/Start Unknown problem situation is shown in the story that is told by the problem. In this story we don't know how many students signed up for the fun run on the first day. But now let's see what operation each student actually uses to solve the problem.

FIGURE 3.20

FIGURE 3.21

STUDENT WORK

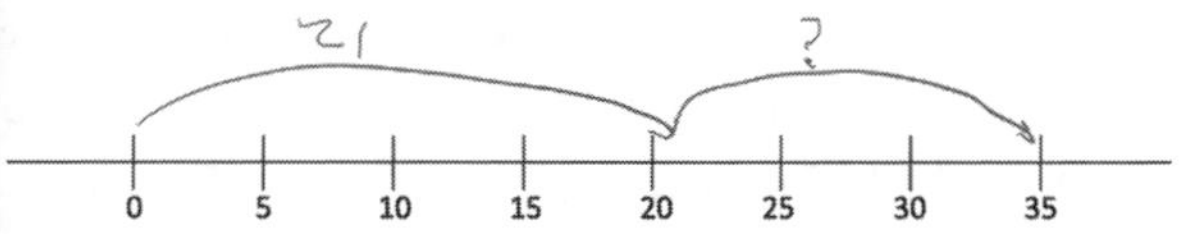

The other day we found out that you can add in either order. I decided to think about it the other way, so I drew the 21 first since I know that and then counted on to see how far it is to 35. It's backward!

Some number plus 21 more makes 35.

I decided to count backward 21 from the 35 runners signed up on the last day. I'm thinking about the problem backward since I'm trying to figure out the beginning of the story.

$$35 - 21 = x$$

35 runners at the end. 21 on the first day. It has to be 14 runners in between.

TEACHER RESPONSE

Devonté's work reminded me of Hannah's solution to the book problem (Figure 3.17). Instead of starting with the start quantity, they both started with the change quantity. I appreciate the flexibility of their thinking. I just want to make sure that they understand that their number line and bar model read "backward." The change comes first, and the start comes second. The strategy works. I just have to watch to make sure that their answers relate to the problem they are solving.

I am happy to see that Devonté is trying out the number line. This is new for the class!

When I saw Jessica start with counters, I wondered how she would represent the story when the starting quantity was unknown. I mean, where would you start? That didn't seem to trouble her at all. She started with the total number of runners and counted back the number of runners who signed up on the second day by flipping the counters. The story reads from the end, back to the beginning!

Now I want to ask her about the equation she wrote. It's subtraction!

VIDEO

Video 3.9

Fun Run With a Number Line

resources.corwin.com/problemsolvingk-2

Video 3.10

Fun Run With Counters

resources.corwin.com/problemsolvingk-2

Devonté's number line in Figure 3.20 might look like he doesn't understand the story in this problem because he starts with the books read in the second month. However, his written words describe the strategy he is using. He has intentionally switched the order of the numbers in the story to make the computation easier, and this makes his solution much more informed than we might have thought. In Chapter 5 we will talk more about using this property of addition (the commutative property) flexibly. In the meantime, we recognize that Devonté understands that when computing the sum of two addends, the two numbers can change places and he still gets the same answer. Devonté also appears to be comfortable counting on with a number line in the same way others have used counters. But, more important, his words tell us that he understands the problem situation.

Like all problems, the fun run problem can be solved using subtraction or addition. When you solved it, did you use subtraction? Or addition? The working backward strategy Jessica used in Figure 3.21 looks like she used subtraction. So, let's look briefly again at the question we posed at the beginning: How is it possible that an Add-To problem situation can be solved with subtraction? In other words, what happens when the operation of the problem situation is not the same as the computational process students (and maybe you, too) used to find a solution? We call those computations addition and subtraction, but for the purposes of discussion we need to distinguish between accurately modeling a problem situation and the computation used to compute an answer. Remember what we said in Chapter 1 about operation sense: Operation sense is not about getting an answer but rather about knowing what work the operation does in the problem.

To find out what work the operation does in the problem, we look at the situation to identify that work. In the case of Add-To problems, this means seeing the action of something coming into the situation. More formally, this is referred to as "joining sets." That's addition, but that doesn't necessarily mean that students need to or even should compute the answer using addition. We have seen throughout this chapter that whether subtraction or addition is used to compute the answer depends on how the equation or number sentence is written (even in verbal form). This is an important idea and bears repeating. Mathematizing the problem situation and identifying the problem situation type is separate and distinct from deciding which computation strategies to use to compute a final answer.

MOVING TO EQUATIONS

The complexity of the Start Unknown variation of the Add-To problem situation gives us the opportunity to begin introducing students to using equations to represent their thinking. In this book we may use a question mark or a variable to show an unknown quantity, but the symbol can be anything, including variables, circles, squares, or other shapes. We are using a question mark in this book because it reminds us that there is normally a question to be asked about the missing quantity.

Figures 3.20 and 3.21 show two different student equations for the fun run problem. In Figure 3.20, we saw an early version of the equation: the mathematical story. Devonté describes the situation in the problem using a sentence with numbers, which could then be translated to symbols:

Some number plus 21 more makes 35

$$? + 21 = 35$$

Start + Change = Result

The problem situation matches this equation. This is true no matter how the student finds an answer.

Devonté showed that he knows that the addends in a problem can be added in any order, and he uses this idea to change the order of the change and the start. His solution therefore looks more like the Change Unknown problem that we saw from Ian in Figure 3.14. Ian's version used base 10 blocks, and he also started with the change instead of the start in order to find the result. Devonté's computation also started with the change, and his equation looked like this:

$$21 + ? = 35$$

Change + Start = Result

In Figure 3.21 we see something very different. The symbolic representation shows subtraction, but this is still an Add-To problem situation. Jessica's computation equation does not match the action in the problem, but instead it describes her choice of computation used to find the answer.

$$35 - 21 = ?$$

Result – Change = Start

The subtraction equation alone does not tell us if the student understands the problem structure: It does not stand alone. We also need to listen to the explanation and look at the other representations to see whether the student understands the problem situation, even if the student has an efficient computation.

Each of these alternatives was created because it is challenging to find a solution to a word problem whose story does not have a starting quantity. As students learn to write equations, they will learn to write equations that represent the actions or relationships in a problem and they will also learn to write equations that are useful for finding an answer. In the problem-solving context, it may be helpful to recognize that these equations may be different from each other, as we saw with the Start Unknown variety. The solution equation and the computation equation may also be the same, which is typically true with the Result Unknown problem situations that we saw in Chapter 2. When the focus is on problem solving, the distinction between the different equations may be critically important for understanding how students arrive at very different solutions to the same word problem, even when their answers are the same.

Having said all that, students really are just starting to make sense of equations, translating their mathematical thinking into symbols. Although you may introduce symbolic equations to your students and use them only at the board at first, encourage students to still say verbal equations and mathematical stories. By doing this, they are learning to put the actions of the problem into their own words.

Modeling problem situations when the start or the change is unknown can be challenging for both adults and children. In general, studies have shown that the challenge isn't necessarily because these problem variations are that much harder; rather, adults and students alike have not done as many of them as they have the Result Unknown variation (Franke, 2018). The only way to address that problem is to practice. If an action problem seems too hard for your students, take a moment to decide if it is too hard or is simply less familiar. Now that you have seen several effective strategies, you can feel more comfortable offering your students the challenge. After all, you've had much more practice yourself, just from doing the problems in this chapter and from seeing how students have solved them.

Finally, although we recognize that students begin working with larger whole-number values, particularly in grade 2, we recommend following our example in this chapter and using lesser values and easier to manipulate numbers when inviting students to explore the connectedness among mathematical representations. There is evidence that when faced with more challenging numbers, students may not apply their understanding of problem situations, even if they already had a firm grasp of them in the first place (Bell, Fischbein, & Greer, 1984; Bell, Greer, Grimison, & Mangan, 1989; Sowder, 2002). Expect this and start with more manageable numbers in the first place.

KEY IDEAS

1. Joining problems reflect action and are called Add-To problem situations.

2. Add-To problem situations follow a common structure in which there is a starting value (the beginning of the story), a change, and a result (the end of the story). Any one of the three parts of the problem may be the missing value.

3. The variations of Add-To have a developmental sequence for fluency. Result Unknown problems are likely the first ones students will be able to handle fluently, followed by Change Unknown problems. The Start Unknown variation is typically the most challenging for students.

4. Students should have experience with *all* problem situations at all primary grades, using the complexity of numbers determined by state standards for each grade.

5. An action problem situation can and should be retold in the student's own words. This "story" simplifies the details of the problem and focuses on the action.

6. For young learners, verbal descriptions will typically be oral rather than written. It will likely be necessary to read the problem to the students more than once so that they can focus on thinking about the mathematics rather than the work of reading it.

7. When focusing on the meaning of word problems, students should focus on creating concrete or visual (often pictorial), verbal, and symbolic representations that closely match the action (or story) in the problem situation.

8. Students' understanding is also displayed through verbal and symbolic representations.

9. Through practice, students can learn to recognize features of each representation and connect them to another representation.

10. To gauge, clarify, and extend student thinking, ask students to share their version of the mathematical story in written or spoken form, and by questions to encourage better descriptions.

TRY IT OUT!

IDENTIFY THE PROBLEM SITUATION

Each of the problems below is an Add-To/Result Unknown situation. Read each problem and rewrite it so that it is either a Change Unknown or a Start Unknown variation. As you are rewriting, think about how you could make this change "on-the-fly" and live with your class, making sure that they have practice with many different variations of problem structures.

1. Maya put 3 hamburgers on the grill. Two friends came over, so she put 2 more hamburgers on the grill. How many hamburgers are on the grill?

2. Arturo cut out 12 biscuits and put them in the oven. When they were done, Arturo cut out and baked 6 more biscuits. How many biscuits did Arturo cut and bake?

3. Austin had $15. He got $40 from the bank. How much money does he now have?

4. Alma's team had 37 points. They scored 46 more points. How many points did the team score?

5. Dipak had 65 building bricks. He got a set of 52 bricks for his birthday. How many building bricks does Dipak now have?

WRITE THE PROBLEM

For each problem situation, write the equation that best describes the action in the problem. Then write the equation that you use to compute the answer, if they are different.

1. There were 3 children on the playground right after lunch. More children came in the afternoon, and now there are 9 children on the playground. How many children came to play in the afternoon?

2. The bakery had some cupcakes on the shelf. The baker baked 24 more and now there are 39 cupcakes. How many cupcakes were on the shelf at the start?

3. Paulette had 4 bottles of fruit juice. She bought some more juice at the store and now there are 15 bottles of juice in the pantry. How many bottles of juice did Paulette buy?

4. The farmer had 75 pigs at the beginning of the year. In the spring more piglets were born. Now there are 102 pigs on the farm. How many piglets were born in the spring?

CHANGE IT UP

Numberless word problems are just as the name suggests: word problems without numbers getting in the way. This isn't a new idea, but Brian Bushart (n.d.) has updated the idea for today. Bushart's model starts with a typical word problem, strips the numbers from the problem, focuses on the relationships, and gradually adds numbers back in. Numberless word problems focus student

The Doorbell Rang

attention on the story, the relationships, and the operations in the problem. Here is the basic process for creating and using numberless word problems:

1. Find any original problem. Without showing it to students, identify the number relationships and operations.

2. Show the problem to students with no numbers and with only one relationship.

3. Add one number to the problem.

4. Add a second number.

5. Reveal the original word problem.

Much of what Bushart is describing in this process is what we call mathematizing in the sandbox. The one suggestion we would add is to incorporate concrete or pictorial models into the process of the slow reveal of the problem. Select a problem from this chapter or from your textbook and try this approach with your students.

REFLECT

1. We are using the "mathematical story" analogy to help students understand the elements of a word problem. What other tools for teaching stories in your English/ Language Arts curriculum can you use to support this thinking?

2. Most teachers find that the Start Unknown situation is the most challenging. What other strategies do you feel you can use right away to help students become familiar with that structure?

3. Look at the word problems in the textbook you currently use and identify 8–10 Add-To problems. Sort them based on which term is missing: start, change, or result. Does the book offer a balance of types? Rewrite some of the problems to move the missing term. For example, Result Unknown problems could be rewritten to be Start Unknown or Change Unknown problems.

NOTES

CHAPTER FOUR

Take-From Problems
Locating the Change

Thinking About Active Subtraction Situations

In this chapter we introduce the second active problem situation, Take-From. These problems follow the same story structure as the Add-To problems we discussed in Chapter 3, but the action is taking away. As with Add-To problems, Take-From problem situations have a starting value, a change, and a resulting value as the main elements of the story, and any one of these can be the unknown in a given problem. The difference can be seen in the action in the story: Something is removed or taken away. In Chapter 2 we explored the Result Unknown variety of this problem type, but in this chapter our focus is on problems with either the change or the start unknown. Let's find out more!

Addition and Subtraction Problem Situations

	Result Unknown	Change Addend Unknown	Start Addend Unknown	
Take-From	There are 19 students in Mrs. Amadi's class. 4 students went to the office to say the Pledge. How many students are in the class now? $19 - 4 = x$ $4 + x = 19$	There are 19 students in Mrs. Amadi's class. Some students went to class to read the Pledge. There were still 15 students in the classroom. How many students went to the office? $19 - x = 15$ $x + 15 = 19$	4 students went to the office. 15 students were still in the classroom. How many students are there in Mrs. Amadi's class? $x - 4 = 15$ $15 + 4 = x$	

Note: The representations for the problem situations in this table reflect our understanding based on a number of resources. These include the tables in the Common Core State Standards for Mathematics (CCSS-M; National Governors Association Center for Best Practices and Council of Chief State School Officers, 2010), the problem situations as described in the Cognitively Guided Instruction research (Carpenter, Hiebert, & Moser, 1981), and other tools. See the Appendix and the book's companion website for a more detailed summary of the documents that informed our development of this table.

ACTIVE SITUATIONS

	Result Unknown	Change Addend Unknown	Start Addend Unknown	
Add-To	Paulo counted 9 crayons. He put them in the basket. Paulo found 6 more crayons under the table. He put them in the basket. How many crayons are in the basket? $9 + 6 = x$ $6 = x - 9$	Paulo counted 9 crayons. He found more and put them in the basket. Now Paulo has 15 crayons. How many crayons did he put in the basket? $9 + x = 15$ $9 = 15 - x$	Paulo had some crayons. He found 6 more crayons under the table. Now he has 15 crayons. How many crayons did Paulo have in the beginning? $x + 6 = 15$ $15 - 6 = x$	
Take-From	There are 19 students in Mrs. Amadi's class. 4 students went to the office to say the Pledge. How many students are in the class now? $19 - 4 = x$ $4 + x = 19$	There are 19 students in Mrs. Amadi's class. Some students went to class to read the Pledge. There were still 15 students in the classroom. How many students went to the office? $19 - x = 15$ $x + 15 = 19$	4 students went to the office. 15 students were still in the classroom. How many students are there in Mrs. Amadi's class? $x - 4 = 15$ $15 + 4 = x$	

RELATIONSHIP (NONACTIVE) SITUATIONS

	Total Unknown	One Part Unknown		Both Parts Unknown
Part-Part-Whole	The first grade voted on a game for recess. 11 students voted to play four square. 8 voted to go to the playground. How many students are in the class? $8 + 11 = x$ $x - 11 = 8$	The 19 first graders voted on a recess activity. 8 students voted to go to the playground. How many wanted to play four square? $8 + x = 19$ $x = 19 - 8$		The 19 first graders voted on a recess activity. Some wanted to play four square. Some wanted to go to the playground. What are some ways the first graders could have voted? $x + y = 19$ $19 - x = y$
	Difference Unknown	Greater Quantity Unknown	Lesser Quantity Unknown	
Additive Comparison	Jessie's paper airplane flew 14 feet. Jo's paper airplane flew 9 feet. How much less did Jo's paper airplane fly than Jessie's? $14 - 9 = x$ $9 + x = 14$	Jo's paper airplane flew 9 feet. Jessie's paper airplane flew 5 feet more than Jo's. How far did Jessie's paper airplane fly? $9 + 5 = x$ $x - 5 = 9$	Jessie's paper airplane flew 14 feet. Jo's paper airplane flew 5 feet less than Jessie's paper airplane. How far did Jo's paper airplane fly? $14 - 5 = x$ $14 = x + 5$	

online resources ⌕ Visit **http://resources.corwin.com/problemsolvingk-2** to download a copy of the full Addition and Subtraction Problem Situations Table.

Sandbox Notes: Explore Your Thinking

As you enter into problem exploration mode, gather your tools, including markers or crayons, base 10 blocks, linking cubes, counters, and any other tools that you routinely have available in your classroom. Try several of the concrete manipulatives and some hand-drawn picture models that reflect the mathematical story in the word problem. If you put the problem in your own words, revisit that rephrasing and specify where you can see each quantity in the problem. Where can you see each quantity in the models you have created? Think about how your work can express your understanding of the problem situation.

Ask yourself these questions to focus your thinking:

- Think about the quantities in each situation. What do they represent? What action is taking place between the quantities in the problem?

- How can you represent the quantities in the word problems with your manipulatives or pictures?

- How can you make a number sentence about the problem?

Read the two problems in Figures 4.1 and 4.2. Remember that the goal is not to solve the problems immediately but rather to consider what your students might do with them. As you put the problems into your own words, think about how the problems are the same and how they are different. You may find a solution path right away, but don't stop there. Find another representation, and think about whether or not it works for both problems. In other words, enter the mathematizing sandbox and explore the many ways these problems could be represented before you move on to the student work and the teacher comments on that work.

FIGURE 4.1

FIGURE 4.2

| Varun had 8 toy cars. He lost some and now he has 5 cars. How many cars did Varun lose? | Austin saved $8. He spent $3 on a toy. How much money does Austin have now? |

ENTER THE PROBLEM

FIGURE 4.3 A MODEL FOR MATHEMATIZING WORD PROBLEMS

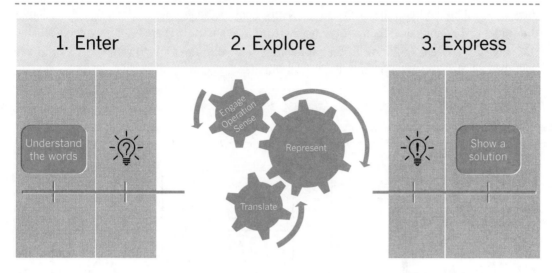

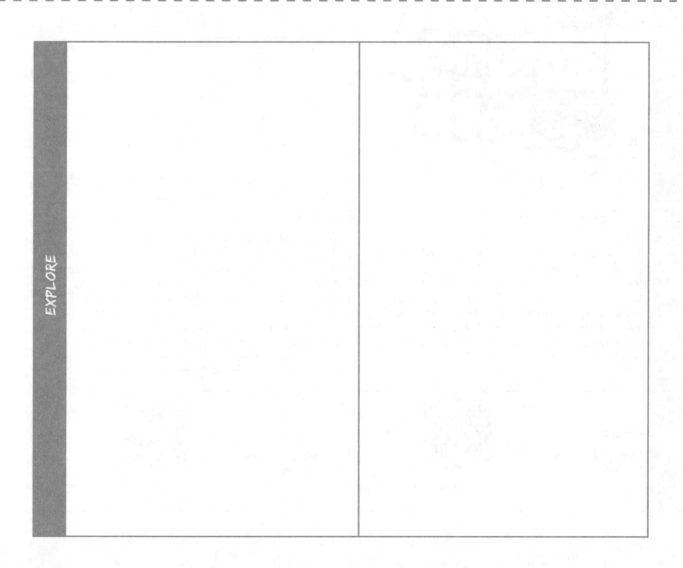

STUDENTS AND TEACHERS THINK ABOUT THE PROBLEMS

Look at the student work in Figures 4.4 and 4.5, and consider how these students describe or draw what is happening in the two word problems. Look at the teacher commentary that follows the student work and consider what the teachers noticed about it. There is also a video available showing each student's solution to the problem, which you may want to watch once you have read through the student work and teacher comments.

FIGURE 4.4   **FIGURE 4.5**

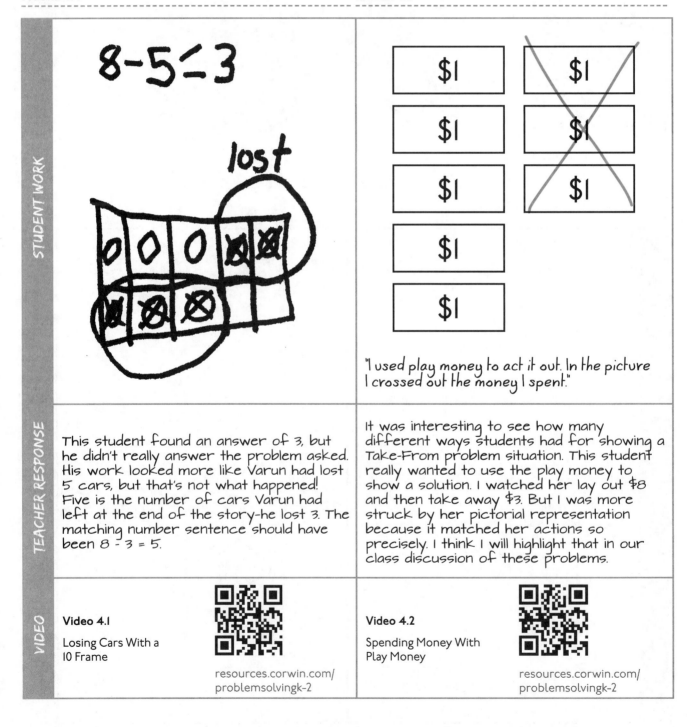

STUDENT WORK

8 − 5 ⊂ 3

lost

"I used play money to act it out. In the picture I crossed out the money I spent."

TEACHER RESPONSE

This student found an answer of 3, but he didn't really answer the problem asked. His work looked more like Varun had lost 5 cars, but that's not what happened! Five is the number of cars Varun had left at the end of the story—he lost 3. The matching number sentence should have been 8 − 3 = 5.

It was interesting to see how many different ways students had for showing a Take-From problem situation. This student really wanted to use the play money to show a solution. I watched her lay out $8 and then take away $3. But I was more struck by her pictorial representation because it matched her actions so precisely. I think I will highlight that in our class discussion of these problems.

VIDEO

Video 4.1

Losing Cars With a 10 Frame

resources.corwin.com/
problemsolvingk-2

Video 4.2

Spending Money With Play Money

resources.corwin.com/
problemsolvingk-2

What do you notice? Did you notice that there is action in both of these problems? The actions of *losing* cars and *spending* money signal a removal situation because something leaves the story in each case. These are both examples of a Take-From situation. We want to highlight an important feature of Take-From problem situations: They all require the action of removing something from the story. In the work shown in Figures 4.4 and 4.5, the change to the problem is losing a value. Despite having the same problem structure, these two samples of student work don't look at all the same. What makes them different? As we explore representations of Take-From problem situations, we will find—as we did with the Add-To problem situation—that the change can be unknown, as can the start or the result. Depending on which value is unknown, the complexity of the problem situation can change significantly. Additionally, we will also look carefully at the difference between the computation used to arrive at the answer and the operation associated with the problem situation as separate ideas.

Take-From: A problem situation that includes an action and a quantity being removed from the original quantity.

FINDING THE UNKNOWN: THREE STORY STRUCTURES

Recall what we learned in Chapter 2. Active mathematical stories have a narrative structure—a beginning, a middle, and an end. In the beginning there is a starting value, and in the case of Figures 4.4 and 4.5, the starting value is 8. The middle of the story brings a change in quantity: Cars are lost or money is spent. In the saving problem, we know the change is $3, but in the car problem the change is the unknown value. The end of the story is the opposite: We know that 5 is the final number of cars, but we don't know how much Austin has left. In most word problems, only one of these three quantities is unknown. Thus, as the table at the beginning of the chapter indicates, the unknown could be the start, the change, or the result, reflecting the arc of the storyline. Identifying the unknown—in other words, the information we need to know—is the first step in problem solving. This is a step we add before even considering the numbers in the problem.

STORY STRUCTURES: IMPLICATIONS FOR TEACHING

Let's look again at the two problems we started with in this chapter, this time considering their different problem structures. The car problem in Figure 4.1 is a Take-From, Change Unknown variation, while Austin's money problem in Figure 4.2 is also a Take-From problem, but it is the Result Unknown variation, the one we are most familiar with. Change Unknown problems represent situations where we know the beginning and end of the story and are asked to work out what happened in the middle.

The student work in Figure 4.4 suggests that this student connects the idea of removal (losing toys) with subtraction but that the student does not yet understand the arc of the start-change-result storyline. The work sample suggests that the student viewed 5 as the quantity of toy cars lost, not as the quantity remaining after some were lost. In other words, this student may have used the quantities in the problem to create and solve a Result Unknown problem rather than solving the problem as the story is told. Since $8 - 5 = 3$ is likely a known fact for this student, the computation may be automatic. In that case, the student might not have paused to think about the structure of the problem. Sometimes we accept correct answers from students without looking at the solution process by which they arrived at that answer. It is easy to accept a correct answer and be happy to see it, but it's more important over the long term to know that students are able to understand a problem situation, represent it appropriately, and use this information to generate a solution and find an answer. In this way, students will be prepared for more challenging problem situations and problems that don't include known facts.

Figure 4.6 shows another student's solution to the problem of Varun losing some cars.

FIGURE 4.6

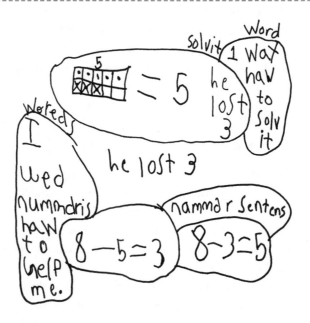

The student whose work is shown in Figure 4.6 uses three different representations to share the solution: a 10 frame (pictorial), a sentence (verbal), and two equations (symbolic). Each of the representations captures a window into the student's thinking. For example, the 10-frame diagram shows 8 cars, which represents the start of the problem. It also shows the 5 cars that remain after the removal of some cars (the change) took place in the problem. What it does *not* say is whether the student put dots in 8 cells and then crossed out 3 of the cells on the 10 frame because the student already knew the answer had to be 3. Or maybe the student started with dots in 8 cells, counted up 5 of the cells, and then crossed out the rest before arriving at an answer of 3. In Video 4.1 you can see both options acted out. In a sense this is a chicken and the egg problem—which came first? The 3 cars or the 5 cars? Does it matter? Yes! The problem asks how many cars Varun lost, leaving him with 5 cars. In the beginning, we don't know that he lost 3. Of course, you might have figured that out right away because you know that fact family, and so would many of your students, but consider what might happen if we change the quantities in the problem:

> Varun had 43,965 cars in stock. He sold some and now he has 27,650 cars in stock. How many cars did he sell?

Clearly this isn't a problem appropriate for primary mathematics, but even you, the reader, don't know the answer at a glance like you knew the answer "3 cars" in Varun's problem. It's reasonable to wonder if the student whose work is shown in Figure 4.6 has developed a strategy for solving *any* Change Unknown problem with a strategy that is still useful without knowing the fact family for the quantities in the problem.

Let's now consider the other representations in the student's solution in Figure 4.6. The student writes, "he lost 3." It is reasonable to assume that the student understands the problem context because he specifically says, "he *lost*," which revisits the words used in the problem context. This statement does not, however, give us any additional information about how the student came up with the answer of 3 cars in the first place.

The student also wrote two number sentences at the bottom of the page: $8 - 5 = 3$ and $8 - 3 = 5$. What information does this give you about the student's understanding? On the one hand, we can be pleased that this primary student correctly wrote two related number sentences (equations). The teacher's emphasis on fact families has paid off. On the other hand, although both of these equations represent the number fact family of $3 + 5 = 8$, only one of them accurately represents the problem situation as it is written. To represent the problem situation more closely, the result of the change should be 5 cars. That equation is $8 - ? = 5$. You may find yourself thinking about how to solve this problem.

To solve the problem, you might restate the problem as $8 - 5 = ?$ so that you can more easily figure out the change value. Years of experience in mathematics have given you the awareness to recognize that strategy. It's important to note that changing the equation this way is done in order to help with computation, rather than to represent the context in an equation.

A context equation represents what happens in the problem situation:

$$8 - ? = 5$$

A computation equation is a version of an equation that allows us to more easily compute the answer to the problem:

$$8 - 5 = ?$$

Now that we are looking differently at students' equations, consider Figure 4.7, another sample of student work on the car problem. Do you think this student understands the problem situation? What does the student understand or not understand about equations? What does the student understand or not understand about the subtraction operation?

FIGURE 4.7

If you are reading this book with a team, this is a good place to stop and consider the challenges of representing Take-From problem situations when the change is unknown, as we see in Varun's car problem. Figure 4.7 has a correct answer, but it's more important to consider whether the student has a strategy that will last beyond problems with known facts.

MODELING THE ACTIVE PROBLEM SITUATION

One thing we know about mathematics is that there is always more than one way to approach a problem. Students can benefit from using concrete and pictorial models where they can show the action unfold in an active problem situation. The models they use can be expressed using *ungrouped* or *grouped* counters to act out a problem situation, or it may be a number line that uses arrows or other marks to show action.

Before we look closely at how the students modeled the problems in Figures 4.8 and 4.9, read through each problem, putting the stories in your own words. Note which quantity is missing in each problem: the start, the change, or the result.

FIGURE 4.8   FIGURE 4.9

| Alfonso picked some pennies up off the floor. He gave 5 of the pennies to his sister. Now he has 9 pennies. How many pennies did he find on the floor? | There were 14 apples in the bowl. Thera and her friends ate 5 apples. How many were left in the bowl? |

The student work in Figures 4.10 and 4.11, and the teacher comments that accompany it, explore a variety of models that students might produce to reflect the action in a Take-From problem situation.

Counters and manipulatives, like the play money and base 10 blocks used for these problems, allow students to act out what happens in the problem. In Figure 4.10, Beth's teacher described her thinking about acting out the story backward as she modeled with the coins. This makes sense when solving a Start Unknown problem since she is working backward to figure out the beginning of the story. Telling the arc of the story forward and in reverse is a strategy that students can understand in the same way they can sequence a story using pictures in an English/Language Arts lesson. As a matter of fact, when introducing this sequencing strategy, it might be helpful to begin the lesson with just such a story-sequencing task.

Although Beth did not write a number sentence, we can translate her words into an equation that represents her thinking:

$$9 \text{ pennies left} + 5 \text{ pennies given away} = ? \text{ pennies picked up}$$
$$9 + 5 = ?$$

The student's solution strategy is to use addition to count up to the original number of pennies picked up off the floor. How surprising! After all, this is a Take-From problem situation. Why is

FIGURE 4.10   **FIGURE 4.11**

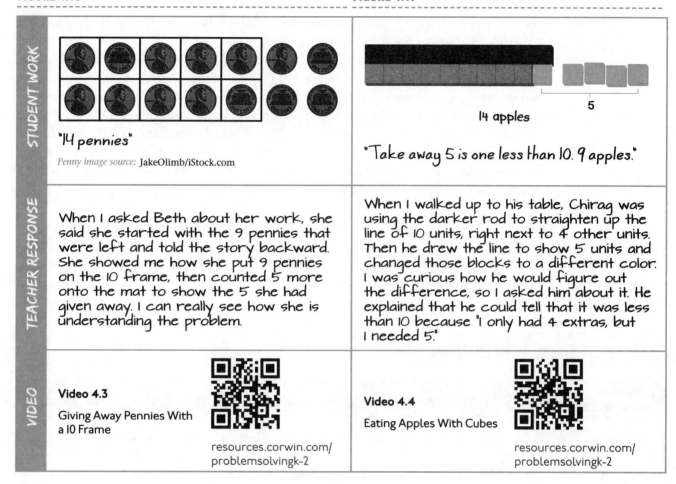

STUDENT WORK

"14 pennies"

Penny image source: JakeOlimb/iStock.com

14 apples

"Take away 5 is one less than 10. 9 apples."

TEACHER RESPONSE

When I asked Beth about her work, she said she started with the 9 pennies that were left and told the story backward. She showed me how she put 9 pennies on the 10 frame, then counted 5 more onto the mat to show the 5 she had given away. I can really see how she is understanding the problem.

When I walked up to his table, Chirag was using the darker rod to straighten up the line of 10 units, right next to 4 other units. Then he drew the line to show 5 units and changed those blocks to a different color. I was curious how he would figure out the difference, so I asked him about it. He explained that he could tell that it was less than 10 because "I only had 4 extras, but I needed 5."

VIDEO

Video 4.3

Giving Away Pennies With a 10 Frame

resources.corwin.com/ problemsolvingk-2

Video 4.4

Eating Apples With Cubes

resources.corwin.com/ problemsolvingk-2

an addition equation an appropriate equation? In this case, the addition equation represents the computation strategy that the student used to find an answer. The problem context situation is still a subtraction equation, reflecting the Take-From action in the story:

$$? \text{ pennies picked up} - 5 \text{ pennies given away} = 9 \text{ pennies left}$$

$$? - 5 = 9$$

Students should have opportunities throughout kindergarten and first and second grades to devise solution strategies for all problem types, but it isn't until the end of second grade that most children are expected to be fluent in a problem like the pennies problem. So we recognize that there is a degree of challenge in working with these Start Unknown or "backward" problems and that some students may not have the sequence skills in place early in their school years to make sense of the problems. But, with exposure and practice, they can gain the experience they need.

The apple problem represented in Figure 4.11 is also a Take-From problem situation structure, but in this case the start and the change in the story are known and the result is unknown. These are the problems introduced in Chapter 2, and they represent the problem structure that students are likely to recognize and use earlier than the others. The student originally showed the 10 units with the dark gray rod and exchanged the grouped rod for 10 individual cubes. But in the final solution we see that the last block is replaced with a colored one instead. The student uses the colors of the base 10 blocks to visually mark the action of 5 apples being eaten. This also allows the change in quantity to be separated from the result quantity. Color can be a useful tool for demonstrating the action in the problem, in this case showing change. Another visual clue that the student leaves is a line that shows 5 units, which separates 5 apples from the quantity of apples left in the bowl after the 5 are eaten. Chirag's narrative also shows that he likely understands the action in the problem, and it gives some insight into how he used a base 10 rod to find the difference of 9 apples. In this problem, the use of color, the student's own grouping symbols, and the student's words help the reader visualize the action in the problem.

To help with your planning, use the chart in Figure 4.12 to make a list of some Take-From action situations that will be familiar to your students. As you read the list, visualize the story and focus less on the quantities and more on the setting and the action. Imagine yourself in that setting, and consider what story you or your students could craft that matches each prompt in the table. The first few have been done for you.

FIGURE 4.12 TAKE-FROM ACTIVE SITUATIONS

CONTEXT	START (Beginning Value)	CHANGE (Action in the Story)	RESULT (Ending Value)
Video game	Points on the board	Points are lost	Final score
Party food	Cookies on the plate	Cookies are eaten	Cookies on the plate
Making a donation	Books on the bookshelf	Books are given away	Books on the bookshelf
Spending money	Money in account	Money spent	Money in account
Trading cards			
			Dirty pots in the sink
	Movies you want to see		

Digging Deeper Into the Start and Change Unknown Situations

As we continue to explore the Start Unknown and Change Unknown variation of Take-From problems, we expand our set of numbers to include values that are less likely to be known facts, which also reflects the range within which many second-grade students are expected to work. The numbers in the problems should not affect students' understanding of problem situations, which is our focus in this book. But in our experience, when the computation itself poses challenges, students cannot rely as much on good or quick calculation estimates to get an answer. If they don't have experience modeling quantities or even problem situations, in particular, they have little else to fall back on. That's when we are likely to hear, "I don't get what they want me to do!"

The two problems featured in Figures 4.13 and 4.14 are Take-From problem situations. When you solve them, pull out a set of manipulatives that are available to you and think about other types of drawings, diagrams, and pictorial images you might use to capture the action in these problem situations. We will share different manipulative models, some of which you may not currently have access to. You may find that you have good substitutes, or you may find a "must-have" tool for next year's supply list.

As you pause before entering the mathematizing sandbox, think about how you can use the manipulatives to focus student attention on the actions taking place in the problem. Act out the problems. Anticipate challenges students might encounter. Remember to focus first on the *context* of the problems and how the manipulative model chosen supports students' understanding of what happens in the problem. Which quantity is missing?

If you get stuck, revisit the Sandbox Notes at the beginning of the chapter for guiding questions and other suggestions.

FIGURE 4.13

FIGURE 4.14

There are some tangerines in the crate. After 25 were sold, 53 tangerines were left in the crate. How many tangerines were in the crate to start?	There are 78 students in second grade. Mr. Bintz's class left to go on a field trip, leaving 53 second graders at school. How many students are in Mr. Bintz's class?

ENTER THE PROBLEM

EXPLORE

The student work in Figures 4.15 and 4.16 shows some possible responses to these typical word problems. The teacher comments in general feature a view into a fellow teacher's practice, and they can help you consider how you might handle similar situations in your own classroom.

FIGURE 4.15

FIGURE 4.16

STUDENT WORK

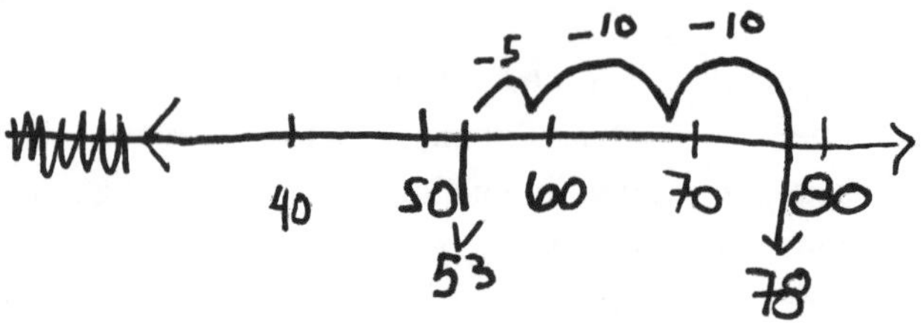

91	92	93	94	95	96	97	98	99	100
81	82	83	84	85	86	87	88	89	90
71	72	73	74	75	76	77	78	79	80
61	62	63	64	65	66	67	68	69	70
51	52	53	54	55	56	57	58	59	60
41	42	43	44	45	46	47	48	49	50
31	32	33	34	35	36	37	38	39	40
21	22	23	24	25	26	27	28	29	30
11	12	13	14	15	16	17	18	19	20
1	2	3	4	5	6	7	8	9	10

First I colored 53. Then I did 25 more. The answer is 78 tangrines.

$78 - 25 = 53$

TEACHER RESPONSE

This student used our new 100 boards to show the story. The student colored the number of tangerines left at the end in one color, and then the number sold in another color. He understands that putting those together makes the total number of tangerines we had at the start. It's interesting that he represented the situation using a subtraction equation but described addition.

I see that she has marked the beginning and ending values of the story on the number line. I asked her about the beginning of her story, and she understood that it is 78 students. I also see that she is using the arrow to show "take-away," or the change in the situation. There is no answer yet, but this is enough for her to start a conversation around the topic with another student.

VIDEO

Video 4.5

Tangerines With a 100 Board

resources.corwin.com/ problemsolvingk-2

Video 4.6

Class Field Trip With a Number Line

resources.corwin.com/ problemsolvingk-2

Before we consider the student work, let's take a moment to identify the problem situations and problem structures for these problems. The word problems in Figures 4.13 and 4.14 are active Take-From problem situations. Both problems even use the same quantities: 25, 53, and 78, but the tangerine problem is a Start Unknown problem and the field trip problem is a Change Unknown problem. Of course, the fact that we are now including greater whole-number values in our problems has no effect on the underlying structure of the problem. It helps to remind students of this and encourage them to look past the more challenging numbers and see that numbers and quantities are not necessarily related to sense-making of the problem situation. To assist students with their sense-making, go back to the mathematizing sandbox, build models, and act out what happens in the problem.

MOVING FROM CONCRETE TO SYMBOLIC REPRESENTATIONS

Acting out problem situations, no matter the quantities involved, is always a good step for students to begin their understanding of a problem situation. Eventually we want them to move to more abstract representations, but never at the expense of understanding what is happening in the problem. Moving to the abstract can be done gradually and in a connected manner. In this section we will follow one problem (Figure 4.17) from an active modeling representation to an abstract representation that is far more flexible and versatile when used appropriately. Follow along as we model a word problem from the most literal and concrete representation to the most abstract representation: symbols.

FIGURE 4.17

Paul is sharing alphabet cookies with his brother, Bob. Paul gave Bob 19 cookies. Then he counted his own cookies. He had 22. How many cookies were in the box to start with?

DIRECT MODELING Direct modeling is a strategy in which students use objects or other realia to act out what happens in the word problem. In the more literal version, the students act out the problem with the objects that are the topic of the word problem. For example, the apple problem in Figure 4.9 can be play-acted using apples and a bowl. In Figure 4.18 we see the progression from an unorganized pile of all of the cookies to one that shows how many were given away to Bob. But the collection remains unorganized, which can easily lead to counting errors. Not only that, realia (real objects) can be problematic simply because they invite complications like cost, hygiene, and sometimes size.

FIGURE 4.18 MODELING A PROBLEM SITUATION WITH REALIA

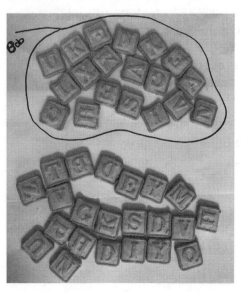

Despite these problems, starting with a problem where the actual objects can be used in the solution may help some students focus on the context of the problem and make sense of it. However, the problems can be easily abstracted with counters like snap cubes or counters standing in for a specific object. In this case, the two-color counters in Figure 4.19 represent a more practical (and flexible) representation of the cookies in Figure 4.18. Another advantage to using a standard-sized object like the counters is that they can help students begin to add structure to their representations.

FIGURE 4.19   MODELING THE COOKIE PROBLEM WITH TWO-COLOR COUNTERS

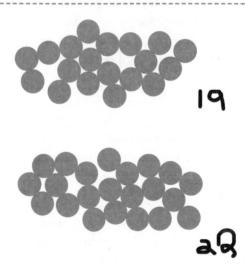

Not only does a more general representation like counters help students focus on making 10, but it can also help students visualize the challenge of a Start Unknown problem. Since this is a Take-From problem, where the amount given away is identified, as is the amount remaining, the only quantity missing is how many cookies were in the box to start with.

STRUCTURES FOR COUNTING AND REPRESENTING There are mathematical tools and structures that can help students organize their thinking when counting and representing. For example, take the 10 frame. Although the 10 frame is not necessarily related to the problem situation itself, it can help students organize their counters as they make sense of the problem. The student work in Figure 4.20 shows the same two sets of counters arranged in the 10-frame structure, using color to distinguish the quantity of cookies Paul gave to Bob and the quantity he kept for himself. The use of 10 frames significantly changes the organization of the problem, which can help students count and add more efficiently, allowing them to focus on the meaning of the problem. Take a look at the 10-frame representation in Figure 4.20. Which color represents Paul's cookies and which represents Bob's? Ten frames can help represent 10 visually, and they may help the student count out 19 and 22 counters and arrive at an answer.

FIGURE 4.20 MODELING THE COOKIE PROBLEM USING 10 FRAMES

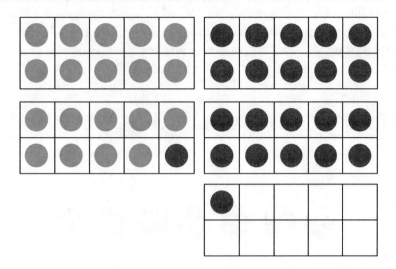

The base 10 blocks in Figure 4.21 serve a similar function. Although acting out the problem with the 10 frame requires the action of placing counters, the base 10 block representation in Figure 4.21 requires the student to exchange 10 units for a rod, a procedure that does not appear in the arc of the problem's story—it is done solely to assist with computation.

FIGURE 4.21 MODELING THE COOKIE PROBLEM USING BASE 10 BLOCKS

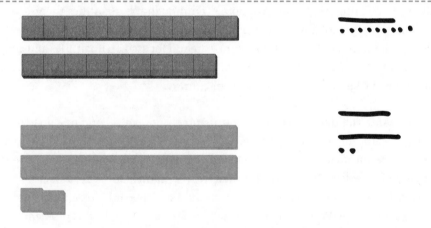

Base 10 blocks are an example of a grouped manipulative. A single rod represents a value of 10 units—in this case, 10 cookies. Similarly, the smaller block is called a unit cube, and here it represents a single cookie. Unlike a dime, the base 10 blocks are proportional, meaning one block in the base 10 set is 10 times as big as another and is 1/10 as big as the larger block. Figure 4.21 shows the same cookie problem situation using base 10 blocks as well as a drawn representation that shares some of the features of the actual base 10 block representation. Now is a good time for your team to stop and consider how the concrete and the drawn representations of base 10 blocks are the same and how they are different.

Place value disks are similar to base 10 blocks in that each block represents one of the powers of 10—that is, 1, 10, 100, 1,000, and so on (including decimal values like 0.1, 0.01, . . .). The place value disks are different because they are not proportional. Compare the image of our two quantities of cookies represented with place value disks in Figure 4.22 to the original photograph of cookies in Figure 4.18. The value of 22 shown in place value disks may make the quantity seem lesser because fewer disks are used.

FIGURE 4.22 MODELING THE COOKIE PROBLEM USING PLACE VALUE DISKS

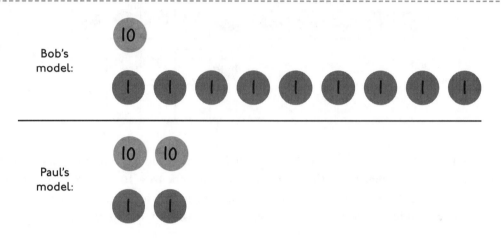

In this set of quantities, it *looks like* Bob has far more cookies (19) than Paul does (22) because there are more disks representing what Paul gave Bob, even though the quantities themselves are the opposite. As students begin to move away from concrete representations to more abstract ones to solve problems, it is important to monitor that they are still focused on quantities and actions and are using the manipulative tools to keep track of quantities and actions rather than using them only to calculate while ignoring the word problem context.

DIAGRAM: 100 BOARD The 100 board is another structure that organizes numbers up to (or beyond) 100. Like a 10 frame, the numbers are organized in groups of ten, and students use crayons, markers, or counters to represent quantities. The 100 board that you see in Figure 4.23 may be different from ones that you have seen in the past. Inspired by two mathematics educators, this version of the 100 board helps make addition and subtraction on the 100 board look and feel more like an Add-To or a Take-From (Bay-Williams & Fletcher, 2017). For example, in this problem, Paul starts with an unknown quantity of cookies and gives his brother 19 of them. The 19 is colored green. The gray represents the 22 more cookies that Paul counts for himself after giving some to Bob. By counting up by tens, from 19 to 29 and from 29 to 39 in gray, the two additional cells are added after to make a total of 41 cookies in the box.

FIGURE 4.23 MODELING THE COOKIE PROBLEM USING A 100 BOARD

91	92	93	94	95	96	97	98	99	100
81	82	83	84	85	86	87	88	89	90
71	72	73	74	75	76	77	78	79	80
61	62	63	64	65	66	67	68	69	70
51	52	53	54	55	56	57	58	59	60
41	42	43	44	45	46	47	48	49	50
31	32	33	34	35	36	37	38	39	40
21	22	23	24	25	26	27	28	29	30
11	12	13	14	15	16	17	18	19	20
1	2	3	4	5	6	7	8	9	10

DIAGRAM: OPEN NUMBER LINES Open number lines are based on a marked number line, but they focus only on critically important numbers in the problem. Marked number lines show precisely placed points on the number line at a certain interval, whether it is relevant to the problem or not. In our sample problem constructed on a number line, Bob's cookies are represented as a bar that stretches from 0 to 19, while the bar for Paul's 22 cookies starts at 19 and moves forward 22. You can see that the two lengths joined together end at 41, representing a starting quantity of 41 cookies in the box.

FIGURE 4.24 MODELING THE COOKIE PROBLEM USING A MARKED NUMBER LINE

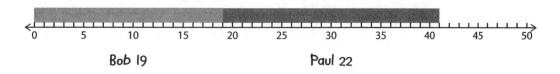

Bob 19   Paul 22

An open number line shows only numbers that either appear in the word problem itself or are included in the student's solution. At this stage of problem solving, students should already have problem-solving and mathematizing strategies in place so that the calculations done on their number lines support computation. If, however, students are still making sense of the action that is happening in a problem situation, an open number line is not likely to contribute to their understanding of the action in the problem. For example, in the open number line in Figure 4.25, the number line starts at 0, a number not mentioned in the problem at all. It is, however, a logical starting point for a solution strategy that includes counting up to the start of the narrative underlying a Take-From problem situation.

FIGURE 4.25 MODELING THE COOKIE PROBLEM USING AN OPEN NUMBER LINE

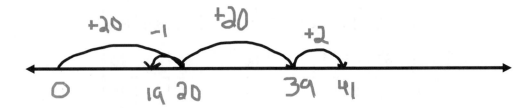

In this open number line solution, also note the student's flexibility in adding the two quantities of cookies. The tens and the ones places are added separately. None of these features is related to the problem situation. Instead, they are features of efficient computation. Students who are focused on modeling a problem situation should use models that support their sense-making of the context, which may mean less focus on abstract strategies and more on modeling the action in the problem situation.

ABSTRACT REPRESENTATIONS The open number line in Figure 4.25 is a pictorial representation, but since it does not represent the real objects presented in the problem situation (e.g., cookies), we call it a diagram. The solution strategy for this problem situation might be written as either one of the following:

Bob's cookies + Paul's cookies = ? cookies

$19 + 22 = ?$

? cookies − Bob's cookies = Paul's cookies

$? - 19 = 22$

On the other hand, the computation presented in the number line would be presented this way:

Bob's cookies

$0 + 20 = 20$
$20 - 1 = 19$

Add Paul's cookies

$19 + 20 = 39$
$39 + 2 = 41$

41 total cookies in the box

We recognize that these final equations represent a computation strategy rather than a context equation. The computation moves match the strategies for computation rather than any actions in the problem. For example, adding 20 and then adding 2 more is an efficient way to add 22; however, nowhere in the problem is there mention of 20 cookies followed by 2 cookies. Students engaging in symbolic work like we see in the open number line and in these equations should engage with these computation strategies to solve a word problem only after they have modeled and understood the actions in the problem situation. The same is true for students building equations. Equations at this grade level should regularly refer back to concrete and understandable situations.

Using Children's Literature to Explore Take-From Situations

Every once in a while, a book is published that not only engages students' attention but also teaches students a lesson for living in the world. *Alexander Who Used to Be Rich Last Sunday* (Viorst, 1978) is one of those books. In this story, Alexander has spent or lost all of the money his grandparents gave him when they came to visit, and he is disappointed that he now has only bus tokens in his pocket. Alexander uses up all of his money in humorous and sometimes impulsive ways, something many students may personally relate to.

There are 12 separate events that cause Alexander to spend or lose his money. These include losing coins in a bathroom and making bets with his brother. Use a 3-Read strategy (Asturius, 2017, n.d.) to engage students with the book. First, read the story as you would for a language lesson. Ask who the characters are and what happened in the story.

During the second reading, begin the process of quantifying what happened in the story. As you read, write the quantities (number and unit being counted) on chart paper or on the board, making sure that students understand what the vocabulary and situations mean. For example, students likely won't know what a bus token is, or they may not know about the appeal of glass marbles. In these instances, you may choose to have students substitute something analogous so that they can relate to the story. A marble is a tool for playing a game. What other tools for playing their own games might students want to purchase? It is helpful to make sure that students understand that the $1 Alexander's grandparents give him is the same as 100¢.

On the third read, students begin to mathematize. They may wonder what might have happened if Alexander did not argue with his brothers and call them names. Or if he didn't kick them. What if he didn't bet his brother and mother that he could beat them at jumping or at holding his breath?

CREATE ANOTHER OUTCOME

Alexander makes some questionable choices with his money. Give students an opportunity to make a change to Alexander's choices. Here are some ideas to engage students in making different choices on Alexander's behalf:

- Pick three events or items that Alexander chooses *not* to spend his money on. Why did he make those different choices? How much money does he have left now that he hasn't spent or lost that money?

- How much would Alexander spend if he didn't get in a fight with his brothers? What could he buy instead? How much would Alexander have if he won the bets? (In this case, you can decide if the bets, the name calling, and the kicking all count, or if just two of these choices counted.)

FIND THE UNKNOWN QUANTITY

This is an activity that you can do with students to model the problem at first, but then encourage pairs of students to do the challenge with other pairs of students. Look at Alexander's list of expenditures and pick one (or two or three), add them together, and subtract the quantity from 100¢. Give students the total and have them come up with the expenditures that Alexander didn't make. For example,

> *Alexander had 100¢. He decided to make different choices and he spent only 80¢.*
> *What did he not spend money on? How much did he save?*

This problem variation has a known start (100¢) and a known result (80¢). Students will find options for combinations of money that will make up part of the change. The change is unknown in this case.

All of the problems in this chapter are about the action of a story with a beginning value (the start), a change in quantity (the change), and an ending value (the result). Specifically, these problems address Take-From situations with a special focus on how to model a problem situation when the start or the change is unknown. In Chapter 5 we will explore problems that do not embody action but instead show a different kind of relationship.

KEY IDEAS

1. Take-From problem situations reflect action happening in the story.

2. Take-From problem situations follow a common structure where there is a starting value (the beginning of the story), a change, and a result (the end of the story). Any one of the three parts of the problem may be a missing value.

3. The Result Unknown variation of the Take-From problem type is typically the easiest, followed by Change Unknown. The Start Unknown variation is typically most challenging for students.

4. Students should have experience with all problem situations at all grades.

5. State standards call for using ever larger numbers as students move up in grades K–2. Changing numbers does not change the problem types in a problem, but it still poses additional challenges for students.

6. An action problem situation can and should be retold in the student's own words. This "story" simplifies the details of the problem and focuses on the action.

7. For young learners, verbal descriptions will typically be oral rather than written. It will likely be necessary to expect multiple readings, including reading the problem to students so that they can focus on thinking about the mathematics.

8. When focusing on the meaning of word problems, students should focus on creating concrete or visual (often pictorial), verbal, and symbolic representations that closely match the action (or story) in the problem situation.

9. Students' understanding is also displayed through verbal and symbolic representations. To gauge, clarify, and extend student thinking, ask students to share the story in written or spoken form.

TRY IT OUT!

IDENTIFY THE PROBLEM SITUATION

Look at the problems below and tell what the Take-From action is in each one. Which term is missing in each problem? The start, the change, or the result?

1. The swim coach had some trophies for the award ceremony. After he gave 6 awards, he had 7 trophies left. How many trophies did the coach have for the ceremony?

2. Linnae had a collection of 7 rocks. She lost 4 of her rocks. How many were left in her collection?

3. There were 7 daffodils blooming in the garden. After Frank picked some for his teacher, there were 3 daffodils left. How many did Frank pick?

4. After the concert there were 10 chairs on the stage. The students put away 6 chairs. How many chairs were still on the stage?

WRITE THE PROBLEM

Write a Take-From word problem represented by each of the equations below:

1. $x - 6 = 2$
2. $28 - 19 = x$
3. $35 - x = 20$
4. $10 + x = 17$
5. $109 - x = 17$

CHANGE IT UP

Read the word problems below. As you imagine what is happening in the story, think about the action that is taking place and how you might model the action in the story for students. What drawings might you make? What marks would help show that there is action in the problem?

1. 20 monkeys were playing in a tree. Some scrambled down the tree trunk and clung to their mothers after a snake was spotted. There were 8 monkeys left in the tree. How many ran back to their mothers?

2. Armando was drinking hot chocolate as he was reading his notebook. His little brother reached for the hot chocolate, and it spilled all over his notebook. 15 pages were ruined, and he had to tear them out. Only 30 pages were left. How many pages did the notebook start with?

3. Mr. Kiernan had collected 134 books for his classroom library. He loaned some of the books his class had already read, but he still counted 96 books on the bookshelf. How many books did Mr. Kiernan loan out?

REFLECT

1. How would your solution strategy change for this version of the field trip problem from Figure 4.14? How is the problem situation different? In what way does your solution strategy change? What kinds of problems can you give students so that they have an opportunity to learn a new strategy?

   There are 83 students in second grade. Mr. Bintz's class left to go on a field trip, leaving 58 second graders at school. How many students are in Mr. Bintz's class?

2. Think about how telling the story in reverse to solve a Start Unknown problem can help students make connections between addition and subtraction. How often do your students count up instead of subtract to solve a Take-From problem situation? What tools or strategies (if any) do they use to make sense of counting up?

3. Look at the word problems in the textbook you currently use and identify 8–10 Take-From problems. Sort them based on which term is missing: start, change, or result. Rewrite the problems to move the missing term. For example, Result Unknown problems could be rewritten to be Start Unknown or Change Unknown problems.

NOTES

CHAPTER FIVE

Part-Part-Whole
Understanding the Relationship

Thinking About Part-Part-Whole Situations

In the last three chapters we explored active addition and subtraction problems and how finding the story and the placement of the unknown—and teaching students to model this using pictorial and physical representations—are all part of developing strong operation sense. In this chapter we explore how students can use equations to represent what they see in a problem and how to model and understand a problem situation that is based not on action but on a relationship: the Part-Part-Whole problem situation. In the beginning of the chapter we will pay special attention to the distinction between these two kinds of problem situations.

Addition and Subtraction Problem Situations

	Total Unknown	One Part Unknown	Both Parts Unknown
Part-Part-Whole	The first grade voted on a game for recess. 11 students voted to play four square. 8 voted to go to the playground. How many students are in the class? $8 + 11 = x$ $x - 11 = 8$	The 19 first graders voted on a recess activity. 8 students voted to go to the playground. How many wanted to play four square? $8 + x = 19$ $x = 19 - 8$	The 19 first graders voted on a recess activity. Some wanted to play four square. Some wanted to go to the playground. What are some ways the first graders could have voted? $x + y = 19$ $19 - x = y$

Note: The representations for the problem situations in this table reflect our understanding based on a number of resources. These include the tables in the Common Core State Standards for Mathematics (CCSS-M; National Governors Association Center for Best Practices and Council of Chief State School Officers, 2010), the problem situations as described in the Cognitively Guided Instruction research (Carpenter, Hiebert, & Moser, 1981), and other tools. See the Appendix and the book's companion website for a more detailed summary of the documents that informed our development of this table.

ACTIVE SITUATIONS

	Result Unknown	Change Addend Unknown	Start Addend Unknown
Add-To	Paulo counted 9 crayons. He put them in the basket. Paulo found 6 more crayons under the table. He put them in the basket. How many crayons are in the basket? $9 + 6 = x$ $6 = x - 9$	Paulo counted 9 crayons. He found more and put them in the basket. Now Paulo has 15 crayons. How many crayons did he put in the basket? $9 + x = 15$ $9 = 15 - x$	Paulo had some crayons. He found 6 more crayons under the table. Now he has 15 crayons. How many crayons did Paulo have in the beginning? $x + 6 = 15$ $15 - 6 = x$
Take-From	There are 19 students in Mrs. Amadi's class. 4 students went to the office to say the Pledge. How many students are in the class now? $19 - 4 = x$ $4 + x = 19$	There are 19 students in Mrs. Amadi's class. Some students went to class to read the Pledge. There were still 15 students in the classroom. How many students went to the office? $19 - x = 15$ $x + 15 = 19$	4 students went to the office. 15 students were still in the classroom. How many students are there in Mrs. Amadi's class? $x - 4 = 15$ $15 + 4 = x$

RELATIONSHIP (NONACTIVE) SITUATIONS

	Total Unknown	One Part Unknown	Both Parts Unknown
Part-Part-Whole	The first grade voted on a game for recess. 11 students voted to play four square. 8 voted to go to the playground. How many students are in the class? $8 + 11 = x$ $x - 11 = 8$	The 19 first graders voted on a recess activity. 8 students voted to go to the playground. How many wanted to play four square? $8 + x = 19$ $x = 19 - 8$	The 19 first graders voted on a recess activity. Some wanted to play four square. Some wanted to go to the playground. What are some ways the first graders could have voted? $x + y = 19$ $19 - x = y$
	Difference Unknown	**Greater Quantity Unknown**	**Lesser Quantity Unknown**
Additive Comparison	Jessie's paper airplane flew 14 feet. Jo's paper airplane flew 9 feet. How much less did Jo's paper airplane fly than Jessie's? $14 - 9 = x$ $9 + x = 14$	Jo's paper airplane flew 9 feet. Jessie's paper airplane flew 5 feet more than Jo's. How far did Jessie's paper airplane fly? $9 + 5 = x$ $x - 5 = 9$	Jessie's paper airplane flew 14 feet. Jo's paper airplane flew 5 feet less than Jessie's paper airplane. How far did Jo's paper airplane fly? $14 - 5 = x$ $14 = x + 5$

online resources ^ Visit **http://resources.corwin.com/problemsolvingk-2** to download a copy of the full Addition and Subtraction Problem Situations Table.

Sandbox Notes: Explore Your Thinking

As you enter into problem exploration mode, gather your tools, including markers or crayons, base 10 blocks, linking cubes, counters, and any other tools that you routinely have available in your classroom. Try several of the concrete manipulatives and some hand-drawn picture models that reflect the mathematical story in the word problem. If you put the problem in your own words, revisit that rephrasing and specify where you can see each quantity in the problem. Where can you see each quantity in the models you have created? Think about how your work can express your understanding of the problem situation.

Ask yourself these questions to focus your thinking:

- Think about the quantities in each situation. What do they represent? What is the relationship between the quantities?

- How can you represent the quantities in the word problems with your manipulatives or pictures?

- How can you make a number sentence about the problem?

The problems in Figures 5.1 and 5.2 highlight the difference between active problem situations and those that show relationship. Keep this in mind as you reformulate the problems in your own words. And remember, your work here isn't to come up with an answer to the problems but to explore the problem situations by engaging in and thinking about how students might use multiple representations to share their thinking.

FIGURE 5.1	FIGURE 5.2
The soccer team has 12 members. 5 players left practice early. How many players stayed until the end of practice?	The soccer team has 12 members. 5 are wearing green shoes and the rest are wearing white shoes. How many team members are wearing white shoes?

ENTER THE PROBLEM

FIGURE 5.3 A MODEL FOR MATHEMATIZING WORD PROBLEMS

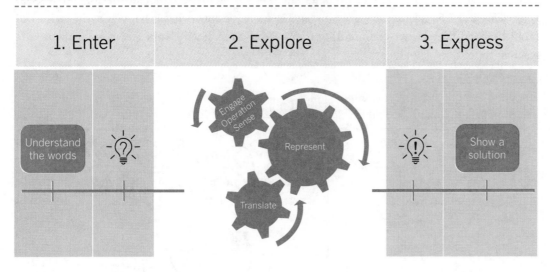

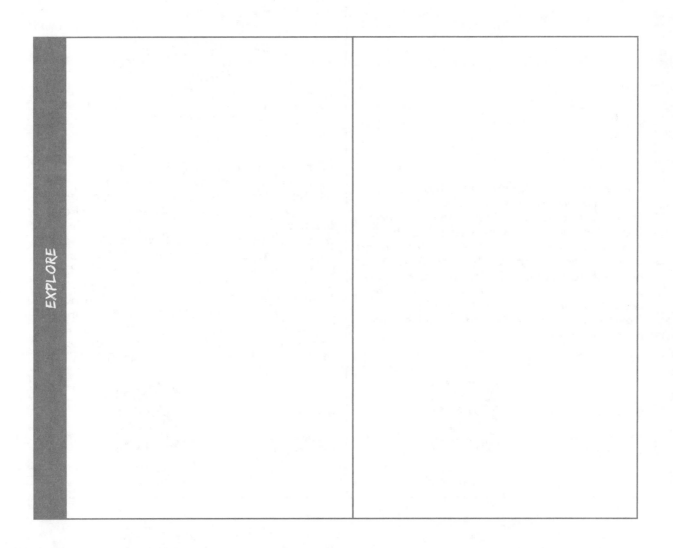

STUDENTS AND TEACHERS THINK ABOUT THE PROBLEMS

Now that you've had a chance to think about your own approach, look at the student work in Figures 5.4 and 5.5 and consider how students describe or draw what is happening in each word problem. Read the teacher commentary that follows the student work and consider what the teacher noticed.

FIGURE 5.4   **FIGURE 5.5**

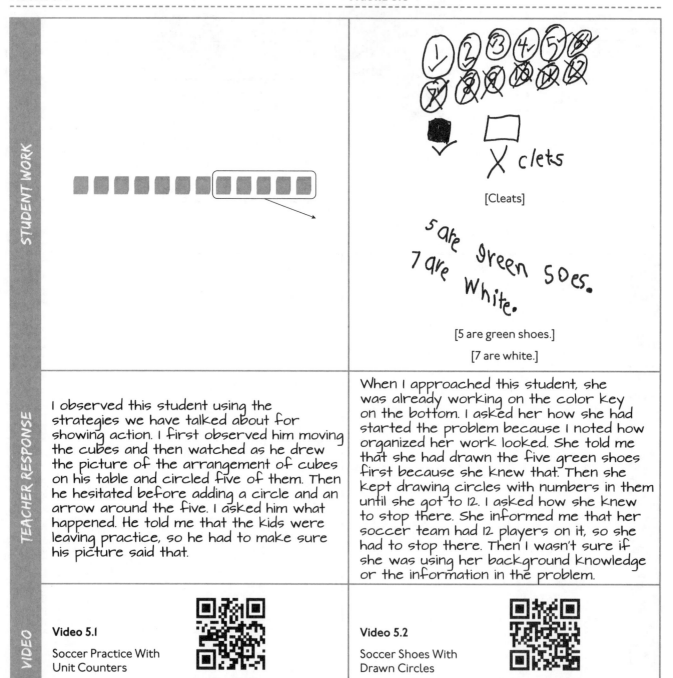

STUDENT WORK

[Cleats]

[5 are green shoes.]

[7 are white.]

TEACHER RESPONSE

I observed this student using the strategies we have talked about for showing action. I first observed him moving the cubes and then watched as he drew the picture of the arrangement of cubes on his table and circled five of them. Then he hesitated before adding a circle and an arrow around the five. I asked him what happened. He told me that the kids were leaving practice, so he had to make sure his picture said that.

When I approached this student, she was already working on the color key on the bottom. I asked her how she had started the problem because I noted how organized her work looked. She told me that she had drawn the five green shoes first because she knew that. Then she kept drawing circles with numbers in them until she got to 12. I asked how she knew to stop there. She informed me that her soccer team had 12 players on it, so she had to stop there. Then I wasn't sure if she was using her background knowledge or the information in the problem.

VIDEO

Video 5.1

Soccer Practice With Unit Counters

resources.corwin.com/ problemsolvingK-2

Video 5.2

Soccer Shoes With Drawn Circles

resources.corwin.com/ problemsolvingK-2

TAKE-AWAY ACTION Look back at your own work. How did you model the "take-away" action of students leaving practice? Did you draw some kind of marks to show that motion? The work sample in Figure 5.4 captured that same kind of action in two ways, one we can see and one we read in the teacher notes and see in Video 5.1. The student first physically moved the five cubes representing 5 students leaving practice and then circled those cubes and added an arrow, using the class's idea about showing action in a picture. As we saw in Chapter 4, this kind of problem is referred to as a Take-From problem situation, and it can be clearly modeled with pictures or manipulatives that display action and show a visible quantity removed.

PART-PART-WHOLE RELATIONSHIP By contrast, the solution to the shoes problem in Figure 5.5 shows 12 students on the team, with 5 wearing green shoes and the rest wearing white. As with the Take-From problem in Figure 5.4, what the student said is just as important as what she drew. Given the color key and what she told the teacher, we see that she is describing the relationship between the two colors of shoes and all of the players, rather than the result of any action. Each group of students represents one *part* of the *whole* team. This problem situation is called **Part-Part-Whole**. Sometimes it's referred to as Put Together/Take Apart, which may cause confusion because it may suggest action where there isn't any. We prefer Part-Part-Whole because it emphasizes the relationships within the problem situation.

> Part-Part-Whole:
> A problem situation that describes the relationship between subgroups (parts) and an entire collection (whole).

Now that we have outlined the difference between the Take-From problem situation that shows actions and the Part-Part-Whole situation that describes relationships, look at the student work in Figure 5.6 and decide if it is a representation of the soccer practice problem or the soccer shoe problem. Be sure to give reasons for your opinion and then think about the questions you might ask this student if you approached her table. This is a good opportunity to discuss your interpretations with a team of colleagues.

FIGURE 5.6 WHICH PROBLEM DOES THIS REPRESENTATION REFLECT?

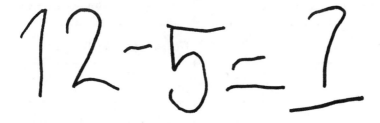

If you and your colleagues could not agree which problem this solution belonged to, you are not alone, because we can't know. When students show us only numbers in an equation, all we know about their interpretation is that they subtracted. But since they don't say why, it's important to follow up and ask for more information in order to assess their understanding of the problem situation.

DEFINING THE PART-PART-WHOLE SITUATION

In this chapter we chose to contrast the Take-From and Part-Part-Whole problem situations because this distinction is particularly challenging for students (and sometimes even adults) to understand. For example, when we ask teachers to describe the differences between the two problems at the beginning of the chapter (Figures 5.1 and 5.2), they say things like:

In the first one, something happened. But in the second one, nothing happened: The problem just described something.

The first one is normal and, I can't describe it, but the second one is different. It's more complicated. The first one is very straightforward.

Though teachers can tell that there is something different about the shoes problem (Figure 5.2), they struggle to find the words to describe it. Acting out problems using physical objects makes sense for modeling players leaving practice, but it just doesn't seem as effective with the shoes type of problem. The shoes problem is an example of a Part-Part-Whole problem situation, and it describes the relationship between the quantity of green shoes and the quantity of white shoes as parts of the whole problem situation. The Part-Part-Whole problem situation doesn't describe an action like the Take-From problem about players leaving practice does.

Before we explore how to model these relationships to improve student understanding, consider some of the Part-Part-Whole situations that might be familiar to your students. Table 5.7 lists some possible "wholes." What parts or subgroups might be included in those wholes? Also listed are some examples of parts. What whole might they be a part of? (Note that Part-Part-Whole problems can have an unlimited number of parts.) The table includes a few examples to get you started, and there are also empty rows so that you can add more examples to use with your students.

FIGURE 5.7 PART-PART-WHOLE SITUATIONS

WHOLE	PARTS IN THE WHOLE
Class	Boys, girls
Stripes in the American flag	Red stripes, white stripes
Pets in the house	Dogs, cats, fish
Colors	
	Soccer, baseball, swimming

MODELING RELATIONSHIPS VERSUS ACTION

Figures 5.8 and 5.9 are representations of the same two problems we saw at the beginning of this chapter. Rather than using two samples of student work this time, we are demonstrating the difference between representations of the Take-From and Part-Part-Whole problem situations using images that are nearly identical. The two-color counters are particularly useful for this demonstration because they allow us to show the two different parts of the whole—in this case, the team of 12 players.

FIGURE 5.8   FIGURE 5.9

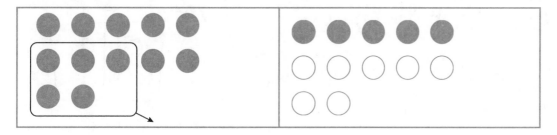

Watch how Video 5.1 models the soccer players leaving practice problem (illustrated in Figure 5.8). How does a video answer change or add to your interpretation of the student's representation and the student's response in general? Does the action in the video make you see the action in the problem differently than you see it in the illustration in Figure 5.8?

Watch Video 5.2 of the green and white shoes Part-Part-Whole problem (illustrated in Figure 5.9). The two-color counters are particularly effective for helping show the difference between two parts of the whole team. Note that each of these videos models a solution showing information about the context of the problem, not just the "answer." If you are reading this with a group, now is a good time to stop and discuss: What is the difference between modeling an answer (like "7") and modeling a solution matching what happens in a problem?

MOVING FROM COUNTERS TO BAR MODELS

As we noted earlier in this chapter, the representations of problem situations that students create can be important sources of information about the depth of their understanding of the problem. As you look at the problem in Figure 5.10, think about the many ways it could be represented. Translate it into your own words and think about the drawings or manipulatives you might use to represent the story in the problem. What representations might your students choose?

FIGURE 5.10

The students had a choice of vanilla ice cream or chocolate ice cream. 8 chose vanilla and 9 chose chocolate.

Look at the two samples of student work in Figures 5.11 and 5.12 and consider how students describe or draw what is happening in the given word problem. Before looking at the teacher commentary that follows the student work, take a moment to discuss these work samples with your partner teachers.

FIGURE 5.11   FIGURE 5.12

STUDENT WORK

0000000o 000 00 0 00
1 2 3 4 5 6 7 8 9 10 11 12 13 14 15 16 17

So iT = 17

[So it = 17.]

I Sartid
at 8 and
Catid
49 9 17

8 9

[I started at 8 and counted up 9.]

[17]

TEACHER RESPONSE

This student started the problem with two-color counters. I asked her if she could draw a picture to show me what the problem was about and how she got her answer from the counters. It's interesting that she has represented and labeled the 9 students who chose chocolate ice cream, and while there are 8 more counters, she has not written the 8.

In other words, I see that she understands that the two ice cream flavor choices are two parts of the whole class's choices. Her counters are even arranged a little like a bar model!

This student created a form of a bar model, showing the two parts, 8 and 9. He also explained his computation strategy, starting with 8, as the problem did, and counting on 9 more to 17. But like the first student, he has not named the quantities in his problem. What is he counting?

VIDEO

Video 5.3

Favorite Ice Cream With Counters

resources.corwin.com/
problemsolvingK-2

Video 5.4

Favorite Ice Cream With a Bar Model

resources.corwin.com/
problemsolvingK-2

The ice cream problem is an example of a Part-Part-Whole problem situation, with the total (whole) unknown. The student work samples in Figures 5.11 and 5.12 show representations of a Part-Part-Whole problem situation in an effective way—two groups that are parts of the whole class. Figure 5.11 is a pictorial representation, but the teacher's words tell us that the student originally used two-color counters to represent her thinking. The student whose work is displayed in Figure 5.12 shows an early version of a mathematical structure called a **bar model**. The two bars with an 8 and a 9 show that the student likely recognizes that those two quantities represent two parts and that they are related to the whole group of students.

Bar model: A visual representation that uses sections of a rectangular bar to represent the quantities in a problem.

How can you help students learn to use an abstract mathematical tool like a bar model effectively while still focusing attention on the context of problems? Start with the concrete example, like we saw the student do in Figure 5.11.

The student whose work is represented in Figure 5.11 used two-color counters to effectively show the correct quantities, lining them up in an organized manner. For some students, two-color counters may be displayed without organization, as you can see in Figure 5.13.

FIGURE 5.13 UNORGANIZED USE OF TWO-COLOR COUNTERS

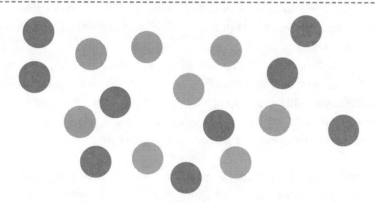

Instead of offering two-color counters, we can make two changes that will help students connect bar models to problem contexts. One, we can give students connecting cubes of different colors, encouraging them to make a colored train for each "part" of the whole. Because the pieces can easily be joined and manipulated, a "bar" is created.

To illustrate a strategy for introducing students to bar models, we are going to change up the ice cream problem a few ways. The first change is to include three addends (or parts) to remind us that Part-Part-Whole isn't always two parts. Second, we can make the difference between the parts more noticeable by presenting a problem with very different quantities separated by color. Third, we are modeling a strategy for modifying a problem context to be more suitable for a group of students' particular needs. In this case, we could, as teachers, change the context from ice cream to smoothies because many students, particularly those of Asian descent, are not accustomed to dairy products. A smoothie can be all fruit and is relatable to most students. On top of that we added mango, a flavor familiar to students from tropical regions. If you worked in a food-insecure community, you might choose to avoid food-based word problems all together. These are small changes, but they show that we acknowledge students' humanity and their membership in our classroom.

Read the problem in Figure 5.14 and note the changes. With your team, talk about the changes you might make in order to adjust this problem to make it familiar to your students, and then discuss how the blocks in Figure 5.15 represent the problem situation.

FIGURE 5.14

The class voted for their favorite smoothie. 3 students voted for mango. 5 students voted for strawberry. 9 students voted for banana. How many students are in the class?

FIGURE 5.15 A PHYSICAL BAR MODEL OF THE SMOOTHIE PROBLEM

As students work with their physical bar models, they have a way to check their quantities. In the smoothie problem, the votes for each fruit are different, and so are the bars that represent them. Students should have opportunities to orally name the parts and name the wholes to which the parts belong. For example, the physical bar model would be identified with the smoothie flavors "Mango," "Strawberry," and "Banana," and by the whole, which is the number of students with votes for their favorite smoothie. Students should have opportunities to create and orally quantify multiple and varied contextual word problems using their linking cubes, even including examples with more than two parts, or even some parts with a quantity of 0.

Once students have engaged with the physical bar models, they can begin to transfer this information to a pictorial model of the linking cubes. To begin with, students can trace their cubes and label each part (Figure 5.16).

FIGURE 5.16 THE BEGINNING OF A PICTORIAL MODEL OF THE SMOOTHIE PROBLEM

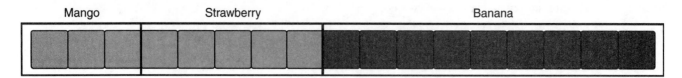

| Mango | Strawberry | Banana |

Because students have had multiple opportunities to explain their parts verbally, this step is grounded in their experiences. Because they have had multiple opportunities to describe and name the wholes, adding the "whole" bar is just one more step in the process that many students will be ready to do (Figure 5.17). Note that the three parts still keep their relative sizes the same.

FIGURE 5.17 THE FINAL PICTORIAL MODEL OF THE SMOOTHIE PROBLEM

| Mango | Strawberry | Banana |

Favorite Smoothie Flavors

Once students have seen many examples of a bar model with real-life problems, they are ready to begin taking away some of the realistic details because the final goal for moving to the bar model is to reduce it to an abstract diagram of the problem situation. The abstract bar model in Figure 5.18 keeps the names and quantities of each part, but each section is roughly the same size. It is important that young students not jump directly to this nonproportional model but instead build their understanding of it with proportional physical models created to represent real-life Part-Part-Whole problem situations.

FIGURE 5.18 A BAR MODEL OF THE SMOOTHIE PROBLEM

3 Mango	5 Strawberry	9 Banana
Favorite Smoothie Flavors		

THE SPECIAL CASE OF BOTH ADDENDS UNKNOWN

A Part-Part-Whole word problem typically has only one element unknown, either one of the parts or the whole, but the addition and subtraction problem types table at the beginning of the chapter also has a fourth column labeled "Both Parts Unknown." This variety of the Part-Part-Whole problem situation is often used as a popular calculation activity for the youngest students. A number of two-color counters (usually 5, 7, or 10) are put in a cup, shaken, and poured out onto the table. Students record the results, sometimes by coloring circles red or yellow to represent the outcome and later by writing number sentences that show the outcome. For example, if 10 counters show 2 yellow and 8 red, the equation would read $2+8=10$. This activity is repeated, reinforcing students' fluency with known facts that add up to 10, among other skills.

This task is not only a good problem-solving task, but it is also good practice in organizing information. It is also inherently a calculation and fluency task with great value. But another variety of this activity can instead emphasize the problem context, still with both addends unknown. Consider the problem in Figure 5.19, and as you do, imagine what each band would sound like with the different configurations.

FIGURE 5.19

There are 10 musicians in the band. Some play the drums and some play the kazoo. How many different ways can they make a band?

drum   kazoo

Image sources: Maksym Rudoi/iStock.com (drum), Suzifoo/iStock.com (kazoo)

This problem is one that your students can act out in your classroom using makeshift or inexpensive instruments. What would the band sound like with 1 drum and 9 kazoos? What if there were 0 kazoos and 10 drums? What about 10 kazoos and 0 drums? Each of these band configurations will produce a different sound. We often give students problems that engage their visual sense, and you could certainly write a variety of this problem that gives students this opportunity, but we rarely write problems that encourage them to listen and discern different sounds. This is especially true in math class. In Figure 5.20 you can see two additional outcomes from the drum and kazoo problem. What would these bands sound like?

FIGURE 5.20 POSSIBLE OUTCOMES FOR THE DRUM AND KAZOO PROBLEM

Image sources: Maksym Rudoi/iStock.com (drum), Suzifoo/iStock.com (kazoo)

When working with a Both Addends Unknown problem situation, students can learn many important mathematical ideas:

- There can be more than one right answer to a problem.

- There are many ways to compose and decompose numbers.

- It takes good organization to be sure you have found *all* of the possible solutions.

- 8 + 2 and 2 + 8 (and other commutative pairs) look different from each other.

- There are lots of ways to make 10, especially if you add a third instrument, like a triangle.

In this particular problem, students are learning all the different ways to make 10 (1 + 9, 2 + 8, etc.). They have opportunities to talk about and see that facts like 2 + 8 and 8 + 2 both have a sum of 10 but the bands nevertheless sound different. The combination of 2 drums and 8 kazoos is certainly not the same arrangement as 8 drums and 2 kazoos, even if both bands have 10 musicians.

For more detailed strategies for teaching tasks centered on Both Addends Unknown problems, please read the helpful article "Variations in Both-Addends-Unknown Problems," by Zak Champagne and two of his colleagues (Champagne, Schoen, & Riddell, 2014).

A NOTE ABOUT THE COMMUTATIVE PROPERTY

The commutative property tells us that the sum of addends is the same, even when two addends are added in a different order. In the preceding example, both 2 + 8 and 8 + 2 have a sum of 10. It is important to recognize that this property applies to computing answers or calculating sums, not necessarily to the problem situations themselves. The two bands (2 drums + 8 kazoos or 8 drums + 2 kazoos) do not have the same sound, though they do have the same number of musicians.

In Chapter 3, we saw Devonté's work on the fun run problem, a Start Unknown situation (see Figure 3.20). Since he did not know the beginning of the narrative, Devonté instead started his computation with the change value given in the problem because it allowed him to use what he already knew. He counted up from 21 (the number of students who joined the fun run on day 2) to 35 (the total number of students who signed up) to find the quantity, which was 14 students who signed up on day 1. Devonté recognized that it was easier to reason about $21+?=35$ than to use the equation that more accurately represents the problem situation ($?+21=35$), and that this process would help him find the answer. Essentially, he used the commutative property when he changed the order of the addends in the equation. But Devonté also recognized that rewriting the equation did not mean that 21 was now the starting quantity in the story.

For Part-Part-Whole situations, the commutative property is nearly invisible because the order in which addends are put together usually doesn't matter. But in active problem situations, this isn't the case, as we saw with Devonté's fun run problem. In this problem there is a narrative sequence, an order in which the action takes place. Devonté used the commutative property only to make calculation easier. But with Part-Part-Whole problems, as long as each quantity reflects the appropriate part of the group (boys and girls or drums and kazoos), they can be named in any order. This is a reminder that we can distinguish between an equation that represents the problem situation and a variation of that equation that makes it easier to compute the answer.

Using Children's Literature to Explore Part-Part-Whole Situations

The town of Puchon in South Korea is known for producing the biggest and sweetest peaches in all of Korea. The peaches are so desirable that the people in the town are not able to afford to eat the peaches themselves. During a strong hailstorm, peaches begin to fall from the mountain and float into the water that is flooding the streets. After feasting on peaches, the townspeople begin to worry about the farmers who lost their crop, so they gather the rest of the peaches, bring them up the mountain, and tie them to the trees for the farmers to retrieve.

There is much about the tale in *Peach Heaven* (Choi, 2005) that can be quantified. How many peaches can one family eat? How many peaches might have fallen because of hail? How many were lost? How many peaches are typically on one tree? How many peach trees are in Puchon?

MAKE PREDICTIONS

The Make Predictions strategy for finding mathematical relationships in children's literature is a good way to dive into this story. If students can't imagine the number of peaches an entire town could eat, consider just what their class might be able to eat. Or predict how many peaches might be on a single tree. If the number of peaches on a single tree is considered the whole, predict how many peaches the class can eat (part). How many would be lost in a storm (part)? How many peaches could be found and returned to the farmers (part)? There is no right answer to these questions, but there are reasonable estimates that help students sort the parts from the whole and consider the quantity of peaches that could be involved in this story.

Tall tales like this one are a good genre for identifying and imagining Part-Part-Whole relationships, but any beloved story has the potential to reveal other opportunities to explore groups that make up a whole collection.

Warning: The next pages include student examples of the next set of problem situations. If you find it difficult to resist looking forward while practicing in the sandbox, consider covering the facing page with a sheet of paper.

Moving Beyond 20

One of the benefits of focusing on context and relationships in a word problem is that it provides everyone access to the problem at the outset, whether they have learned to calculate the numbers or not. Thus, students who haven't mastered the calculation of larger whole numbers can still take a problem into the mathematizing sandbox, find the story, and express it through different representations. In this section, we explore problems involving whole-number values as great as 120, the upper range typically expected of primary students.

As you reflect on the problems in Figures 5.21 and 5.22, pause before entering the mathematizing sandbox. Look for models that closely represent the Part-Part-Whole problem situation, and think about whether and how the introduction of greater quantities affects your exploration. For example, do larger quantities affect your choice of grouped or ungrouped units?

Remember to revisit the Sandbox Notes at the beginning of the chapter for suggestions and guiding questions.

FIGURE 5.21

FIGURE 5.22

One of Mrs. Masuda's students brought her tulips on the first day of spring. Everyone noticed how tall the flowers were and wanted to measure them. The bud of the tulip was 9 centimeter cubes tall and the stem was 29 centimeter cubes tall. How tall is the whole flower?

Image source: VIDOK/iStock.com

mi cuaderno

Juan brought a new notebook to measure on the class's measurement day. The soccer ball part measured 29 cm tall. The whole notebook measured 38 cm tall. How tall is the top part that says "mi cuaderno"?

Image source: traffic_analyzer/iStock.com

ENTER THE PROBLEM

EXPLORE

STUDENTS AND TEACHERS THINK ABOUT THE PROBLEMS

Sometimes student thinking surprises us because they think of things that we ourselves might never have thought of. The work samples in Figures 5.23 and 5.24 surprised the teacher who was looking at them. Now that you've had a chance to solve these problems yourself, look at the solutions and the teacher's responses and consider what is similar to your thinking and what is different.

FIGURE 5.23

FIGURE 5.24

STUDENT WORK

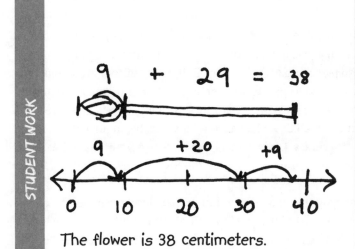

The flower is 38 centimeters.

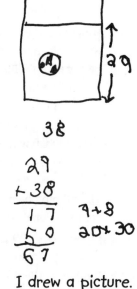

I drew a picture.
I like to play soccer.

TEACHER RESPONSE

This student was working in a group with a parent volunteer today. When I walked by, I heard the student describe her calculation strategy and saw the volunteer draw the number line to support her thinking. I am not sure what else happened, honestly, but when I passed by, the flower drawing was not yet there. I wonder how they got that flower drawing.

Later on, I asked the parent volunteer about the flower. She said that they had finished the number line together and that the student was very disappointed that it didn't look like the flower anymore. So, they worked together to figure out which of the number line jumps was the bud and which was the stem.

After we did Measurement Day in class, I was sure that the students would have enough experience with measurement to do these problems. I was surprised that this student added the measurement of one part to the measurement of the whole. The fact that the 38 is written without any connection to the drawing tells me that he may not have understood the problem his partner posed.

VIDEO

Video 5.5

Tulip Height With a Number Line

resources.corwin.com/
problemsolvingK-2

Video 5.6

Notebook Height With a Sketch

resources.corwin.com/
problemsolvingK-2

One of the challenges in the primary grades is making sense of a variety of different models and tools for representing numbers. When learning to work with greater values, students learn to use not only standard tools like rulers but also nonstandard tools like cubes or paper clips for measuring. Making a connection to a number line encourages students to recognize that numbers measure real and tangible quantities. As we will discuss in the next section, the models that students draw can influence their understanding of the problem situation and how that connects to the real-world context.

MODELING MEASUREMENT PROBLEMS

Often we see measurement story problems in more active problems, representing situations where something is changing. It might be an Add-To situation, when a tree grows, or a Take-From situation, when a piece of something is cut away. But as we saw in the preceding set of problems, measurement problems can also be nonactive, making comparisons in the problem or describing a part of a whole, like a flower with two parts: its bud and its stem. Tulips are not complicated-looking flowers, and it is easy to recognize the bud as part of its overall length in a naturally interesting real-world context for students. What we are striving for are models that most accurately reflect a context. As the student examples in Figures 5.23 and 5.24 show, it is possible to solve the problem using models with varying degrees of accuracy. Let's take a look at these two solutions and see what might be lost in focusing just on getting an answer.

The tulip problem (Figure 5.23) is an example of a representation that closely matches the child's computational strategy. The problem itself is of the Part-Part-Whole type, with the whole length unknown. During their work time, the parent volunteer and the student who created the number line showed $9 + 20 + 9$. Interestingly, without the drawing created after the number line, we would not know which 9 was the centimeters of the bud and which was the 9 centimeters that is part of the stem, decomposed into 20 cm and 9 cm for easier computation. With the drawing the reader can more easily recognize the parts of the flower and match them to the number line. Maybe you are thinking that this calculation would have been far easier if the student had added 9 and 9 to get 18 and added that to 20. That is certainly an easier calculation! But for students who are just starting to focus on problem solving separately from their computation skills, it is helpful to match the relationship in the problem to the representation used to find a solution. This supports students' operation sense as they learn to build meaning of addition and subtraction as operations.

The solution in Figure 5.24 shows an efficient and accurate calculation, but the calculation doesn't represent the problem presented in the notebook context. Like the first problem of the set, the notebook problem is also a Part-Part-Whole situation, this time with one of the parts unknown. The problem context can be represented by the following equation:

$$29 + ? = 38$$

soccer part + top part = whole notebook

Our student, the efficient calculator, does not appear to have made sense of the problem context before picking out the numbers and calculating. Perhaps it's no surprise that the student lost focus on the details of the problem situation too quickly before moving to do the calculation, particularly if he just learned how to add two-digit numbers. As you have likely seen, students will often use their most recent math lesson as inspiration for what calculation to choose to do. At the same time, this may be an error related to the challenge of the Part Unknown version of the Part-Part-Whole situation in general: A missing part is a more challenging variation of the problem type. It may just be a matter of handing the student a ruler and asking, "How tall is the notebook?" and see how he addresses the fact that he has two answers: 39 cm in the problem and 67 cm in his answer.

Maintaining students' focus on the problem situation before moving quickly to computation can help students build those skills alongside their computation skills. This is doubly true when they are trying to understand problem situations that can be more challenging, such as the missing part variation of the Part-Part-Whole problem type. What other ideas do you have for focusing student attention on the context of the problem? If you are reading this with a team, now is a good time to stop and discuss your ideas.

WRITING EQUATIONS: ADDITION OR SUBTRACTION

In the previous section we introduced an equation that shows the missing part of a Part-Part-Whole situation using a question mark standing in for the missing value. You may have noticed that this is an addition equation. Look back at your own solution to this problem. Did you use subtraction or addition to solve it? Most adults use subtraction to solve a problem like the notebook problem, using "take away" to find the missing length, like this:

$$38 - 29 = ?$$

whole notebook – bottom part = top part

Of course, there is no "taking away" going on in this problem. It is not an active problem type. Instead, the subtraction represents the relationship between the measurements of the bottom part and the top part of the notebook. Together these both make the whole length of the notebook. So why do we often use subtraction to find the solution to this problem? To make sense of this we have to expand our definition of subtraction to include more than just "take away." This new model of subtraction is often called the "difference model," because we are looking for the difference between the length of the whole notebook and the bottom part. We will see this model of subtraction again in Chapter 6, when we explore comparisons.

We can also use equations to represent any Part-Part-Whole situation, using both addition and subtraction variations to describe the same relationship. One benefit of representing a relationship as subtraction is that it sets up the calculation strategy that we already discussed. By contrast, an addition equation representation gives students the opportunity to learn to use counting-up calculation strategies. Either way, we emphasize again that assessing students' calculation strategies or their computing of an answer has to be separate from assessing students' understanding of the relationships in any problem situation. The calculation strategies make up a separate but important skill set. Understanding the problem situation is yet another set of skills.

As you read the Part-Part-Whole word problem in Figure 5.25, think about an equation that best represents the relationships in the problem. Again, do not rush to find an equation that would simply work to calculate an answer. Instead, start by focusing on the relationships in the problem and write an equation that would be the best illustration of the relationships.

FIGURE 5.25

- -

Jian had 20 grapes for snack. 14 of the grapes were green. The rest of the grapes were red. How many grapes were red?

Look at the models in Figures 5.26 and 5.27 and think about which equations most closely match the student's interpretation of the problem situation. After studying the student work, read the teacher's comments and consider what is challenging the teacher's thinking.

FIGURE 5.26   **FIGURE 5.27**

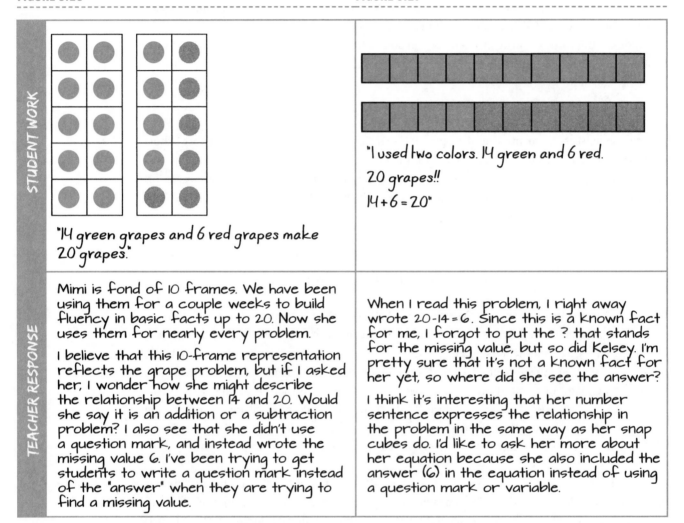

STUDENT WORK

"14 green grapes and 6 red grapes make 20 grapes."

"I used two colors. 14 green and 6 red.
20 grapes!!
14+6 = 20"

TEACHER RESPONSE

Mimi is fond of 10 frames. We have been using them for a couple weeks to build fluency in basic facts up to 20. Now she uses them for nearly every problem.

I believe that this 10-frame representation reflects the grape problem, but if I asked her, I wonder how she might describe the relationship between 14 and 20. Would she say it is an addition or a subtraction problem? I also see that she didn't use a question mark, and instead wrote the missing value 6. I've been trying to get students to write a question mark instead of the "answer" when they are trying to find a missing value.

When I read this problem, I right away wrote 20-14 = 6. Since this is a known fact for me, I forgot to put the ? that stands for the missing value, but so did Kelsey. I'm pretty sure that it's not a known fact for her yet, so where did she see the answer?

I think it's interesting that her number sentence expresses the relationship in the problem in the same way as her snap cubes do. I'd like to ask her more about her equation because she also included the answer (6) in the equation instead of using a question mark or variable.

Both students put the answer of "6" in their equation instead of using a placeholder, like a question mark or variable, to stand in for the unknown quantity. Their teacher had been trying to introduce the question mark to them as a placeholder to use when they didn't yet know the answer to a word problem. This may not seem like a big problem, but it depends on how the students actually found the answer. If they found the answer by counting the spaces (or cubes) between 14 and 20, they are fully relying on the physical model to find the answer. At this age (early primary), this is perfectly acceptable, but as students move into second and third grades and beyond and start moving away from physical models to symbolic representations, they won't have the skills they need to find answers that are not known facts. For example, what if there are 91 grapes and 63 of them are green and the rest are red? Students not only need a strategy in place to figure out the computation procedure, but, more important, they also need a strategy for making sense of the problem situation and representing it in a way that suggests the calculation that will solve it.

It is important that students be able to use both addition and subtraction equations to represent a variety of situations and model them effectively. Often children will let the order in which the numbers are presented in the problem guide the structure of their equations (De Corte & Verschaffel, 1987). In this case, students would be more likely to present the 20 first, followed by the 14 green grapes, and then the rest. The equation would look like this:

total grapes = *green* *grapes* + *red grapes*

$$20 = 14 + ?$$

But this strategy might easily have led the students astray. They might have written this equation instead:

$$20 + 14 = ?$$

The numbers are presented in the equation in the same order that they are given in the problem. But with this equation we add, which gives us an incorrect interpretation of the problem situation.

Notice that the equation could also show students focused first on the two kinds of grapes rather than on the total number of grapes. For a student who sees the situation this way, this equation might make more sense:

green *grapes* + *red grapes* = *total grapes*

$$14 + ? = 20$$

A student who writes the following equation is likely already familiar with the efficient computational strategy mentioned by the teacher in her response to the student work in Figure 5.27, recognizing that an efficient way to calculate a Part Unknown problem like this one is to subtract:

total grapes − *green* *grapes* = *red grapes*

$$20 - 14 = ?$$

At the beginning of this section we asked you to write the equation that you feel best represents each of the first two problems. In the grape problem, we saw that the *best* equation might not be a single version. The *best* equation may vary from student to student, but the *best* equation should represent the student's understanding of the context. When students write equations, ask about the reasoning for their choices, whether the equations look accurate to you or not. Their reasoning may surprise you.

FINDING THE EQUATION IN THE MODEL

As you read the Part-Part-Whole word problem in Figure 5.28, think about the equation and the pictorial or concrete model that best represents the relationships in the problem. Again, do not rush to find an equation that would simply work to calculate an answer. Instead, start by focusing on the relationships in the problem and write an equation that would be the best illustration of these relationships.

FIGURE 5.28

Tyler works at an amusement park. His job is to empty all of the trash and recycling bins. He has 95 bins to empty. If 63 of these bins are trash bins, how many recycling bins does he have to empty?

Take a look at the student models in Figures 5.29 and 5.30 and think about how the equations closely match the student's interpretation of the problem situation. After studying the student work, read the teacher's comments and consider what is challenging the teacher's thinking.

FIGURE 5.29   **FIGURE 5.30**

STUDENT WORK

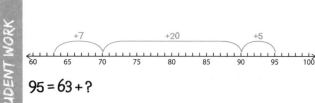

$95 = 63 + ?$

$7 + 20 + 5 = 32$ recycling bins

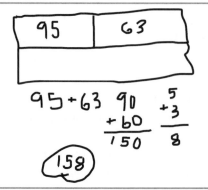

TEACHER RESPONSE

I am pleased to see that Cecilia is trying out the number line strategy. I keep a collection of number lines on the math tools table and encourage students to use them to assist with their calculations.

In this case, it looks like she chose to add up from 63 to 95, although I can see that the jumps on her number line could have also represented a counting-down strategy since they didn't have arrows. In this case, the equation clears it up.

Then I decided to pair her with Tito, who had drawn a bar model, also with no reference to the problem situation. In this case, I want to see if together they can figure out why they have different answers.

When I walked by, Tito had just started drawing the bar model. This was the first time I had seen him attempt the bar model without starting with the blocks first. I chose this problem (using larger quantities) so that I could see what students would do.

I walked by later and saw that he had put numbers in his bar model. But he smiled confidently back at me, proud of the work he had done. "Look, Mrs. M! I took the numbers apart!"

Yes, he had. His calculation was perfect, and I was very happy to see that, but I wasn't sure how to handle the fact that he added the wrong numbers.

I wanted to ask him to explain the relationship between the two kinds of bins to see if he understood the problem situation.

Cecilia's number line in Figure 5.29 represents an accurate and effective calculation strategy using a number line, yet we can't tell if she understands the problem situation even though she has an accurate answer and recognizes that there are 32 recycling bins. Her teacher is pleased with Cecilia's efficient use of the number line but points out that the 95 and the 63 are not labeled. Maybe Cecilia does understand the problem situation, but there isn't enough evidence here to tell us for sure.

Tito used a bar model in his answer. However, he drew the bars and then placed the numbers. It seems like he may have put the numbers into the spaces in the order in which they appear in the problem: 95 went into the first space and 63 went into the second. This is not an uncommon approach, and it means that Tito is likely not taking time to rephrase, model, and make sense of the relationships in the problem situation. Instead, he is entering numbers without the sense-making step and then moving straight to the calculation.

When Cecilia and Tito teamed up to work on this problem, they were able to explore the differences between their representations. The teacher encouraged them to revisit the problem situation, label the numbers as quantities, and describe the relationship between those quantities. Together they created a more complete solution and a single answer to the problem.

Although the bar model is a good fit for representing Part-Part-Whole situations, without first making sense of the problem situation, it holds no more value than using no pictorial model at all. Because the bar model can visibly show the relationship between the parts and the whole, it has the potential to be a useful tool. But it is no substitute for sense-making.

We have one final note about bar models. Many instructional resources recommend bar models for any subtraction or addition computation. It is definitely possible to do so. But remember that the goal in this book is to maintain focus on using representations to show *what happens* in the problem situation, rather than on effective computation strategies. Since bar models do not show any kind of action, we suggest reserving those only for nonactive problem situations, like Part-Part-Whole and Additive Comparisons (see Chapter 6), when the focus of instruction is on understanding the context of word problems. Chapters 2, 3, and 4 offer a variety of other models and representations that highlight what happens in active problem situations.

KEY IDEAS

1. Part-Part-Whole problem situations are nonactive. There is no beginning or end of a story because no changes are taking place.

2. The Part-Part-Whole problem situation describes a relationship, rather than an action, between the parts and the whole.

3. A Part-Part-Whole situation can be represented by either an addition or a subtraction equation without changing the meaning of the problem.

4. Effective models and representations of Part-Part-Whole problem situations have an attribute that helps distinguish one part from another part. This may be color, size, or pattern, or another recognizable attribute.

5. Use the commutative property carefully. It can be helpful in calculating answers, but we should be sure students understand and can represent the original problem situation first.

6. Students don't need to focus on classifying problem situations, but one research team discovered that using simple language like "something happened" to describe active problems and "altogether" to describe Part-Part-Whole problem situations was helpful information for students posing their own problems (Rudnitsky et al., 1995).

7. Equations that represent problem contexts are different from equations that represent efficient computation strategies. The equation students share is likely the one that represents how they are thinking about a problem or context.

8. Bar models should be built from concrete models and related to problem contexts. Often bar models are used for active problem situations, but they may be more effective in showing relationships like Part-Part-Whole problem situations.

9. The Both Addends Unknown problem situation not only provides good practice in recognizing problem situations, but it is also good practice for computation and fact fluency.

TRY IT OUT!

IDENTIFY THE PROBLEM SITUATION

Look at the problems below and decide which ones have action (Take-From or Add-To) and which ones are about relationships (Part-Part-Whole). Write an equation that represents each situation.

1. There were 12 people listening to the puppet sing; 10 of the people were children, and the rest were adults. How many adults were listening to the puppet sing?

2. The pet store donated a bag of 75 dog bones to the shelter. Some of the dog bones were round, and some of them were long. What possible combinations of round and long dog bones could be in the bag?

3. There were 36 bicycles parked at school. After some fifth graders left early, there were 14 bicycles left at school. How many fifth graders left early on bicycles?

4. The farmer sold 3 pounds of apples and 2 pounds of cherries at the market. How many pounds of fruit did the farmer sell?

5. There were 115 books donated for the used book sale: 86 of the books were children's books, and the rest were adult books. How many adult books were donated?

6. On Saturday, parents donated 86 children's books for the library's used book sale. They also donated some adult books. At the end of the day, 115 books had been donated. How many adult books were donated?

WRITE THE PROBLEM

Create a Part-Part-Whole word problem that could be represented and/or solved by each equation below. (For younger grades, translate into a verbal number sentence first.)

1. $? = 7 - 2$

2. $19 = ? + 5$

3. $20 - ? = 11$

4. $12 = 31 - ?$

5. $55 + ? = 72$

6. $23 + 45 + ? = 90$

CHANGE IT UP

Sorting activities help primary students develop their early algebraic-thinking skills by encouraging them to focus on the many attributes a single object can have. Draw two large circles on a sheet of construction paper, one near each edge (top and bottom) of the page. Give each pair of students a scoop of countable objects and ask them to sort the objects into two groups according to a sort criterion that they decide on.

(continued)

(continued)

This is a common activity in many mathematics curricula, but you can expand the activity by asking students to write equations to describe their parts and their wholes. For example,

12 red bears + 13 blue bears = 25 bears

Differentiate this task by varying the quantity of sort characteristics, or by the number of objects to be sorted, or by changing the complexity of the set of objects. It would be far more challenging to do this task with an old box of buttons than with the set of attribute bears that are readily available from teacher supply vendors.

REFLECT

1. In this chapter, we have emphasized the distinction between problem situations that include action and those that are about the relationship between quantities. What classroom routines can help your students notice this distinction in their everyday lives?

2. Part-Part-Whole situations in which both addends are unknown are excellent opportunities to develop number sense as students compose and decompose numbers to make various combinations. What situations can you use in your classroom to extend this experience from the classic "ways to make 10" to experiences including greater values like 20 or 30 or even 100 or 120?

3. Using a copy of the Addition and Subtraction Problem Situations table (available for download from http://resources.corwin.com/problemsolvingk-2), examine the textbook you use for the grade you teach and read the word problems. Look for examples of addition and subtraction word problems. As you classify the word problems you find, make a tally on the table for each example. If you encounter a multistep problem, classify it by the first action that should take place in the problem.

NOTES

CHAPTER SIX

Additive Comparisons
Another Kind of Relationship

Thinking About Additive Comparison Situations

In Chapter 5 we explored Part-Part-Whole problem situations and highlighted the difference between these problem types, which describe relationships, and those such as Add-To and Take-From problem situations, which describe actions. Now we turn to Additive Comparison problems, which also describe relationships. Comparisons are the last of the addition and subtraction problem types.

Addition and Subtraction Problem Situations

	Difference Unknown	Greater Quantity Unknown	Lesser Quantity Unknown	
Additive Comparison	Jessie's paper airplane flew 14 feet. Jo's paper airplane flew 9 feet. How much less did Jo's paper airplane fly than Jessie's? $14 - 9 = x$ $9 + x = 14$	Jo's paper airplane flew 9 feet. Jessie's paper airplane flew 5 feet more than Jo's. How far did Jessie's paper airplane fly? $9 + 5 = x$ $x - 5 = 9$	Jessie's paper airplane flew 14 feet. Jo's paper airplane flew 5 feet less than Jessie's paper airplane. How far did Jo's paper airplane fly? $14 - 5 = x$ $14 = x + 5$	

Note: The representations for the problem situations in this table reflect our understanding based on a number of resources. These include the tables in the Common Core State Standards for Mathematics (CCSS-M; National Governors Association Center for Best Practices and Council of Chief State School Officers, 2010), the problem situations as described in the Cognitively Guided Instruction research (Carpenter, Hiebert, & Moser, 1981), and other tools. See the Appendix and the book's companion website for a more detailed summary of the documents that informed our development of this table.

ACTIVE SITUATIONS

	Result Unknown	Change Addend Unknown	Start Addend Unknown	
Add-To	Paulo counted 9 crayons. He put them in the basket. Paulo found 6 more crayons under the table. He put them in the basket. How many crayons are in the basket? $9 + 6 = x$ $6 = x - 9$	Paulo counted 9 crayons. He found more and put them in the basket. Now Paulo has 15 crayons. How many crayons did he put in the basket? $9 + x = 15$ $9 = 15 - x$	Paulo had some crayons. He found 6 more crayons under the table. Now he has 15 crayons. How many crayons did Paulo have in the beginning? $x + 6 = 15$ $15 - 6 = x$	
Take-From	There are 19 students in Mrs. Amadi's class. 4 students went to the office to say the Pledge. How many students are in the class now? $19 - 4 = x$ $4 + x = 19$	There are 19 students in Mrs. Amadi's class. Some students went to class to read the Pledge. There were still 15 students in the classroom. How many students went to the office? $19 - x = 15$ $x + 15 = 19$	4 students went to the office. 15 students were still in the classroom. How many students are there in Mrs. Amadi's class? $x - 4 = 15$ $15 + 4 = x$	

RELATIONSHIP (NONACTIVE) SITUATIONS

	Total Unknown	One Part Unknown	Both Parts Unknown
Part-Part-Whole	The first grade voted on a game for recess. 11 students voted to play four square. 8 voted to go to the playground. How many students are in the class? $8 + 11 = x$ $x - 11 = 8$	The 19 first graders voted on a recess activity. 8 students voted to go to the playground. How many wanted to play four square? $8 + x = 19$ $x = 19 - 8$	The 19 first graders voted on a recess activity. Some wanted to play four square. Some wanted to go to the playground. What are some ways the first graders could have voted? $x + y = 19$ $19 - x = y$

	Difference Unknown	Greater Quantity Unknown	Lesser Quantity Unknown	
Additive Comparison	Jessie's paper airplane flew 14 feet. Jo's paper airplane flew 9 feet. How much less did Jo's paper airplane fly than Jessie's? $14 - 9 = x$ $9 + x = 14$	Jo's paper airplane flew 9 feet. Jessie's paper airplane flew 5 feet more than Jo's. How far did Jessie's paper airplane fly? $9 + 5 = x$ $x - 5 = 9$	Jessie's paper airplane flew 14 feet. Jo's paper airplane flew 5 feet less than Jessie's paper airplane. How far did Jo's paper airplane fly? $14 - 5 = x$ $14 = x + 5$	

online resources 📄 Visit **http://resources.corwin.com/problemsolvingk-2** to download a copy of the full Addition and Subtraction Problem Situations Table.

Sandbox Notes: Explore Your Thinking

As you enter into problem exploration mode, gather your tools, including markers or crayons and counters. Save the base 10 blocks, linking cubes, and any other tools that you routinely have available in your classroom for the remaining problems in the chapter. Try several arrangements of the counters, and create hand-drawn picture models that reflect the mathematical relationship in each problem. Where can you see each quantity in the models you have created? Think about how your work can express your understanding of the problems and the questions that go along with the task.

Ask yourself these questions to focus your thinking:

- Think about the quantities in each situation. What do they represent? What is the relationship between the quantities?

- How can you represent the quantities in the word problems with your manipulatives or pictures?

- How can you make a number sentence about the problem?

As you read through the tasks and questions in Figures 6.1 and 6.2, think about the similarities and differences between the two sets of questions. Should the representations look the same or different? How do the questions themselves change the task?

FIGURE 6.1

FIGURE 6.2

Put 10 two-color counters in a cup. Spill the counters onto the table.
How many counters are white?
How many counters are red?
How many counters are there altogether?

Put 10 two-color counters in a cup. Spill the counters onto the table.
Is the number of red counters greater than, less than, or the same as the white counters?

ENTER THE PROBLEM

FIGURE 6.3 A MODEL FOR MATHEMATIZING WORD PROBLEMS

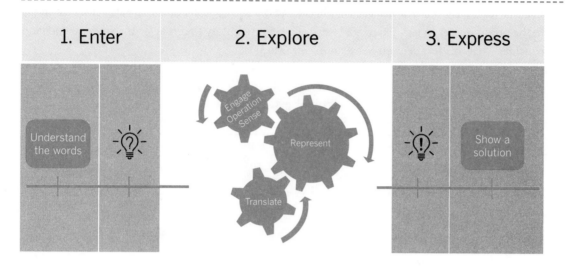

EXPLORE

STUDENTS AND TEACHERS THINK ABOUT THE PROBLEMS

Now that you've had a chance to try out the task and think about how the questions asked change the task, look at the student work in Figures 6.4 and 6.5 and consider how these students responded to the prompts in each task. Then read the teacher commentary that follows the student work and consider what this teacher and her teammate noticed.

FIGURE 6.4   **FIGURE 6.5**

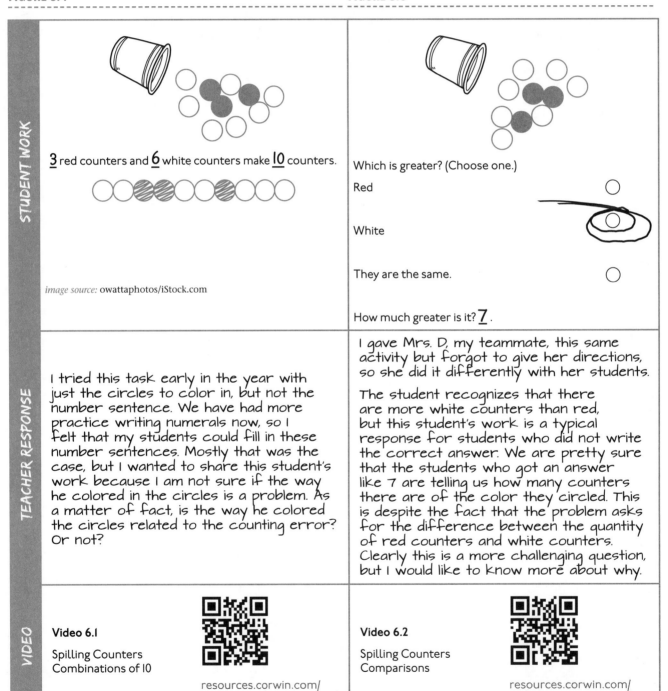

STUDENT WORK

3 red counters and **6** white counters make **10** counters.

image source: owattaphotos/iStock.com

Which is greater? (Choose one.)

Red

White

They are the same.

How much greater is it? **7** .

TEACHER RESPONSE

I tried this task early in the year with just the circles to color in, but not the number sentence. We have had more practice writing numerals now, so I felt that my students could fill in these number sentences. Mostly that was the case, but I wanted to share this student's work because I am not sure if the way he colored in the circles is a problem. As a matter of fact, is the way he colored the circles related to the counting error? Or not?

I gave Mrs. D, my teammate, this same activity but forgot to give her directions, so she did it differently with her students.

The student recognizes that there are more white counters than red, but this student's work is a typical response for students who did not write the correct answer. We are pretty sure that the students who got an answer like 7 are telling us how many counters there are of the color they circled. This is despite the fact that the problem asks for the difference between the quantity of red counters and white counters. Clearly this is a more challenging question, but I would like to know more about why.

VIDEO

Video 6.1

Spilling Counters Combinations of 10

resources.corwin.com/
problemsolvingk-2

Video 6.2

Spilling Counters Comparisons

resources.corwin.com/
problemsolvingk-2

EARLY YEARS COMPARISONS

The two Counter Spill tasks in Figures 6.1 and 6.2 are very similar—they start with 10 two-color counters spilling onto the table, and students are asked to record an answer. Although these are not technically word or story problems, they are a common task for kindergarten students. More important, they use a familiar activity to illustrate the difference between two problem situations. The task in Figure 6.1 resembles a Part-Part-Whole problem situation. When students color the 10 circles representing counters, they will use one of two colors to represent each of the two parts. The fact that an incorrect quantity of 6 white counters is noted instead of 7 counters likely does not reflect a misunderstanding of the problem. We can't know this based on the evidence here, but it is more likely a counting error.

The task shared in Figure 6.2, by contrast, is an example of a comparison problem situation. At the kindergarten level, comparisons are expressed using language that identifies and compares attributes of objects, for example, "lighter than" and "heavier than" or "more than" and "less than," as seen in Figures 6.2 and 6.5. In this case, the student circled "White" to say that there are more white counters than red. The teachers recognize that the student has identified the greater quantity, reflecting the relationship that is always present in an **Additive Comparison** relationship. The final question of this task appears to be more problematic. The student responds with "7" to the question "How much greater is it?" That is the correct answer to "How many white counters are there?" but it isn't an answer for "How many more white counters are there than red?" The problem situation posed by the task is a comparison, and the student is responding with thinking related more to a Part-Part-Whole problem situation. This is understandable in the early part of the primary years. You can see and hear solutions to both problems in Videos 6.1 and 6.2.

> **Additive Comparison:** A problem situation that describes the difference in value between two quantities.

When children shift to a comparison, they are engaging with a new kind of relationship between two quantities. To make this transition, students might benefit from learning different models for comparison. For example, lining up the counters next to each other, matching a red two-color counter to a white counter, may help students understand comparisons by providing a structure, as we see in Figure 6.6.

FIGURE 6.6 A STRUCTURE FOR UNDERSTANDING COMPARISONS

With the counters lined up, it is easier to see that the difference between the two quantities in the Counter Spill problem in Figure 6.5 is 4. Keep in mind that identifying the difference in a comparison problem is challenging because the difference itself doesn't actually exist. It is the empty space that separates the two quantities. We might even call it an imaginary space. Comparing the heights of two people makes it easier to see why (Figure 6.7).

FIGURE 6.7 DIFFERENCE: AN IMAGINARY QUANTITY

Image source: MicrovOne/iStock.com

The line shows that the difference between their two heights is measurable, yet the difference is not part of the shorter child, nor is it part of the taller child. It is the gap between the two quantities. Because the structure of the two-color counters allows us to focus students' attention on the space between the two quantities, it is easier to discuss the difference.

ADDITIVE COMPARISON SITUATIONS

As with other rows of the table, the Additive Comparison problem situation has three elements. Because it is a comparison, the difference between two quantities is one of the elements that may be missing. In the problems that we have seen so far, the difference is the missing element. The other two quantities in the relationship are the greater and the lesser quantities. In the Counter Spill problem, the greater quantity is 7 white counters, and the lesser quantity is 3 red counters. You should know that other interpretations of the Additive Comparison problem situation label these two elements differently, but most standards in the United States refer to the greater and lesser quantities.

Pause for a moment to think about problems where your students would encounter Additive Comparison situations. What quantities might they compare? What kinds of questions might they pose and answer? Figure 6.7 provides space for you to list potential Additive Comparison situations in the first column and possible difference and quantity combinations to match the situations. We have listed a few to get you started, but there is space to add more problem contexts.

FIGURE 6.8 ADDITIVE COMPARISON SITUATIONS

CONTEXT	LESSER QUANTITY	DIFFERENCE	GREATER QUANTITY
Weight of pets	Weight of kitten		Weight of adult cat
Score of the game	Points for the loser		Points for the winner
Snowfall	Dusting of snow		Enough snow to block a doorway
Number of people in the classroom	2 adults		25 children
Money spent on a toy		5 dollars	$30 video game
Children on the playground equipment	5 boys	10 children	
Hours of sleep in a night		4	
Children in your family			
Days of the week			
	1		2
		5	

Warning: The next page includes student examples of these problem situations. If you find it difficult to resist looking forward while practicing in the sandbox, consider covering the facing page with a sheet of paper.

Building Models for Comparisons

Most of this chapter explores the relationships contained in Additive Comparison problems, using structures like a bar model to highlight the relationships. In this section we consider strategies that students can use to model their understanding of comparisons. Using these tools in the same way we use buckets and shovels in the sandbox allows students to explore problems and find different solutions and an answer for the missing element.

Before we do that, take the Additive Comparison problem situation in Figure 6.8 into the mathematizing sandbox by trying out different physical and pictorial models. As you restate the problem and then engage in your exploration, consider what is similar between the representations you create and how they allow you to find the missing element.

If you get stuck, revisit the Sandbox Notes at the beginning of the chapter for guiding questions and other suggestions.

FIGURE 6.9

Jessie's paper airplane flew 14 feet. Jessie's paper airplane flew 5 feet more than Jo's paper airplane. How far did Jo's paper airplane fly?

ENTER THE PROBLEM

EXPLORE

Look at the student work in Figures 6.10 and 6.11 and consider how the students' representations are used to address the problem situation.

FIGURE 6.10

FIGURE 6.11

STUDENT WORK	⑨⑧⑦⑥ ⑤ ④③②① ⓧⓧⓧⓧⓧ $14 - 5 = 9$	J̶~̶𝙸𝙸𝙸𝙸 𝙸𝙸𝙸𝙸 𝙸𝙸𝙸𝙸 feet 𝙸𝙸𝙸𝙸 5 feet more Jo's Paper airplane Fly 5 feet $14 + 5 = 19$

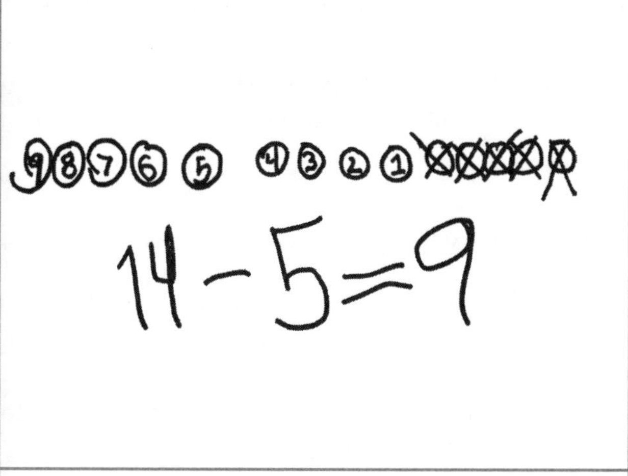

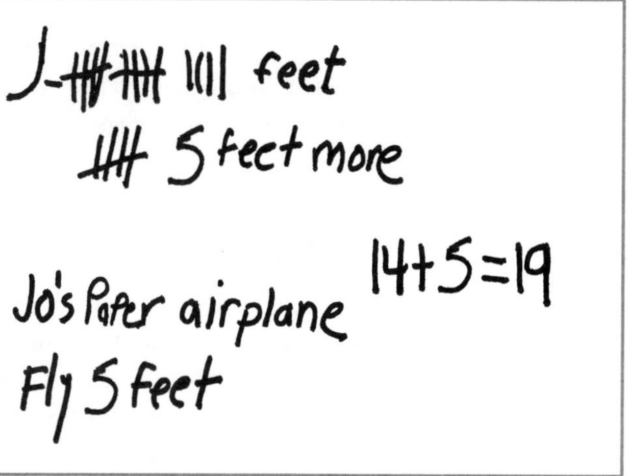

STUDENT WORK — Figure 6.10: ⑨⑧⑦⑥ ⑤ ④③②① ⓧⓧⓧⓧⓧ $14 - 5 = 9$

STUDENT WORK — Figure 6.11: tally marks "feet", "5 feet more", "Jo's Paper airplane Fly 5 feet", $14 + 5 = 19$

TEACHER RESPONSE (Figure 6.10):

I noted right away that Maya had a correct answer and that her equation was accurate as well. Then I was sorry I didn't see her actually work on her solution because I wanted to hear her explanation for why she crossed out 5 circles. That feels more like a Take-From action, so I want to clarify. I guess I could assume that she understood that Jessie's distance was 14 feet, that 5 feet is the difference between Jessie's and Jo's flights, and that Jo's distance was 9 feet, but I didn't want to assume–I wanted to hear from her. Is that too much to ask for when she has a right answer already?

TEACHER RESPONSE (Figure 6.11):

Arturo's solution made me question my own at first. After all, he noted that the problem said "5 feet more," so he did just that–he started with 14 feet and did 5 feet more to get 19 feet. There is some logic to that!

After looking carefully, I realized that he did 5 feet more than Jessie instead of recognizing that Jessie's distance itself was 5 feet more than Jo's distance.

But now what should I tell him? How can I help him see that it's a different relationship?

VIDEO

Video 6.3

Paper Airplane Flights With Counters

resources.corwin.com/
problemsolvingk-2

Video 6.4

Paper Airplane Flights With Tally Marks

resources.corwin.com/
problemsolvingk-2

STUDENTS AND TEACHERS THINK ABOUT THE PROBLEMS

The student work samples for the paper airplane problem in Figure 6.9 show two similar representations, one using circles (Figure 6.10) and the other using tally marks (Figure 6.11). Despite these similarities, the students arrived at different answers to the same problem. The teacher focuses her thinking on the students' work, trying to understand how students made sense of the problem. It is clear to her that both students identified the 14 feet that Jessie's plane flew as an important starting point for the problem. The difference of 5 feet is where the students' understandings diverge. Maya's work from Figure 6.10 recognizes the 5-foot difference as separating Jessie's 14-foot flight from Jo's shorter flight. She subtracts to find how many feet Jo's paper airplane flew. At the same time, the teacher recognizes that Arturo responded to another part of the problem. He made a note that the second airplane was associated with 5 more feet, even writing the phrase "5 feet more" next to his tallies. We aren't sure why Arturo labeled Jo's flight with 5 feet and would certainly want to ask him more about it. In either case, the answer he gets for Jo's flight length is shown as longer than Jessie's. Because this is partially a result of the language used in the original problem, we address the language of comparisons later in the chapter. For now, we will focus on strategies to help students use models to make sense of the problem situations.

MAKING USE OF MODELS FOR THINKING

Model *of* thinking: When a student's model of a problem situation describes how the student interprets and solves a specific task.

Model *for* thinking: A model that emerges as a student's model for understanding a mathematical idea is no longer tied to a specific problem or task and becomes a tool for reasoning about a new mathematical task.

Dutch researcher Koeno Gravemeijer (1999) makes an interesting distinction between models *of* thinking and models *for* thinking in relation to models students create while mathematizing. A model *of* thinking is a representation students produce to reflect their ideas. Most likely this is an image taken either at the beginning or at the end of the solution process. We like to think of it as a presentation of a mathematical idea, or what students have shared after working in the mathematizing sandbox. Alternatively, a model *for* thinking becomes a tool, a working "holder" and "displayer" of thoughts for students as they puzzle through the mathematics. It's a tool that students can use while in the mathematizing sandbox.

Arturo's solution might be considered a model *of* his thinking because he represents the first distance of 14 tally marks and then he represents the difference of 5 feet using a separate set of tally marks. He either does not understand or does not accurately represent the relationship between Jessie's 14-foot flight and the 5-foot difference. Because his tallies remain separate from each other, they do not help him to strengthen his understanding of the relationship between the two flights. He appears to rely solely on the words "5 feet more" but not what distance it is 5 feet more than.

By contrast, we could argue that Maya is using the pictorial representation in her solution as a model *for* thinking. The circles that represent each foot of distance start with 14, and the difference of 5 feet is crossed out to show 9 feet. In this case, the tools become part of Maya's thinking process as she manipulates them to explore an idea. In some cases, students may use tools to reset and start a new strategy. Essentially the tools become tools for mathematizing. However, since we do not have the opportunity to speak with these students, we really are making educated guesses from the written evidence in their work. One strategy you can use to promote students' intentional tool use is to provide them with ways to structure their thinking so that they are more able to capture the relationships within a problem situation.

NUMBER TRACKS AND NUMBER LINES The number track (Figure 6.12) is one way to assist younger students. The number track is an early alternative to a number line, used primarily because it resembles a model that students might make of quantities using linking cubes. Besides its resemblance to a concrete tool for counting, another advantage of using number tracks is the ease with which students can count off a quantity, even a linear quantity like we see in Figure 6.12. Touching 14, the student can count back to 9 on the number track.

FIGURE 6.12 MODELING THE PAPER AIRPLANE FLIGHT PROBLEM WITH A NUMBER TRACK

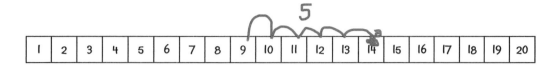

As students gain experience, they can transition to number lines, which you can see in Figure 6.13. The number track and the number line may look similar, but as you may have found with your classes, students will often count using the numbers on the number line tick marks instead of the space between them (the intervals), ending up with the incorrect difference. But the number track outlines the interval in a box, keeping students' attention focused on the space, or distance, covered rather than the labels on either end of the interval. In the paper airplane problem, for example, students might start at 14 and count that mark as one, move to 13 and count it as two, etc. Given this pattern, the student would identify the difference between the 14-foot flight and the 10-foot flight as 5 feet.

FIGURE 6.13 A COMMON ERROR IN USING A NUMBER LINE

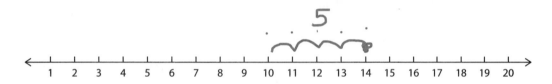

Number lines are now included in most state standards as a critically important tool, one of the few models specifically named as important tools for learning. As students move into the higher grades, the number line becomes even more important. Although it may pose challenges for your students, a number line (and the number track early in their schooling) is an important tool over the long term. In the next section we will explore ways that students can use this tool to make sense of the relationships in Additive Comparison problem situations.

As you look at the models in the next section, ask yourself if the students have made the Additive Comparison elements (lesser quantity, greater quantity, difference) and the relationships between them evident in their representations.

ANCHOR-JUMP STRATEGY The **Anchor-Jump strategy** for making sense of an Additive Comparison problem is a way to record the thinking process as students locate one quantity, identify the difference, and use that information to find the remaining quantity.

In the paper airplane problem in Figure 6.9, the anchor was 14 feet. After reading the problem, we want students to recognize that two students are comparing the flight lengths of their paper airplanes. Since Jessie's flight was 14 feet, this becomes our anchor, which we marked on the number line as the starting point. After we anchor the problem with a known value, we identify the difference. In this case, it was 5 feet. As we discussed in detail in relation to this problem, Maya correctly recognized that Jessie's plane flew 5 feet more than the other plane and she *jumped* that distance down the number line. Arturo also *anchored* at 14 feet and *jumped* 5 feet, but his interpretation of the problem incorrectly identified the direction of the jump. Let's look at an example that uses a different tool to see how the Anchor-Jump strategy works.

Anchor-Jump strategy: A problem-solving strategy in which you identify one quantity in the problem situation, mark (anchor) it, and then move back or forward (jump) to the other quantity.

Take a moment to consider what tool you would take with you into the mathematizing sandbox in order to make sense of the Additive Comparison problem in Figure 6.14.

FIGURE 6.14
- -

> Nia scored 11 points in the basketball game. Eddie scored 7 more points than Nia scored. How many points did Eddie score?

Now consider how the group of students whose work is shown in Figure 6.15 made sense of the same problem. If you are reading this book with a team of teachers, talk about how the students anchored the comparison and how they represented the jump.

FIGURE 6.15
- -

18 points

We looked at the number grid and we stardid at 11 and cawnted up 7.

[We looked at the number grid and we started at 11 and counted up 7.]

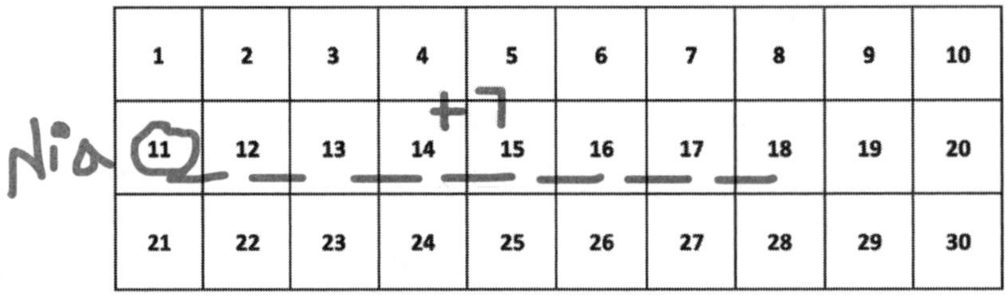

1	2	3	4	5	6	7	8	9	10
11	12	13	14	15	16	17	18	19	20
21	22	23	24	25	26	27	28	29	30

In this partner effort, the students share their thinking both using their written words and on a "number grid." They anchored (or "started") at 11 and jumped (or counted up) 7 to find an answer of 18 points for Eddie's score. Note that the students used marks that made sense to them: They circled 11, and then they made 7 lines to illustrate the jumps made to reflect the difference between Nia's and Eddie's points.

The Language of Comparison Problems

As you enter the problems in Figures 6.16 and 6.17 and work to restate them in your own words, think about the relationships in the problems and how the language used describes the relationships. How might your restatement help you clarify the nature of these relationships? Remember the three elements of Additive Comparison situations: the lesser quantity, the difference, and the greater quantity. Which are given, and which is missing in each problem?

If you get stuck, revisit the Sandbox Notes at the beginning of the chapter for guiding questions and other suggestions.

FIGURE 6.16

FIGURE 6.17

Andrea and Karen both collect baseball cards. Andrea has 53 cards, and Karen has 18 more cards than Andrea has. How many baseball cards does Karen have?

The animal shelter houses 71 cats. There are 18 more cats than dogs at the shelter. How many dogs are at the shelter?

ENTER THE PROBLEM

EXPLORE

Look at the student work in Figures 6.18 and 6.19. How do the students' responses compare to your own solution strategies?

FIGURE 6.18   FIGURE 6.19

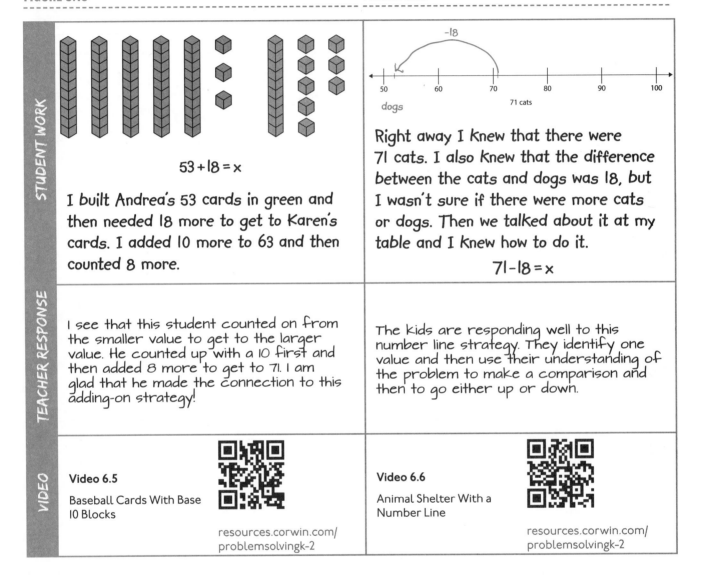

STUDENT WORK

$53 + 18 = x$

I built Andrea's 53 cards in green and then needed 18 more to get to Karen's cards. I added 10 more to 63 and then counted 8 more.

Right away I knew that there were 71 cats. I also knew that the difference between the cats and dogs was 18, but I wasn't sure if there were more cats or dogs. Then we talked about it at my table and I knew how to do it.

$71 - 18 = x$

TEACHER RESPONSE

I see that this student counted on from the smaller value to get to the larger value. He counted up with a 10 first and then added 8 more to get to 71. I am glad that he made the connection to this adding-on strategy!

The kids are responding well to this number line strategy. They identify one value and then use their understanding of the problem to make a comparison and then to go either up or down.

VIDEO

Video 6.5

Baseball Cards With Base 10 Blocks

resources.corwin.com/ problemsolvingk-2

Video 6.6

Animal Shelter With a Number Line

resources.corwin.com/ problemsolvingk-2

The solutions shown here draw on a strategy we just discussed, Anchor-Jump, although we see it differently when using these models. Before this strategy can be employed, students must identify the three essential elements: the lesser quantity, the difference, and the greater quantity.

In the baseball cards problem (Figure 6.18), the student anchored his work on the 53 cards Andrea has. Then he used the information that Karen has more—18 more, to be precise—to create the second part of the model, adding more base 10 blocks. This is the jump from one value to the other. Once the anchor point and jump are placed, the relationship is now shown in a visual form so that students can reason about the comparison and the solution. Video 6.5 shows this thinking in action.

The number line visual in Figure 6.19 is effective because it allows students to focus on one quantity in the problem situation first. First, *anchor* one value. In this example, the problem is anchored on 71 (the number of cats), so it is the first point placed on the number line. Next, the student reasoned about whether the comparing quantity is greater than or less than the first one. The next sentence in the problem reveals the next move: There are fewer dogs, so the difference of 18 *jumps* down to a lower value. Once the anchor point and the jump are labeled, the relationship is now translated into a visual form that the student can use as a model for thinking about the comparison. The student can make decisions about the best calculation strategy using the number line as a source of information. Video 6.6 shows this thinking in action.

LANGUAGE CAN GET TRICKY

As with each of the problem situations we have examined so far, there are variations of Additive Comparison problems based on which of the three terms is unknown in the given problem. In the active problem situations like Add-To and Take-From, the three possible elements are the start, the change, and the result. For the Additive Comparison problem type, we don't have a story arc, so we are exploring the relationship between the elements of the problem. In the table at the beginning of the chapter, the unknown terms are referred to as *lesser quantity*, *greater quantity*, and *difference*. Where these unknowns appear and how they are expressed in the language of the problem can greatly affect students' understanding. Consider this variation of the baseball cards problem:

> *Andrea and Karen both collect baseball cards. Andrea has 53 cards, 18 fewer than*
> *Karen has. How many baseball cards does Karen have?*

Does this new version seem more difficult or less difficult than the original problem in Figure 6.16?

For many students, a problem may be more challenging because of the language used to present the situation (de Koning, Boonen, & van der Schoot, 2017). For example, the word *fewer* in a word problem might indicate subtraction to students who are taught to use key words as clues. Students may also write equations based on the order in which information is shared (De Corte & Verschaffel, 1987). If you combine both the word *fewer* and the tendency to write equations relying on the order in which the numbers appear in the problem, some students will inevitably generate the following expression: 53 – 18. Because 53 is the first number given in the problem, and 18 is the second, along with the word *fewer* in the problem, an incorrect equation is created. Have you observed students rushing to create an equation like this one?

Instead of jumping to quick conclusions, let's think about the problem in terms of operation sense rather than key words, focusing on the relationships expressed in the words—*more than* (or *greater than*) and *fewer than* (or *less than*)—rather than on the specific words identified as key words. As we have noted throughout this book, by engaging in exploration and modeling a problem situation, students can develop a sense of what is happening in a problem. Although there are three possible missing terms in comparison problems (the difference, the lesser quantity, and the greater quantity), there are even more ways to write these problems because we can approach them from both *greater than* and *less than* perspectives.

Addition and subtraction are **inverse operations**, which generally means that one will "undo" the other. In active problem situations, like Add-To and Take-From, an inverse operation shows that actions can be undone or reversed. In nonactive problem situations, the addition and subtraction equations are just different ways to describe the same relationship between the

Inverse operations: Operations that "undo" or reverse the effects of each other.

quantities. Thinking about and comparing different language versions of a comparison word problem may help students understand how addition and subtraction could say the same thing. Keeping students' attention focused on the relationship between the quantities in the problem will help. Once these relationships are clear, students can use them to work through any Additive Comparison problem, no matter how complex the language. As long as students can identify the three elements and the relationships among them and build a model, they can write an accurate equation and solve the problem.

Young learners come to Additive Comparison problems from more general comparisons involving the question, "Which one has more?" The balance board situation in Figure 6.20 illustrates this bridge. Will everyone have a balance board? How many children will not get a balance board? This second question is the foundation for Additive Comparison—the difference between the lesser and greater quantities. One-to-one correspondence is a powerful strategy for students beginning to understand comparison situations because it is possible to see the quantity that is the same (children standing on the balance boards) and the difference ("extra" children or balance boards).

FIGURE 6.20

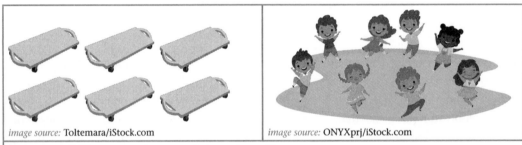

image source: Toltemara/iStock.com   image source: ONYXprj/iStock.com

Question I: Will every student get a balance board?

Question 2: How many more children are there than balance boards?

Question 3: There are six balance boards. There are two more children than balance boards. How many children are there?

Question 4: There are six balance boards. That is two fewer balance boards than children. How many children are there?

Students who can easily answer question 1, recognizing that there are not enough balance boards to go around, may still not be able to answer question 2. In other words, identifying how many boards are missing is different from simply saying that the quantities are not the same (Riley, Greeno, & Heller, 1983).

It is important for students to see Additive Comparison problems written in a variety of ways. Questions 3 and 4 offer two different ways to ask the same question about the balance board situation. Straightforward language such as the wording used in question 3 might be considered "friendly language" because the phrase "more children than" is included in the problem and it matches the action of adding the two quantities given, which will yield the correct answer. More complex language, as in question 4, might be considered "less friendly language" because matching the word *fewer* in the question to a subtraction operation doesn't describe the correct relationship in the comparison. These are the problems many students find "tricky," but it's important to include both friendly and less friendly versions of problems in your lessons. Most standards call for fluency with the friendly version in first grade and with the less friendly version in second grade (McCallum, Daro, & Zimba, n.d.). This does not mean that we shouldn't give students opportunities to learn both versions at the same time. We should. But it does mean that we can expect students to work harder on the less friendly versions. With experience, students can learn to put their attention on the relationship between the two quantities and apply a structure like the bar model or a strategy like Anchor-Jump to support their thinking and understanding.

Figure 6.21 illustrates both "more than" and "less than" language for the same problem situation. This means that students might see as many as six possible word problems derived from a single relationship. The figure offers another Additive Comparison problem, first sharing an example of the potentially tricky "less than" language. Use the spaces in the figure to craft the other versions students might encounter based on the same story.

FIGURE 6.21 LANGUAGE VARIATIONS IN ADDITIVE COMPARISON PROBLEM SITUATIONS

	Friendly Language	Less Friendly Language
Greater Quantity Unknown		Kim's cat weighs 8 pounds. That is 3 pounds fewer than Sara's cat. How much does Sara's cat weigh?
Lesser Quantity Unknown	Sara's cat weighs 11 pounds. Kim's cat weighs 3 pounds fewer than Sara's cat. How much does Kim's cat weigh?	
Difference Unknown	Sara's cat weighs more than Kim's cat. Sara's cat weighs 11 pounds and Kim's cat weighs 8 pounds. How many fewer pounds does Kim's cat weigh than Sara's cat?	

Once you have crafted these variations, talk with your colleagues about how your students might respond to them. Which variations will your students consider most straightforward? Which are likely to be more challenging? You may decide to ask your students to restate a problem using "less than" rather than "more than" to express the same relationship, as we did here. Or you may speak directly to students about the use of language in "less than" word problems. What support will *your* students need to recognize related problems and represent them accurately?

BUILDING BAR MODELS FOR COMPARISONS

Although there are many representations that can effectively express the Additive Comparison problem situation, bar models can be particularly useful in highlighting the relationships in comparison problems. Figure 6.22 presents a bar model used for a comparison.

FIGURE 6.22 USING A BAR MODEL

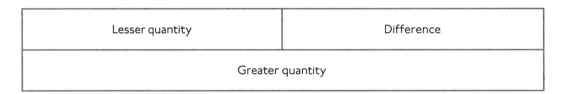

Displaying quantities in a bar model offers a visual structure that makes it easier for students to see that the difference from Figure 6.21 (3 pounds) combined with the lesser quantity (8 pounds) makes the greater quantity (*x* pounds). In this way, the bar model offers a structure that supports thinking about the mathematical relationships within the context of the story. The structure also works against a peculiar English language turn of phrase that can easily derail a student's interpretation of the problem. For example, we may say "3 less than 11," but mathematically this is written as 11 – 3, which is the reverse of the order in which it is said in English. Unfortunately, this is a pretty common use of language in word problems. Overall the language challenge is one of the difficulties of Additive Comparison problems, and it illustrates one of the risks of relying on key word strategies to help students solve word problems: Sometimes they simply don't work, and sometimes key word strategies are downright deceptive. Focusing on the relationships in the problem situation sidesteps the language complications and focuses instead on meaning. The bar model can help sort out these relationships.

FROM COUNTERS TO BAR MODELS

Moving from concrete models to abstract models like a bar model is important at every grade level. Look at the student work in Figure 6.23. It was done in response to this version of the cat problem: *Sara's cat weighs 11 pounds. Kim's cat weighs 3 pounds less than Sara's cat. How much does Kim's cat weigh?*

The teacher guided her students through this process when they were learning to use bar models. Because operation sense is about the relationships themselves, not the computation, a physical model like the two-color counters can also show these relationships. The lined-up counters show the relationship between 3 pounds (the difference) and 11 pounds (the larger quantity) clearly, and the model is proportional to the cats' actual weights. The transition to a proportional bar model starts with removing the counters and leaving behind the bars. We can see an example of this transition in the third bar model: The bar for 3 pounds is approximately one-quarter the size of the bar that represents 11 pounds. The newly created bar model is proportional, and it also has the units labeled to keep students focused on the relationships in the problem. Not only does this retain features of the concrete model, but it also has the benefit of providing a bar model diagram that can be represented easily with only paper and pencil.

We recommend that students who are learning to recognize and describe the relationships in an Additive Comparison problem spend time modeling the relationships with concrete objects before transitioning to the bar model. The bar model shows that the lesser quantity plus the difference is equivalent to the greater quantity, whether the bar model is proportional or not.

FIGURE 6.23

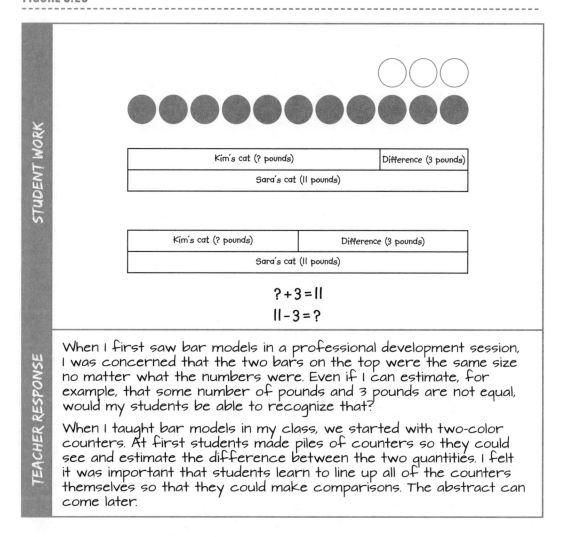

When we make instructional decisions on providing access to manipulatives and structural models, we are obligated to make sure that students have a variety of experiences and can make these decisions based on their own understandings. When students are encouraged to create representations that reflect their own thinking about a comparison relationship, the potential for great variety in the classroom increases. In this chapter alone we have seen an extensive collection of concrete models, pictorial models, and mathematical structures that can not only help students make sense of problem situations but also spark discussion and productive mathematical discourse as students make sense of each other's models. The result is a more engaging and productive classroom environment.

PROBLEM POSING AS AN INSTRUCTIONAL STRATEGY

Word problems ask students to make sense of a context that someone else thinks is important. Word problems may also focus students' attention on real-life situations, but sometimes focusing on imaginative situations can achieve the same goal. A group of educators noted how often we pose problems to students but wondered what would happen if the students posed the problems themselves (English, 1998).

Interestingly, one finding from this study is a strategy that most inspired students to think about and write their own problems: reading picture books. Children love stories, and they love to compare things. Fables compare good behavior with bad. Tall tales force us to compare larger-than-life characters with ourselves and our own world. Even when a story doesn't include comparisons, young children will share them anyway: "I have *three* cats!" "I'd give a mouse *five* cookies!" Students' personal comparisons are evidence that they are internalizing the story and are making sense of it on their own terms. In this respect, pulling comparisons out of your class's favorite stories is a perfect introduction to problem posing.

Anything that can be counted or measured or otherwise quantified can be compared. Counting is a natural choice for this age group, but don't forget to include quantities that are not countable, such as length, weight, height, temperature, and much more. Students may choose to make comparisons with numbers that are beyond their current standards. For example, your class may want to compare the weight of two dinosaurs, or the length of two butterflies measured in fractions of an inch, bringing up larger numbers than their standards cover, or even fractional units of measure. If the students' interest is there, you can help them use the skills they already have to try to figure it out. If not, it's all right to let it go unresolved. Honoring the students' interests is what's important.

Using Children's Literature to Explore Additive Comparison Situations

As with other problem situations, using beloved books is a fun way to explore the mathematics in the story. *Alma* (Martinez-Neal, 2018) is the story of a curious girl who wants to know where she got her very long name. Since her first name is only four letters long, everyone at first wonders why she says she has a long name. The story is an inspirational account of Alma's amazing ancestors, telling us how her full name is a reflection of her family's rich history. Students can use this as a starting point for comparing the length of their own names to Alma's and exploring their identities as well.

CREATE ANOTHER OUTCOME

Creating a different outcome is an idea that you can use in your classroom right away. As usual, all lessons begin with a reading for the sheer pleasure of the story. You may choose to ask your students how many names they have, recognizing that it is quite common for Hispanic children to carry names as long and meaningful as Alma's. Students then use snap cubes to make a tower as long as their own first name, one block per letter. The teacher uses a tower that represents "Alma" and asks students to compare, side by side if necessary. Using a sentence frame to support comparison language, students say one of the following:

> *My name is _____ letters. My name is _____ letters longer than Alma's name.*
> *My name has _____ letters. Alma's name is _____ letters shorter than my name.*

The second sentence frame reflects the more challenging sentence structures used in English for comparisons. In either case, students are finding the difference between their name and Alma's name. Of course, if you have names shorter than Alma's in your classroom, you would need to include (or discuss) a sentence frame for those students.

After reading the book once, return to full names. Show students a tower as long as your full name and ask them how they could create a tower as long as Alma's full name. Depending on students' ages, this may be work for a group of students to do together as a problem-solving task. Ask students to write out their own full names and decide whose name is the longest. Compare one of the names to Alma's full name and return again to the sentence frames.

Alma is a good book to look for or request from your school library. If none of the libraries you have access to have it on their shelves, you can do a similar lesson with *Chrysanthemum*, by Kevin Henkes (1991). Chrysanthemum, too, worries about her unusual name.

KEY IDEAS

1. Comparisons are a nonactive problem situation. They describe relationships, not actions.

2. The language in an Additive Comparison problem can be a roadblock. Exposing students to many different ways to talk about comparisons can help them sort out the root relationship.

3. Abstract models (or diagrams) of additive comparisons, like bar models, number tracks, number lines, and so on, can become models *for* thinking and help students organize their comparisons.

4. The bar model, number track, and number line structures can help students organize the relationships among the quantities in a comparison.

5. The Anchor-Jump strategy can help students identify one quantity and consider its relationship to the other quantity and the difference in a problem.

6. The difference between two quantities is a value that does not correlate with anything concrete. It measures a space between two real objects but is not real itself. This can sometimes make it challenging for students to recognize it.

7. Problem-posing activities can help students identify and mathematize examples of comparisons in their own environment.

TRY IT OUT!

IDENTIFY THE PROBLEM SITUATION

Decide if each of the following is an example of a Part-Part-Whole or Additive Comparison problem type. Draw a bar model or other pictorial representation of the situation. Remember to explain the reasoning for your decision.

1. Mom put jelly beans in both of her girls' baskets. Kimmy counted 22 jelly beans in her basket. Lauren is older, so she got 15 more jelly beans than Kimmy got. How many jelly beans did Lauren get?

2. The front patio measures 300 square feet. The back patio measures 830 square feet. How much tile is needed to cover both patios?

3. The cafeteria at school expects to sell 65 cartons of milk each day to the first grade class. It normally sells 41 chocolate milk cartons, and the rest are cartons of plain milk. How many cartons of plain milk does the cafeteria sell?

4. Write an Additive Comparison word problem for each of the bar models below:

3 seconds	x
7 seconds	

x pounds	5
14 pounds	

112 people	24
x people	

WRITE A PROBLEM

1. Gather a collection of whiffle balls or crumpled balls of scrap paper. Give students the opportunity to throw the ball twice. Use a ruler to measure the two distances and find the difference between the distances.

2. Ask older students to figure out how many months old they are. (You can structure this lesson as a rigorous task-based lesson as well.) Record their responses and ask groups of students to make additive comparisons about their ages: *Preetika is z days older than Franco.*

3. Give students a number and tell them that it is the difference between two quantities. The students then name the unit being counted and two numbers with that difference. Ask students to create visual and/or concrete representations for their comparisons.

4. The book *Actual Size* (Jenkins, 2011) shows actual-size illustrations of some body parts of interesting animals. Hand out rulers and ask students to make additive comparisons between, for example, the width of their eye and the width of the eye of the giant squid!

CHANGE IT UP

As we noted earlier, addition and subtraction are inverse operations, which generally means that one will "undo" the other. Thinking about and comparing different language versions of a comparison word problem may help students understand how addition and subtraction could say the same thing. Keeping students' attention focused on the relationship between the quantities in the problem will help.

The first word problem in the matching exercise below matches the equation opposite it. The rest are mixed. Connect the word problem to the equation in the opposite column that best matches it. There will be one equation left at the end for you to craft a word problem to match it.

Example	Kyle can write his name 11 times in one minute. Cristina can write her name 2 more times in one minute. How many times can Cristina write her name in one minute?		$11 + 2 = x$ (lesser + difference = greater)
1.	In one minute, Cristina can write her name 13 times and Kyle can write his name 11 times. How many fewer times can Kyle write his name than Cristina?	a.	$13 = x + 2$ (greater = lesser + difference)
2.	In one minute, Kyle can write his name 11 times. That is 2 times fewer than Cristina. How many times can Cristina write her name in one minute?	b.	$13 - 11 = x$ (greater – lesser = difference)
3.	In one minute, Cristina can write her name 13 times. Kyle writes his name, too, but Cristina writes her name 2 more times than Kyle. How many times can Kyle write his name in one minute?	c.	$11 = x - 2$ (lesser = greater – difference)
		d.	$x + 2 = 13$ (smaller + difference = larger)

REFLECT

1. When children pose problems, they like to make them "harder" by adding more steps (English, 1998). However, posing problems that instead require additive comparisons may be even harder for them. Think of some contexts in your classroom or school that can encourage students to compare quantities regularly.

2. The bar model is a useful tool for students to add structure to an Additive Comparison problem. Think of ways you can introduce the bar model as a tool to understand these problem situations. How can you help students use a bar model for both Part-Part-Whole and Additive Comparison problems but still recognize the problem situations as different?

NOTES

CHAPTER SEVEN

Early Multiplication and Division

Patterns and Predictions

Thinking About Early Multiplicative Thinking

In Chapters 2–6 we focused on the addition and subtraction problem situations and addressed all four rows of the table that appeared in those chapters. We noticed that addition and subtraction problem situations can be characterized as either active or nonactive and that the models and representations we choose to represent them matter. In this chapter we will see how the important work your students already do to understand addition and subtraction sets the stage for learning about the multiplication operation in third grade and beyond. We will briefly explore key ideas—reflected in the Multiplication and Division Problem Situations table—that your students will learn as soon as next year and also describe how the ideas are related to important ideas from most primary standards.

Students in kindergarten through second grade are not typically expected to meet standards related specifically to multiplication or division; nevertheless, ideas emerge that can be developed in order to set the stage for students to have a strong start in multiplicative thinking in third grade.

As you put the problem in Figure 7.1 into your own words, think about the models your students might generate to represent this problem. Consider what an appropriate model looks like and the words students might use in their responses. Because this is an open-ended problem, there are many possible responses and approaches to solving it. Think about how this feature changes how you, as the teacher, would use this problem in your class.

Multiplication and Division Problem Situations

	Product Unknown	Multiplier (Number of Groups) Unknown	Measure (Group Size) Unknown
Equal Groups	Mayim has 8 vases to decorate the tables at her party. She places 2 flowers in each vase. How many flowers does she need? $8 \times 2 = x$ $x \div 8 = 2$	Mayim has some vases to decorate the tables at her party. She places 2 flowers in each vase. If she uses 16 flowers, how many vases does she have? $x - 2 = 16$ $x = 16 \div 2$	Mayim places 16 flowers in vases to decorate the tables at her party. There are 8 vases and each vase has the same number of flowers. How many flowers will be in each vase? $8 \times x = 16$ $16 \div 8 = x$

	Product Unknown
Area/Array	Bradley bought a new rug for the hallway in his house. One side measured 5 feet and the other side measured 3 feet. How many square feet does the rug cover? $5 \times 3 = x$ $3 + 3 + 3 + 3 + 3 = x$ $3 \times 5 = x$ $5 + 5 + 5 = x$

Note: In the upper elementary grades, students begin the long journey of learning to think multiplicatively and proportionally. Part of this process involves moving away from counting and repeated addition to represent ideas that are better expressed with multiplication, but the primary years are still focused mostly on counting and adding. Some standards leverage that strength to introduce early ideas of multiplication: Counting squares in an array is one of them, and skip counting is another. We have included multiplication and division equations for our adult readers. K–2 students are not typically expected to represent these operations in equation form.

The representations for the problem situations in this table reflect our understanding based on a number of resources. These include the tables in the Common Core State Standards for Mathematics (National Governors Association Center for Best Practices and Council of Chief State School Officers, 2010), the problem situations as described in the Cognitively Guided Instruction research (Carpenter, Hiebert, & Moser, 1981), Heller & Greeno (1979), and other tools. See the Appendix and the book's companion website for a more detailed summary of the documents that informed our development of this table.

ASYMMETRICAL (NONMATCHING) FACTORS

	Product Unknown	Multiplier (Number of Groups) Unknown	Measure (Group Size) Unknown	
Equal Groups	Mayim has 8 vases to decorate the tables at her party. She places 2 flowers in each vase. How many flowers does she need? $8 \times 2 = x$ $x \div 8 = 2$	Mayim has some vases to decorate the tables at her party. She places 2 flowers in each vase. If she uses 16 flowers, how many vases does she have? $x - 2 = 16$ $x = 16 \div 2$	Mayim places 16 flowers in vases to decorate the tables at her party. There are 8 vases and each vase has the same number of flowers. How many flowers will be in each vase? $8 \times x = 16$ $16 \div 8 = x$	
	Resulting Value Unknown	**Scale Factor (Times as Many) Unknown**	**Original Value Unknown**	
Multiplicative Comparison	Amelia's dog is 5 times older than Wanda's 3-year-old dog. How old is Amelia's dog? $5 \times 3 = x$ $x \div 5 = 3$	Sydney has $15 to spend at the movies. Her sister has $5. How many times more money does Sydney have than her sister has? $x \times 5 = 15$ $5 = 15 \div x$	Mrs. Smith has 15 puzzles in her classroom. That is 3 times as many puzzles as are in Mr. Jackson's room. How many puzzles are in Mr. Jackson's room? $3 \times x = 15$ $15 \div 3 = x$	

SYMMETRICAL (MATCHING) FACTORS

	Product Unknown	One Dimension Unknown	Both Dimensions Unknown
Area/Array	Bradley bought a new rug for the hallway in his house. One side measured 5 feet and the other side measured 3 feet. How many square feet does the rug cover? $5 \times 3 = x$ $3 + 3 + 3 + 3 = x$ $3 \times 5 = x$ $5 + 5 + 5 = x$	The 12 members of the student council lined up on the stage to take yearbook pictures. The first row started with 6 students and the rest of the rows did the same. How many rows were there? $6 \times x = 12$ $x = 12 \div 6$	Daniella was building a house foundation using her building blocks. She started with 20 blocks. How many blocks long and wide could the foundation be? $x \times y = 20$ $20 \div x = y$
	Sample Space (Total Outcomes) Unknown	**One Factor Unknown**	**Both Factors Unknown**
Combinations (Fundamental Counting Principle)	Karen has 3 shirts and 7 pairs of pants. How many unique outfits can she make? $3 \times 7 = x$ $3 = x \div 7$	Evelyn says that she can make 21 unique and different ice cream sundaes using just ice cream flavors and toppings. If she has 3 flavors of ice cream, how many kinds of toppings does Evelyn have? $3 \times x = 21$ $21 \div 3 = x$	Audrey can make 21 different fruit sodas using the machine at the restaurant. How many different flavorings and sodas could there be? $x \times y = 21$ $x = 21 \div y$

online resources ↘ Visit **http://resources.corwin.com/problemsolvingk-2** to download a copy of the full Multiplication and Division Problem Situations Table.

Sandbox Notes: Explore Your Thinking

Remember that the focus of exploration for any problem isn't simply to find any workable way to represent the problem but, rather, to try out multiple representations in the search for the ones that most accurately represent the problem situation. By paying attention to the quantities and articulating to yourself the work each does—in short, by following the guiding questions—not only will you be solving the problem, but you will also be building an understanding of the concept of even and odd numbers.

As you have done in previous chapters, ask yourself these questions to focus your thinking:

- *Think about the possible quantities that might be part of this situation. What are they, and what do they represent?*

- *How can you represent the quantities in the word problem with your manipulatives or pictures?*

- *How can you describe what is happening in this problem?*

FIGURE 7.1

Ms. Fong, the principal, passed our class in the hall. She smiled and said, "I see that you have an even number of students in the class today!" How does Ms. Fong know that there is an even number of students?

ENTER THE PROBLEM

FIGURE 7.2 A MODEL FOR MATHEMATIZING WORD PROBLEMS

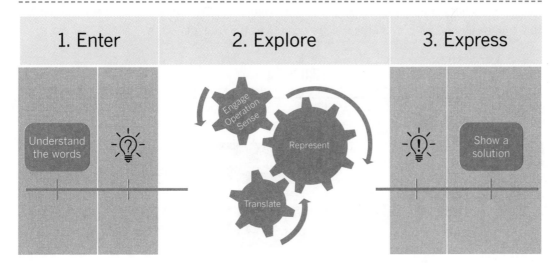

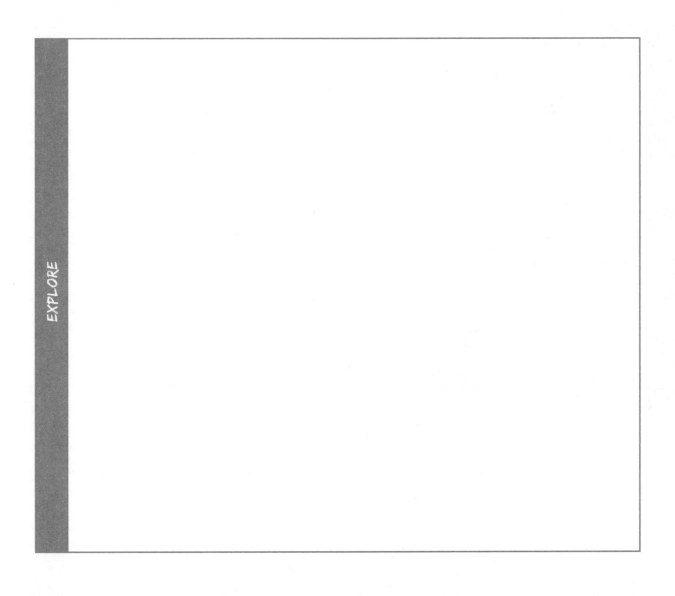

STUDENTS AND TEACHERS THINK ABOUT THE PROBLEM

Look at the student solutions in Figures 7.3 and 7.4 and consider how the students describe or draw what is happening in the word problem in Figure 7.1. Then read the teacher commentary that follows and consider what the teacher noticed in the students' work.

FIGURE 7.3   **FIGURE 7.4**

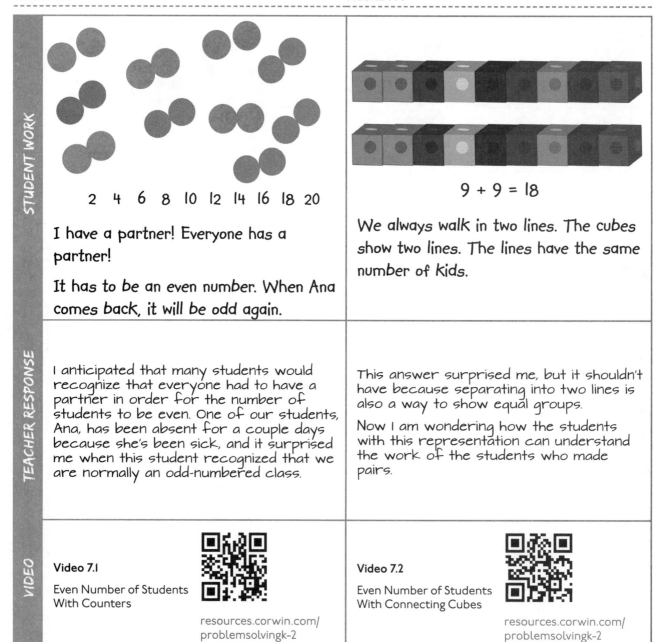

STUDENT WORK

2 4 6 8 10 12 14 16 18 20

I have a partner! Everyone has a partner!

It has to be an even number. When Ana comes back, it will be odd again.

$9 + 9 = 18$

We always walk in two lines. The cubes show two lines. The lines have the same number of kids.

TEACHER RESPONSE

I anticipated that many students would recognize that everyone had to have a partner in order for the number of students to be even. One of our students, Ana, has been absent for a couple days because she's been sick, and it surprised me when this student recognized that we are normally an odd-numbered class.

This answer surprised me, but it shouldn't have because separating into two lines is also a way to show equal groups.

Now I am wondering how the students with this representation can understand the work of the students who made pairs.

VIDEO

Video 7.1

Even Number of Students With Counters

resources.corwin.com/ problemsolvingk-2

Video 7.2

Even Number of Students With Connecting Cubes

resources.corwin.com/ problemsolvingk-2

This is an open-ended problem, which gives students many options to represent their answers. It also gives the teacher many opportunities to see how students interpret and approach the problem. The student work samples in Figures 7.3 and 7.4 share two distinctly different approaches, and the teacher wonders how to help her students make sense of each approach and see that they represent the same idea: evenness.

MODELING EVEN AND ODD NUMBERS

Complicating matters is the fact that students might give examples of classes with different quantities of students, as we saw in these samples. For example, the student whose work is shown in Figure 7.3 emphasizes the fact that even numbers always come in pairs. It is as if the student could determine evenness while skip counting by twos. In this case, she notes "2, 4, 6, 8, 10, 12, 14, 16, 18, 20," marking off each pair of students. She recognizes that every student must have a partner in order for the quantity of students to be even. We can reasonably make this assumption because she also mentions that, when Ana returns, the quantity will return to an odd number. You can hear this thinking in Video 7.1.

Skip counting—in particular, counting by familiar numbers like 2, 5, and 10—is a skill introduced in most second-grade standards. Skip counting by fives and tens relies on, and further develops, students' understanding of the base 10 number system. Skip counting by twos is not only accessible for most students, but it is also an efficient way to determine if a number is even. One way to help students make these connections is to continually relate the multiples of two to a pair of objects, whether it is pairs of students, eyes, legs, or arms, or of counters or other common classroom objects. Students may also discover that adding a single object, or taking away a single object, reinforces the idea that no odd number is ever more than one away from being an even number.

The student whose work is featured in Figure 7.4 and Video 7.2 sees the hallway situation differently. He makes two lines of students using cubes and notices that the two lines have the same number of students. In this case, the students are represented by cubes, and the two trains of cubes are the same length. Unlike the first student, this student does not describe what would happen with an odd number of students, but he does clearly say that the lines are the same length. As part of the study of evenness, most standards recognize that two equal addends are one representation of even numbers, just as this student did ($9 + 9 = 18$). It's possible that some students will recognize that a number is even by showing two equal lengths, which we see in the towers made from cubes. However, comparing two lengths and finding them to be equal is a kindergarten standard. To encourage students to address this same idea from the second-grade perspective, two understandings should accompany the comparison. The first is to represent the two equal lengths with an addition sentence with two of the same addends, as we see in the student work in Figure 7.4. Recognizing that two equal lengths and two equal addends will make an even number rounds out an appropriate second-grade understanding of evenness. In the future, students will add "divisible by 2" as another feature of "evenness."

As adults, we are more likely to think of evenness in terms of numbers "ending in 2, 4, 6, 8, or 0." This generalization is accurate, but it is also based far too much on the outward appearance of the number than on the divisibility of the number by 2. Eventually students will recognize even numbers as "divisible by 2," but our primary students don't yet know this about divisibility. Notice how the idea of "two-ness" is still a part of their solutions. The student who created pairs to show evenness is making groups of two: Each pair is a group of two students matched together. However, the student who presented the second solution sees "2" differently. He sees two as the number of equal groups it takes to show evenness: He divides the class into lines that form two equal groups. The idea of equal groups is also an early introduction to multiplication.

EQUAL GROUPS PROBLEM SITUATION

In previous chapters we explored each row of the Addition and Subtraction Problem Situations table because it governs much of the work students do in the primary grades. However, before students leave second grade they learn certain ideas, such as equal groups and skip counting, that foreshadow multiplication, which will be a large part of what they learn in the next few years. You saw at the beginning of this chapter that multiplication and division are covered by another table of problem situations. The first line of the Multiplication and Division Problem Situations table is called "Equal Groups" and it is part of second-grade learning.

An **Equal Groups** problem situation has two **factors** and a **product**. Each of the two factors is different in an Equal Groups problem situation because each factor has a different role. In other words, each factor does different work. One factor is the **multiplier factor** and the other is the **measure factor**. The multiplier factor describes *how many groups* there are in the problem while the measure factor tells *how many are in each group*. The images in Figures 7.5 and 7.6 illustrate the difference between the two types of factors. Notice how the quantity of kittens in both representations stays consistent at 12, even when the situation changes. In Figure 7.5, there are 2 cats (number of groups) and each has 6 kittens (number in a group). Figure 7.6 shows 6 cats and each has 2 kittens. Notice again that each situation shows the same quantity of kittens: 12. We have shown the multiplication equation below each image so that you can see how the equations will differ as well.

FIGURE 7.5   **FIGURE 7.6**

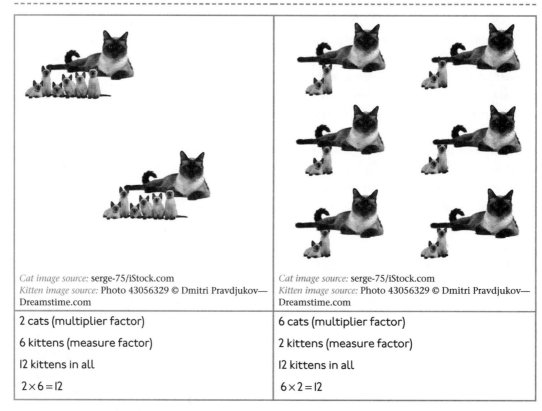

Cat image source: serge-75/iStock.com *Kitten image source:* Photo 43056329 © Dmitri Pravdjukov—Dreamstime.com	*Cat image source:* serge-75/iStock.com *Kitten image source:* Photo 43056329 © Dmitri Pravdjukov—Dreamstime.com
2 cats (multiplier factor)	6 cats (multiplier factor)
6 kittens (measure factor)	2 kittens (measure factor)
12 kittens in all	12 kittens in all
$2 \times 6 = 12$	$6 \times 2 = 12$

Although this is not content your students learn in the primary grades, notice the similarities between the cat/kitten contexts and the even number problem that opened the chapter. The first student (Figure 7.3) modeled pairs of classmates to show there was an even number of students

Equal Groups: A multiplication problem situation in which one of the factors states the number of groups and the other factor states how many objects are in each group.

Factor: In a multiplication problem, one of the numbers multiplied together.

Product: The answer or result of multiplication.

Multiplier factor: The factor in an Equal Groups problem situation that answers the question, "How many groups?"

Measure factor: The factor in an Equal Groups problem situation that answers the question, "How large is each group?"

in the class. Similarly, the kittens in Figure 7.6 come in pairs and there are two kittens for each mother cat. In this case, we have called the 2 a measure factor because it tells us how many are in each group. We could say the same thing about the students grouped in pairs: We know there are two students in each group. By contrast, the second student's work on the evenness problem (Figure 7.4) shows the classmates in two lines to illustrate evenness, which we might also call *groups*. This is similar to the cat/kitten problem in Figure 7.5 because it shows the kittens in two groups equally divided between the two mother cats.

Evenness can be modeled using the same forms of models and representations that students will use in third grade to model the Equal Groups problem situation. Why should primary teachers learn this? When you recognize a connection to a major idea of a later grade, you can design your lessons not only to teach your standards but also to put new ideas in place that will serve students later. As we have seen, focusing on the odd and even properties of numbers can be an opportunity to begin to model Equal Groups problem situations in preparation for third grade. Modeling even and odd contexts can also broaden students' conceptual understanding of the idea as they learn to recognize both models of "two-ness" that we saw in the student samples.

USING PATTERNS TO IDENTIFY EVEN AND ODD NUMBERS

Often when we teach even and odd numbers, we focus on identifying "evenness" and "oddness" based on the digit in the ones place. In our work in schools we often observe students counting a collection and checking the number against an anchor chart showing numerals with a list of odd digits (1, 3, 5, 7, 9) and a list of even digits (0, 2, 4, 6, 8) in order to determine if the number itself is even or odd. These even/odd lessons can be effective, to a point. Sometimes a student overgeneralizes the rule and points to 32, calling it an odd number because it has a 3 in it. In this case, the student may have decided that the odd number 3 in the tens place is enough reason to identify the number as odd. This is not an uncommon misconception, and it is important to recognize that it is based on logical reason, even if that reason is applied incorrectly to the digit in the tens place.

If students rely only on the procedure of using a single digit in the number to determine if it is odd or even, they can be misled. As students get older, a different overgeneralization of the rule may occur. Figure 7.7 shows the work of an older student. Think about how she might have thought through this problem.

FIGURE 7.7

Even! It ends in 4.

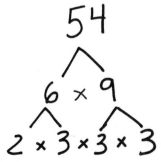

But, there are more threes. The number has to be odd.

This misconception can emerge when students are asked to say whether 54 is odd or even. The student whose work is shown in Figure 7.7 produces a quick procedural answer, recognizing that the digit in the ones place is 4. But then she appears to think a little more and explore the number using new ideas she has learned, in this case, finding the prime factorization of the number. She recognizes that three of the prime factors of 54 are odd, and she believes that this somehow makes the number more odd than even. This is just another example of how students' over-application of a rule can become misleading as they learn more about numbers. In this example, it's an error that has some logic behind it. When students have strong physical models of evenness, like forming pairs or making two equal groups, as seen in Figure 7.8, they can use those strategies to verify their thinking before coming up with answers.

FIGURE 7.8 PHYSICAL MODELS OF EVENNESS

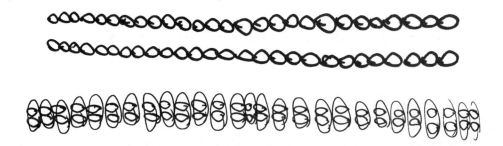

Building models of odd and even numbers to represent real problem contexts and situations in order to learn about even and odd problem situations will help students recognize that "odd" and "even" have real meaning in context. Some students will begin to recognize that "pairing" up or "making two equal groups" can be done even for quantities greater than 100 or more. If the pairings include every item in the set, the number is even. If there is one left over, the number is odd. By doing enough of these examples, some students will eventually observe that we can predict whether a number is odd or even simply by looking at the digit in the ones place. In this chapter we emphasize that the *outcome* of a series of lessons on even/odd numbers is the understanding that the digit in the ones place can tell us whether a number is even or odd. It is not the *starting point* of the first lesson, nor is it the singular goal of teaching the concept.

Using Children's Literature to Explore Early Multiplication

For the most part, in this book we chose not to access the amazing collection of books in lists of picture books that explicitly feature mathematics, simply because so much has been written about them in the past. Our goal in this book was to offer classroom teachers like you four strategies that you can use to mathematize any book that your class loves.

However, a quick library search for odd and even numbers will show you a variety of books that quite explicitly teach the concepts of odd and even. To start, there is *Missing Mittens* (Murphy, 2000) and *Even Steven, Odd Todd* (Cristaldi, 1996), two of our favorites.

TRANSCRIBE THE ACTION OR RELATIONSHIP

One book captures the mathematical idea of evenness and oddness in an unexpected place: *The Snowy Day*, by Ezra Jack Keats (1962). Peter wakes up on a snowy day, excited to explore the world covered in crunchy white snow. As Peter walks across the snow-covered sidewalk, we see his footprints in the snow, appearing only in pairs, whether his toes are pointed in or pointed out. Then Peter tries another way to move through the snow. He drags his feet, leaving two parallel tracks in the snow behind him. In these two visual images, we see the two models of evenness that were also seen in the principal's observation problem that opened the chapter (Figure 7.1): the pairs of objects and the two matching lines. Then, Peter picks up a stick and drags it through the snow, and there are no longer two tracks in the snow, but three. What a lovely way to visualize how "even" can quickly change to "odd"!

The artwork in *The Snowy Day* is composed of collages and torn paper images that are embellished with painted details. Peter's footsteps in the snow look very much like they were stamped. Make footprint stamps using wood or plastic blocks and adhesive foam available from the craft section of your local superstore. Students can use white paper to create a snow scene, adding their own footprints across the snow with the stamp. Give students a cotton swab to paint the tracks Peter's feet make as he drags his feet through the snow. Then, add the stick to see what happens! Round out a creative lesson like this one by leading students to act out making footprints and making tracks. Bring the mathematical idea of evenness back into the discussion by posting a sentence frame that helps students capture their mathematical thinking about how they know Peter has two feet.

Bringing in Another Dimension With Arrays

Students in kindergarten through second grade learn many strategies for structuring the numbers they encounter. In Chapter 4, we saw how 10 frames support students' focus on our base 10 system, teaching them to "make tens" or even "make fives." We also saw how base 10 blocks and place value disks reinforce students' understanding of our base 10 system by providing placeholders that help them think about numbers in terms of ones, tens, and hundreds. As students prepare to expand their understanding of how numbers are organized to include multiplication and division, they learn to form equal groups with quantities other than 10 to organize their counting.

Before we look closely at how the students modeled the problem in Figure 7.9, read through it carefully, putting the story in your own words. Use the workspace to sketch your own representation of the problem before looking at the student work. Note that this story only gives the final product, and both factors change. This makes the task more open ended, which gives it the added benefit of having a "lower floor" for access to the problem but also a "higher ceiling," meaning that there are many ways to approach the problem and expand on it. If carpet squares are unfamiliar to your students, think of something else that students might recognize as being arranged in squares and substitute it in the problem.

Warning: The next page includes student examples of this problem situation. If you find it difficult to resist looking forward while practicing in the sandbox, consider covering the facing page with a sheet of paper.

FIGURE 7.9

Mr. D asked students to bring 12 carpet squares to the front of the room. He challenged them to use the squares to make a rectangle.

As you examine the student work in Figures 7.10 and 7.11 and read the teacher comments that follow, consider how the teacher focuses students' thinking on the one thing each of these responses has in common: There are 12 carpet squares, no matter how the arrangement of the carpet squares changes.

YOUR WORKSPACE

FIGURE 7.10　　　　　　　　　　　　**FIGURE 7.11**

STUDENT WORK

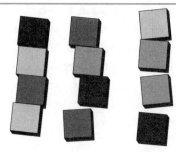

We see 12 squares. We counted by threes.

After talking to the teacher …

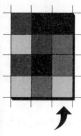 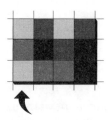

Jennifer's view　　　Carlos's view

Every time we counted 12 squares!
Carlos is right. Jennifer is right!

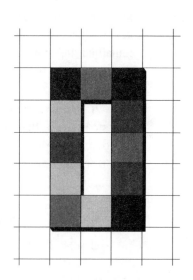

Our rectangle has 12 squares inside!

TEACHER RESPONSE

When I walked by this group, I noticed that they had created something close to a three-by-four array. I asked the group how they knew that there were 12 squares. Jennifer counted by threes to prove it to me ("3, 6, 9, 12"). The other students nodded.

But Carlos said, "I see fours, not threes!" I looked at where he was standing, looking at the carpet squares from the other side, and I could see why he thought that!

So, I handed the group two sheets of 1" grid paper and asked them to make a smaller representation with square tiles of what Jennifer sees and of what Carlos sees. You can see their models and their words in the second set of images, including their surprise when both Carlos's and Jennifer's interpretations are correct.

I have to admit I was surprised by this group's array! There were 12 squares, and it was a rectangle! Of course, the three squares in the middle matter, but I wasn't sure right away how to address it with students.

VIDEO

Video 7.3

Creating a Rectangle With Color Tiles

resources.corwin.com/
problemsolvingk-2

Video 7.4

Creating a Rectangle With a Gap in the Center

resources.corwin.com/
problemsolvingk-2

RECOGNIZING AREA/ARRAY AS A PROBLEM SITUATION

Earlier in the chapter we introduced the Equal Groups problem type, noting that the two factors each have a different role in understanding the problem situation. One is the measure factor, and the other the multiplier factor. The Area/Array problem situation addressed in this section is different in that the factors don't have entirely different roles in the problem. We saw this in the group solution in Figure 7.10. Jennifer and Carlos were able to interpret the same arrangement of carpet squares differently, counting by threes or counting by fours, while the shape of the carpet remained the same. In terms of multiplication, if we labeled the carpet rectangle 3 × 4 or 4 × 3 the arrangement of the carpet wouldn't change in any way.

But our second graders are not representing their thinking using multiplication. Instead, we are encouraging them either to count the squares individually or to use repeated addition, as Carlos and Jennifer's group did. We want to see that second graders recognize how both of these equations represent the same rectangle yet also recognize how the equations (and counting) are different:

$4 + 4 + 4 = 12$ squares

$3 + 3 + 3 + 3 = 12$ squares

Note that the students might have made four other array arrangements that are not represented in the student work samples in Figures 7.10 and 7.11:

$6 + 6 = 12$ squares	*or* $2 \times 6 = 12$
$2 + 2 + 2 + 2 + 2 + 2 = 12$ squares	*or* $6 \times 2 = 12$
$1 + 1 + 1 + 1 + 1 + 1 + 1 + 1 + 1 + 1 + 1 + 1 = 12$ squares	*or* $12 \times 1 = 12$
12 squares	*or* $1 \times 12 = 12$

BUILDING AN UNDERSTANDING OF ARRAYS AS STRUCTURES

Earlier in this section we described arrays as another tool that is important for helping students structure an understanding of numbers. In third and fourth grades, arrays are often used to build models of multiplication fact families. Before students can do that, they must first recognize the row and column organization that forms an array. As you can see from the two third grade examples in Figure 7.12, this structure is not always solidly in place. Understanding the regular structure of an array is not automatic, and not all students naturally draw the perpendicular and parallel lines that make up the rows (Battista, 2004).

Area/Array: A problem situation where the factors can be swapped (interchanged) without changing the meaning of the situation.

FIGURE 7.12 UNORGANIZED ARRAYS

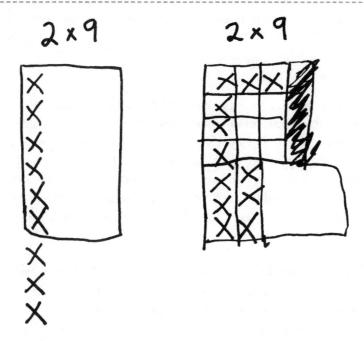

The student work for the carpet problem solution in Figure 7.11 also shows that the array structure develops in different ways (Battista, 2004). The group of students who worked on this problem do not yet recognize that an array should count every "cell" where a row and a column meet. None of these cells can be empty. Similarly, none of the cells can be counted twice, or extend beyond the array. Leaving empty squares and counting a square twice are common errors that students make when learning to draw arrays. In the case of Figure 7.11, it would be important to ask the class to discuss what is happening in the empty squares inside the rectangle. Someone can make the observation that there are no carpet squares there at all.

We considered carpet squares in Figures 7.9–7.11, but any situation in which we find the area of a space or arrange objects in rows and columns can be an example of an Area/Array problem situation. The fact that we can show arrays from different points of view while they remain essentially the same separates arrays from the Equal Groups problems we saw earlier in the chapter. Equal Groups problem situations are not as flexible.

Using Children's Literature to Explore Area and Array Situations

Ruby's Wish (Bridges & Blackall, 2002) tells the story of a plucky young girl who always wears red, which in China is the color of celebrations. She lives in a large household made up of connected buildings, arranged five houses wide and seven houses deep. In old China, families often lived close together like this. Despite being one of more than 100 children in her grandfather's household, Ruby captures her grandfather's eye as exceptional. Her wish is to go to the university, and Grandfather grants her wish. For students who do not live near their grandparents, aunts and uncles, or cousins, the household in which Ruby lives will be new and interesting. At the same time, these close familial living arrangements may be familiar to students who come from other countries.

TRANSCRIBE THE ACTION OR RELATIONSHIP

As usual, read the book first for the story and for its literary value. On the second read, focus attention on Ruby's family situation in order to understand how Ruby's family lived. Read the passage that describes what the large household looked like: "five houses wide and seven houses deep." What does that mean? How many houses do you think would be on that city block? After students understand the story and what "deep" and "wide" mean in this context, offer them square tiles to recreate Grandfather's household. How many buildings are there in Ruby's grandfather's household? Record their solutions and their answers on graph paper. If there are 100 children, where might they all live?

We know that multiplication will solve this problem quickly, but most state standards invite second graders to get to know arrays like this one and use structured counting strategies like skip counting or repeated addition, supported by the arrays, to introduce counting the squares in an array. Look for students who recognize that it is easier to count by rows rather than one by one. Look also for students who recognize that counting by fives rather than sevens is much easier but that they can choose which method to use.

Setting the Stage for Division

Students in kindergarten through second grade are not typically expected to meet standards related explicitly to division; nevertheless, ideas emerge that can be developed in order to set the stage for students to have a strong start in multiplicative thinking. In most cases, these second-grade-level ideas are embedded in standards from other domains of mathematics, like geometry or measurement.

Rather than avoiding these ideas because they don't directly address primary standards, recognize that the tasks and problems shared in this section can be taught as higher-level problem-solving tasks: Students can make sense of what is happening in the problems and devise strategies to solve them. As the teacher, you can focus your attention on the standards for mathematical practice instead, like problem solving or noting evidence that students are looking for and making use of the structure in the task. Do not feel the need to introduce the symbolism of equations if it doesn't seem appropriate for your students.

Before we look closely at how the students modeled the problems in Figures 7.13 and 7.14, read through the problems carefully, putting the stories in your own words. Think about the kinds of manipulatives you might provide to help students model the problem situations and reasons for selecting those tools. Use the workspace to show your representations of the problems.

FIGURE 7.13

FIGURE 7.14

Ashley volunteered to pass out raffle tickets at the school's Indigenous Peoples' Day celebration. The teacher printed 42 tickets on a sheet. Raffle tickets were given away 3 tickets at a time. How many students got tickets from one sheet of paper?	The second-grade teachers want to divide all of their 42 students into 3 equal groups to study the Navajo, Inuit, and Powhatan tribes. Afterward, students will share what they learned. How many students should be in each group?

Using the information on multiplier and measure factors introduced earlier in this chapter, identify which factor is unknown in each problem: the multiplier (number of groups) or the measure (size of each group) factor, as described in Figures 7.5 and 7.6. If you are reading this book with a team of teachers, discuss your reasoning for the choices, using physical objects to illustrate your reasoning.

YOUR WORKSPACE

FIGURE 7.15

FIGURE 7.16

STUDENT WORK

Image source: vector illustration/iStock.com

We gave away 3 tickets. Some people didn't get tickets.

Navajo	Inuit	Powhatan
Tony	Nan	Arjun
Greg	Kelly	Jessalyn
Sunil	Ben	Matilde
Arjun	Padhu	Nathalie
Tami	Spencer	Jordan
Anthony	Juan	Noah
Lisa	Jennifer	Denia
Joey	Ellie	Jamison
Mia	Alex	Michal
Maricella	Gurshawn	Ana
	Brooke	Jose
	Makoa	Camryn
	Olivia	Jennifer
	Maddie	Mason
	Diep	
	Lemar	
	Angel	
	Shruti	

We made three lists. Everybody got the one they wanted.

TEACHER RESPONSE

Once we read through the problem, each group was able to figure out that they had to give away three tickets at a time. They gave away the tickets in groups of three, as you can see in the picture. Interestingly, I asked how many people got tickets, which is the question in the problem. Not only did the students not know how many people got tickets, but they also weren't immediately sure how to figure that out!

As you can see from their writings, they were definitely sure that not everybody could get tickets with just one sheet, though!

This group understood right away that the goal of the task was to make three groups of students. They started with the class lists and asked everyone which tribe they wanted to study. Someone mentioned that the Inuit lived in the Arctic and then everyone wanted to be in that group!

Someone else said that being cold all the time isn't all that fun, so some students' interest waned a bit. When the time for the task was nearing the end, I asked the group to tell me about their lists.

The group knew that their lists were not the same length, but they didn't see a problem with that.

VIDEO

Video 7.5

Distributing Tickets in Groups of Three

resources.corwin.com/
problemsolvingk-2

Video 7.6

Creating Three Groups of Students

resources.corwin.com/
problemsolvingk-2

The ticket problem and the student group problem are each an example of an Equal Groups problem situation. Think back to the way you decided to model a solution to these problems. For example, how did you distribute the tickets? Did you give them away three at a time as the students did? You may have figured out that the sheet of tickets included enough sets of 3 for 14 students, but this group of students did not arrive at an answer at all. It isn't uncommon for students first learning to model Equal Groups division to go through the actions correctly yet fail to come up with a final quotient (Mulligan & Mitchelmore, 1997). Coordinating quantities and keeping track of how many groups of three is part of the learning process. Even if students are skip counting as they give out the groups of 3 tickets, they may count up to 42 (3, 6, 9, 12, . . ., 42) and still not know how many counts it took to get there. In other words, they know the measure factor of 3 tickets but don't recognize that they had counted out 14 groups and that the multiplier factor was 14.

In all honesty, students will have time to master the coordination of all of those skills in later grades, but as your students do these tasks in the primary grades, their focus is on skip counting as well as on building an understanding of division as a distribution into equal groups as they are skip counting. Skip counting also builds on students' early understandings of one-to-one correspondence. Some students might skip count accurately but tag only one object in the collection as their numbers get higher. For example, it isn't unusual for a student to pick up on the skip-counting rhythm and then tag one snap cube for each number! After all, that worked just fine when the student first learned to count. The student who is tagging one cube per count, rather than one group per count, counts 14 snap cubes as 3, 6, 9, 12, 15, 18, 21, 24, 27, 30, 33, 36, 39, 42. In this case, 42 is the answer announced, not the 14 represented right in front of the student. This may persist into third grade or beyond.

EQUIPARTITIONING

In the work shown in Figure 7.16, more students wanted to study the Inuit tribe than the other tribes. Young students may not be troubled by the different-sized groups and must learn that division requires *equal* groups. This will also be an important concept for them to understand in relation to partitioning a whole into fractional parts. The problem in Figure 7.17 looks specifically at the development of this skill.

Before we look closely at how the students made sense of the problem, read through it, recording your solution in the workspace. Consider which tools you would likely provide for your students, and think about similar problems that build the same conceptual idea.

Warning: The next pages include student examples of the next problem situation. If you find it difficult to resist looking forward while practicing in the sandbox, consider covering the facing page with a sheet of paper.

FIGURE 7.17

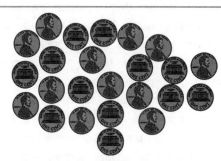

Four people are going to share these pennies. Show how they can share them equally.

Image source: JakeOlimb/iStock.com

YOUR WORKSPACE

The problem we are demonstrating here is built around a countable model that is familiar to students: pennies. As you examine the students' solutions and the teacher's comments, think about how the evidence in the students' visible work reflects their thinking about the problem.

FIGURE 7.18	FIGURE 7.19

STUDENT WORK

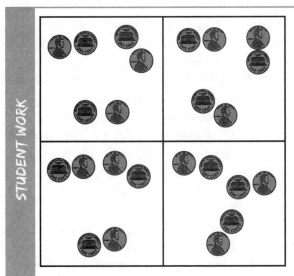

"I have 6 pennies!"

"Each person gets this* many."

*(points at a row and drags her finger across the bottom row)

TEACHER RESPONSE

I had never done this activity with students before, so I wasn't sure how they would organize it. I provided four squares on a piece of paper so that they would be able to figure out how many pennies each person would get. After seeing how one group solved the problem while they were working alone with me, I realized that I had made it too easy for them to do. Providing four squares took some of the productive struggle away.

Some kids put two pennies in a square at a time and others put just one at a time, but I think it went too easily. I decided to try to do it differently the next day with the other groups.

This time I gave the students paper, a marker, and 24 pennies and then asked them to share the pennies between 4 people, showing their thinking on the paper. Some students drew a grid much like the one I had made the day before (see Figure 7.18). Other students put the pennies into the four corners of a piece of paper, and others did what Sujin did here.

I watched as Sujin picked up the pennies one at a time and carefully laid them into rows. None of the rows you see in her work was ever more than one penny longer than the others as she distributed the pennies to each of the four rows, one at a time.

VIDEO

Video 7.7

Sharing Pennies With Groups

resources.corwin.com/
problemsolvingk-2

Video 7.8

Sharing Pennies in an Array

resources.corwin.com/
problemsolvingk-2

To equipartition is to break something apart into equal-sized portions. In the case of fractions, equipartitioning consists of making equal portions of a whole, like halves or quarters. With whole numbers, the task is making equal groups from a quantity. When students are learning to equipartition, sometimes they don't split up the collection equally or they leave out part of the collection. We saw unequal partitioning in the class groups problem in Figure 7.16.

Interestingly, equipartitioning can be achieved by students who have not, or cannot, yet count the collection. The student whose work is shown in Figure 7.18 has successfully partitioned the collection of pennies, but she has not identified the number of pennies she started with. She has, however, recognized that one of the four equal parts contains 6 pennies. By contrast, the student whose work is shown in Figure 7.19 has not identified any quantities at all. The fact that this student has successfully equipartitioned the collection of 24 pennies, yet has assigned no value to any part of the task, is important. It suggested to one researcher that equipartitioning is an understanding that develops early and that it can be entirely separate from an understanding of the cardinality of the set, or how many pennies there are (Confrey, 1994). If you have ever observed preschoolers sharing fruit, small toys, or snacks, this likely is not surprising to you. Children know when they are not getting a fair share, even if they cannot name the quantity they have or the quantity they are missing.

It's important to recognize that the set of equipartitioning skills develops separately from counting and measuring. This means that not only can we broaden what it means to count a collection, but we are also making a conceptual link between counting objects and equipartitioning two-dimensional geometric shapes, like squares and triangles, according to their area. After all, students can find half of a square or triangle long before they can calculate their areas. Since finding and demonstrating half or a quarter of a shape like a square or triangle is a standard included in most second-grade state standards, equipartitioning sets of objects helps students develop partitioning strategies and makes connections with the similar task done with fractions of a shape.

TWO MODELS OF DIVISION

In the tickets problem (Figure 7.15), students typically will make a group of three tickets and give them away one group at a time. One study found that acting out a problem situation like this one was accessible to students in grades 1 and 2 (Kouba, 1989). However, when faced with a similar situation, a group of preservice teachers were able to find correct solutions to similar problems but did not recognize the context as an example of a division problem. They did not represent, for example, giving away tickets in sets of three using ÷3, but instead with –3, repeated until all of the collection was given away (Graeber, Tirosh, & Glover, 1989). As a matter of fact, repeated subtraction is one way in which this type of division is often modeled. More formally, this model of division is known as measurement division, but it wouldn't be wrong to think of it as repeated subtraction division. The situation with the preservice teachers is a perfect example of how someone could easily solve a problem yet still not understand how to represent the actions with the best choice of operator. Eventually everyone needs experience to connect the action and the operator that represents it.

When we teach division, it is often done through a strategy called "fair share." This type of division is referred to as partitive division. If you have never taught division in your teaching career, instead think back to how you learned it long ago. The fair-share (or partitive division) strategy "deals out" the quantities in the problem so that each person has the same quantity as another person.

Measurement division: A model of division focused on the formation of equal portions of a known size. This model is sometimes thought of as *repeated subtraction.*

Partitive division: Also known as fair-share division; most commonly represented by the equal distribution of objects into a known number of sets.

In the case of the class groups problem, a fair share of the students in the second grade is expected to be distributed to each of the groups studying a tribe's history and culture. The penny-sharing problem is also a typical example of a partitive division problem situation.

Why does the model of division matter? It matters for three reasons. First, if we as teachers recognize that there is more than one model of division, we can intentionally select a variety of contexts within tasks that include both models. Second, a problem is represented differently depending on the division model, including how we make sense of it. Just looking at how different the solutions to the tickets (Figure 7.15) and class groups (Figure 7.16) problems are shows that very different actions are happening in each problem, despite their having the same answer. Third, both models of division mimic innate ways that children share collections of objects. Being purposeful about developing both models will help build students' skill sets for modeling division operations later, because in later grades the modeling matters much more. In essence, primary students are just beginning to understand that sometimes problems can be solved with a fair-share action (dividing the classes into groups) and sometimes with a distribution action (giving away groups of tickets).

Using Children's Literature to Explore Early Multiplication and Division

As mentioned previously, the collection of lists and annotated bibliographies of books specifically supporting mathematical ideas is large. *The Doorbell Rang* (Hutchins, 1986) is a picture book that often makes an appearance on these lists, and it's an "oldie but goodie," if you will. *The Doorbell Rang* captures a clear representation of an Equal Groups problem situation.

TRANSCRIBE THE ACTION OR RELATIONSHIP

The story starts with two children about to enjoy 12 of their grandma's cookies. The doorbell rings, again and again, and more and more guests come to the door, until each child has only one cookie. Things get suspenseful when the doorbell rings one more time. How will they share the cookies now? But instead, at the door is Grandma, with more cookies to share.

You can read this book and leave out the children's announcement of how many cookies each child will get, asking students instead to make good guesses. You might also decide to represent the cookies using magnets on a white board or large cookie sheet, inviting students to come up and rearrange the "cookies" on the board after each new group of children arrives. Depending on your students and your lesson goal, you might choose to introduce students to the new symbols like $12 \div 2 = 6$ or $2 \times 6 = 12$. You may even represent the Equal Groups situation using addition if it is more appropriate: $6 + 6 = 12$.

In this case, the important task is for students to see that they can reorganize the cookies each time more children come to share Grandma's cookies.

A Final Word on Introducing Early Multiplication and Division

The mathematical thinking from kindergarten through second grade is concerned primarily with the development of students' understanding of the base 10 number system so that they can efficiently decompose numbers and do computations. These are important skills. At these same grade levels, it is also critically important for students to develop their understanding of the common addition and subtraction problem situations that form the basis of just about every additive word problem or real-world situation they will ever encounter. The goal of this book has been to explore the Addition and Subtraction Problem Situations table in depth. However, as students move into second grade, most standards begin to introduce early concepts that build students' capacity to think multiplicatively. Some examples include counting areas, dividing up collections, identifying equal parts of geometric figures, skip counting, and the idea of identifying even and odd numbers. For this reason, Chapter 7 focuses on some of the multiplication and division ideas that are introduced before third grade, and it leads you as the teacher to a broader and more detailed understanding of these conceptual ideas so that you can identify your role in developing them.

KEY IDEAS

1. Recognizing even and odd numbers involves much more than identifying the final digit of a number.

2. Even numbers can be represented as grouped in pairs, or they can be shown as forming two equal groups.

3. Odd numbers are always one less or one more than an even number.

4. Students' understanding of even and odd numbers is often not as stable as adults think it is.

5. In an Equal Groups problem situation, one factor tells how many groups there are (the multiplier) and one factor tells the size of the groups (the measure).

6. Students must develop an understanding of the row/column structure of an array.

7. An Area/Array problem situation explores multiplication as covering (area) or organizing in a rectangular pattern.

8. Equipartitioning can be done without naming specific quantities, an understanding even young preschoolers have.

9. Very young students can easily model both kinds of division problems—fair-share (partitive) and distribution (measurement) division—without using the formal symbols.

10. Many older children and adults often do not recognize measurement division as a model of division. They see it as a kind of subtraction. They may recognize only partitive (fair-share) division as "real" division.

TRY IT OUT!

IDENTIFY THE PROBLEM SITUATION

Decide if each problem situation is an example of an Equal Groups or Area/Array problem situation.

1. There are 5 baskets at the farmers' market, and all together they hold 30 apples. Each basket holds the same number of apples. How many apples are there in each basket?

2. There are 4 pieces of art in each display area at the school art show. There are 28 pieces of art all together. How many display areas are there at the school art show?

3. The groundskeeper noticed that the 6 trees along the river have a total of 24 eggs in nests about to hatch. An equal number of eggs is hatching in each tree. How many eggs are in each tree?

4. There are 36 packets of nuts in the box. Adara took 3 packets and gave them to the teacher next door. If she continued giving away packets of nuts 3 at a time, how many teachers would receive a portion?

If you are reading this book with a team of teachers, discuss your answers together. For more than one of these situations, you might be able to make the case for both problem types.

WRITE THE PROBLEM

Decide if the quantity in each of the following Equal Groups problem situations is odd or even:

1. The students in second grade are going to the zoo today. Each student got on the bus and sat with a friend. There are no leftover seats. Is there an even number of students in the grade or an odd number of students in second grade? How do you know? Draw a picture of the full bus.

2. Marlena passed out two graham crackers to every student at her table. In the end she had one cracker left over. Did she start with an odd number of graham crackers or an even number of graham crackers? How do you know? Draw a picture.

3. Mario and his partner Luis poured a bag of candies onto their paper so they could share. Mario made a circle for himself and one for Luis. Mario put one candy in his circle. Then Luis put one candy in his circle. They continued taking turns sharing all of the candies. Mario was the last one to put a candy in his circle. Is there an odd number of candies or an even number of candies?

4. Sergei was making sandwiches for a picnic. When he finished, there were no slices of bread left in the bag. Did the bag have an even or an odd number of slices in it? Draw a picture that explains your answer.

(continued)

(continued)

CHANGE IT UP

This task is adapted from a study of how students develop their understanding of arrays and area as rows and columns arranged as a grid. First, look at the task and think about what students must understand to successfully complete it.

Student Task

Directions: Estimate how many squares it takes to cover the rectangle with square tiles. Complete the grid.

Materials: A copy of the partially erased grid below, a pencil (but NO square tiles).

Source: Based on Battista (2004).

Take a look at the student work samples. What do you notice? What do you wonder? What are the students' understanding of rows and columns? What would you want to teach next?

A follow-up to this activity is to ask students to complete the array using square tiles to check their estimates.

REFLECT

1. How has your thinking about odd and even numbers changed since reading this chapter? What will you do differently when teaching it the next time?

2. Equipartitioning is a skill that starts developing in the toddler years and continues through fair sharing, to division, and even into the study of exponential operations in middle school. What are some examples of lessons you have taught, in any grade, that are related to this important idea?

3. Look at the word problems in the textbook you currently use and identify where in your book the topics in this chapter are addressed. They will not be identified by the name of the problem situation, because that table isn't used until the third grade. Instead, look for the standards in your curriculum that address these topics and use that information to find the lessons in your current curriculum.

4. Once you find the lessons, discuss how you see those lessons differently after reading this chapter. How will you teach them differently? How will your emphasis change?

CHAPTER EIGHT

Changing How You Teach Word Problems

Think back to the first-year teacher's classroom we visited at the beginning of this book. She asked her students to solve two word problems:

> *Daphne has 35 shells in her collection, 4 more than Nathan. How many shells does Nathan have?*

> *Raphine had 18 books. He bought 13 more at the library book sale. How many books does Raphine have now?*

This teacher realized that her students were misled in the first problem by the word *more*, treating it as a key word and thinking that addition was the right approach to the problem. Knowing what you know now, what guidance would you give this new teacher if she were your colleague?

Getting Into the Mathematizing Sandbox

Problem-solving protocols are not a new idea. Certainly you have seen models for problem solving in your mathematics textbook, and many books have been written on this subject. Perhaps the most influential problem-solving protocol was written in 1945 by Pólya. His general plan included four steps: understand, devise a plan, carry out a plan, and look back. If this protocol were enough to resolve all difficulties with problem solving, there would be no need for this book or any other book on problem solving. Of course, this issue is far from being resolved. We offer in this book a model that targets the space somewhere between "understand" and "devise a plan" with the belief that there is a need to explore more deeply what it means to understand a problem mathematically.

The mathematizing sandbox model emphasizes the power and importance of play and interaction with mathematical tools and ideas. Problem solving doesn't ride on a train and barrel through to the end of the track. Sometimes it needs to meander and rest and sit idle to allow thoughts to coalesce into working theories. We chose the metaphor of a sandbox with intention. What do we do in a sandbox? We play, construct, take down, and reconstruct. We get our hands dirty as we pick up new tools and move things around. We shake off the old and use the grains to form new ideas. When we emerge from the sandbox, we take away nothing tangible. But the play has done its work forming ideas in the child's mind. That is the takeaway. When we are young, we don't solve problems so that we can find the answer. We solve problems so that we learn to solve bigger and more important problems. This is how real problem solving works. Figure 8.1 reviews the steps in the mathematizing sandbox model, giving you a chance to think about it again after having applied it multiple times in your own work on the problems in the book.

FIGURE 8.1 A MODEL FOR MATHEMATIZING WORD PROBLEMS

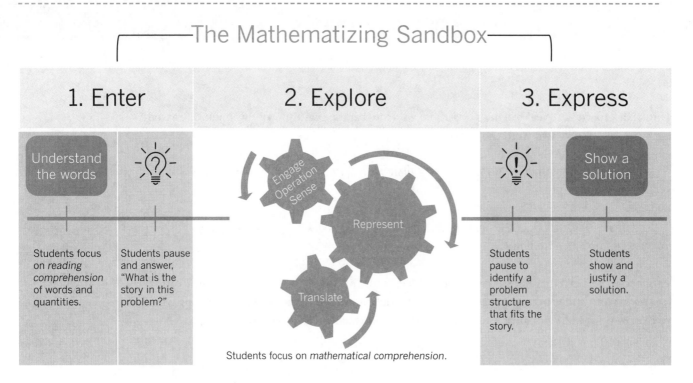

ENTER:	In this problem-solving model we acknowledge the importance of language and literacy strategies in making sense of the words that frame a problem situation: Understanding what is happening in the problem is a ticket into the sandbox. If the problem is one that the students have identified and posed themselves, this is less of a concern. But for a traditional word problem, it is important to help students decipher the language.
💡	Teachers tell us, and we know from our own work with students, that rushing into a problem often results in "number plucking and plugging" (SanGiovanni, 2020), a haphazard application of operations that involves little sense-making. Here we stop to tell the story in our own words. What is happening? Between each set of word problems and a workspace given to you to write down your own solutions, we stepped in and included questions that helped to guide your thinking or to give you an idea to focus on as you did your own work. In this respect, we intended to model the Pause step of this model.
EXPLORE:	The three parts of Explore are the core content of this book, the place where operation sense is built. Each problem exploration included multiple representations and deliberately made connections (translations) between each of those representations. Sometimes, like in Chapter 2, the same problem was explored using five or more representations, all in the interest of revealing more details about the relationships in the problem and figuring out the right operation to use to find a solution. Sometimes we encountered a solution in the sandbox, but that was not the primary goal. Our goal was to learn more about the problem, the problem situation, and how to use multiple representations to understand the work of the operation in the problem.

Chapter Eight. Changing How You Teach Word Problems

175

	The pause on the way out of the sandbox gave us the opportunity to generalize what was learned during exploration. For students, we recommend that they spend time deciding which problem situation applies, what element is missing, and then how they will calculate an answer.
EXPRESS:	Finally, students can compute an answer. That's a long process just to get to the answer, right? Yes. That is intentional. As the teacher, you decide what you would like to see your students express. What evidence from their sandbox work is important to you? Do you want to see an equation? A drawing? Just an answer? We decided not to make that decision for you because you know your students best and you know the contexts in which they will need to show their solutions.

Eight Shifts in Instruction for Building Students' Problem-Solving Skills

In this book we've presented an approach to problem solving that comes from a sense-making point of view. Recognizing that calculation and computation skills are important for student success, we also realize that computation alone is not very effective for preparing students to make sense of word problems or to pose and solve real-world problems. In the discussion that follows, we suggest eight changes that you can make in your teaching practice that will help build strong problem solvers in your classroom.

DO WORD PROBLEMS FOR SENSE-MAKING

Word problems are typically organized in textbooks to give students the opportunity to practice a computation strategy. This can be done meaningfully. But we have used word problems as a tool throughout the book to highlight the problem situations and many of their variations. Through this very familiar tool, you have had the opportunity to explore common solution approaches, some of which are precisely efficient and others of which are inefficient. But unpacking word problems is not the goal of this book. Building operation sense is. The problem situations that we explored are present in any everyday situation that you and your students wish to mathematize. Do your students want to keep track of who chooses what activity at recess? Their discussions won't be about "plus" or "minus." Instead, they will talk about comparisons, measurements, and the different groups of students on the playground (parts and a whole). They focus their problem-solving discussion on the actions they wish to accomplish. The problem situations and the ideas behind them give them tools to *do*. That is operation sense. Tools for calculation, like addition and subtraction, will follow the need for them.

Shift #1: Use word problems to help students learn to recognize the properties of the problem situations that represent a wide range of contexts. Word problems are not just tools for practicing computation.

TREAT CONTEXT AND COMPUTATION SEPARATELY

Separating context from computation is a consistent theme throughout the book. Chapters 3 and 4 focused on the power of concrete and visual representations to show the action in a problem situation. Across the book, we distinguish between using tools such as number lines or 10 frames to structure numbers and using those same tools to make sense of problem situations. The motion on a number line to show that 7 crayons have been lost (an arrow jumping left 7 spaces) might be represented differently if we are focusing on the computation of subtracting 7. In the latter case, we might make two jumps, stopping on a friendly value along the way. By keeping context and computation separate, we focus on understanding the meaning of the situation before we decide what computation strategy to use. Focusing on context has its own challenges, and they are not insignificant. It is our goal to raise your awareness of the many ways you can subtly but directly make instructional changes in order to hone students' focus on what is happening in a problem, any contextual problem. To be clear, computational skills are critically important, but that's not what this book set out to address.

Shift #2: Focus instruction on finding and explaining the meaning of a problem situation. Figuring out how to calculate an answer comes second.

CREATE MORE AND VARIED REPRESENTATIONS

Representations of mathematical ideas take many forms. In Chapter 1 we outlined five different modes of representation and the ways each mode can help describe what is happening in a problem situation (Figure 8.2). And throughout the book we have urged you to try out multiple representations in your own explorations of the problems presented. In Chapter 3 we saw, for example, how a concrete model composed of two-color counters to represent people participating in a fun run could be translated into a representation of the same problem using a formal symbolic equation. The power of mathematics is in its capacity to capture and manipulate abstract thoughts and ideas. Students need plenty of experience describing and connecting real-life contexts to the symbolic representations before they can deal wholly within the abstract. Multiple, and connected, representations add shading and nuance to students' understandings, which leads to greater mathematizing power.

Shift #3: Match multiple representations to the details of a problem context. Translating between representations strengthens this understanding.

Chapter Eight. Changing How You Teach Word Problems

177

FIGURE 8.2 FIVE REPRESENTATIONS: A TRANSLATION MODEL

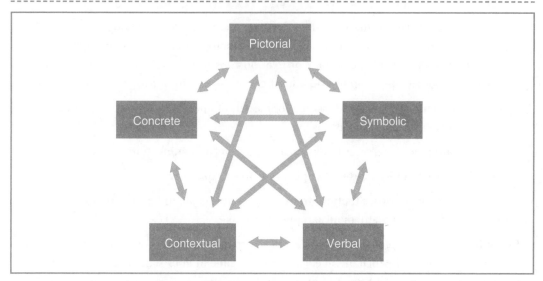

Source: Adapted from Lesh, Post, and Behr (1987).

EXPLORE ALL THE WORK OPERATIONS CAN DO

Each person has an intuitive mental model for each of the operations (+ − × ÷). Sometimes students' mental models are limited to only one or two of the "jobs" that an operation can do. We saw in Chapter 5 that subtraction can do more than just "take away." It can also describe the relationships among the parts and the whole of a set. This latter model of subtraction often surprises learners. In Chapter 7 we began to explore some of the work multiplication and division can do as we examined situations of sharing fairly and the characteristics of sets of odd or even numbers. Using the chapter-opening problem situation tables as a guide, this book exposes some of the lesser-known work that the operations can do.

Shift #4: Focus student attention on the actions or relationships in a problem situation. When students know what they need an operator to do, they are better able to make a good choice.

ADD OPERATION SENSE ROUTINES TO THE SCHOOL DAY

Operation sense is part of the sense-making stage of any problem-solving protocol you might already use. It includes the ability to mathematize a problem situation, to create multiple representations of the actions or relationships in the problem situation, and to assign an appropriate operation to find a solution. Students with a strong operation sense

- Understand and use a wide variety of models of operations beyond the basic and intuitive models of operations

- Use appropriate representations of actions or relationships strategically

- Apply their understanding of operations to any quantity

- Can mathematize a situation, translating a contextual understanding into a variety of other mathematical representations

In this book we have explored a wide variety of informal models and commercially available manipulatives, most of which are likely already available in your school or have digital or print alternatives. None of these is appropriate all the time, but part of operation sense is selecting the right tool for the job and using it to make sense of a problem situation.

Shift #5: Build operation sense routines into your normal instructional time. Operation sense routines might include problem posing, numberless word problems, and acting out problems.

OFFER STUDENTS EXPERIENCES WITH A VARIETY OF PROBLEM SITUATIONS

When focused on context-based instruction, the value or form of the numbers in the problem should not matter. But in some ways they do. For example, it matters which quantities are known and unknown, and students need practice with unknown elements in different parts of the problem. Changing number categories—for example, from small whole numbers to larger quantities (or even fractions in the upper grades)—is like putting a wrench in the gears of a machine: It can cause a multitude of problems (Figure 8.3). As students experience new number categories, let them wrestle with problem contexts that arise, and observe carefully both the roadblocks they hit and the creative solutions they find. This productive struggle will improve their capacity to solve problems and your capacity to challenge and support them. Remember that students' ability to pose and solve mathematical problems reflecting all of the different problem situations is based on experience. If they never solve additive comparisons using larger values, they will never be comfortable with this structure. Experience matters.

Shift #6: Anticipate that the introduction of a new category of numbers will require a review of the problem situation variations, but don't back away from the challenge.

Chapter Eight. Changing How You Teach Word Problems

179

FIGURE 8.3 THE CHALLENGE OF NEW NUMBER CATEGORIES LEADS TO GROWTH

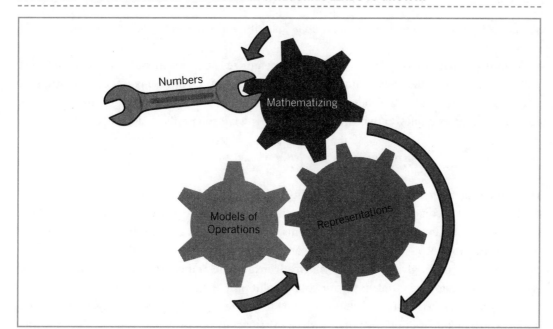

LISTEN TO STUDENTS AND BE CURIOUS

We used dozens of work samples throughout this book to illustrate some of the ways that students might grapple with a focus on context in a problem. Sometimes these examples are chosen specifically to feature the teacher's response to the student work. Often this is because the teacher has made an insightful observation about the student's work, one that helps the reader make sense of the new information. Throughout the book we worked to use qualified, non-evaluative language, recognizing that we can only interpret the student work based on the evidence before us. This is also true for you in the classroom. Even when you know your students well, continue to ask for clarification and evidence in your assessment procedures.

Shift #7: Don't assume you know what students are thinking. Be curious! Ask questions!

MAKE TIME FOR MATHEMATIZING IN THE SANDBOX

The mathematizing sandbox is a state of mind more than it is a place to go. The sandbox shows that your priority is exploration and learning. Failed models are expected, but replacement ideas are also expected. For this reason, we would never grade work done in the sandbox. Of course, this means that time will need to be carved out for students to engage in this thinking time. To make the time, do fewer problems. Do more problems that are in response to questions or concerns your students have posted and fewer randomly assigned problems.

Shift #8: Take time for students to explore and learn to problem solve.

Guidance for Moving Forward: FAQs

Should my students have to memorize the kinds of problems in the tables and their definitions?

We consider it inappropriate to ask students to memorize the problem situation tables and sort problems into those categories accurately. Use the language in the problems and even let students create class anchor charts that describe the characteristics of the problem types that your class encounters. Post examples so that they can remember what the problems look like.

How do I find more high-quality problems of different types?

The most valuable resource you have might be your textbook and your creativity! Textbook publishers have become much more intentional since 2010 in the word problem types that they include in chapter exercises. Read the problems available to you, classify them according to the problem situation tables, and plan your lesson with supports for that problem situation. Often, minor variations in the given problems will greatly extend their range. You can change which term is unknown or adapt the numbers to suit your current unit of study, for example. Overall, choose problems carefully so that students have exposure to different problem situations over time. If you find the textbook doesn't offer enough variety, other resources are available. One of our favorite sources for word problems is Greg Tang. He has included a word problem generator on his website that will generate lists of problems, and you have the opportunity to select the problem type and which element is unknown (Tang, n.d.): https://gregtangmath.com/wordproblems.

What about those kids who are always racing to finish?

Sometimes the same students who race to finish their work are able to come up with a correct answer. Other times, they are not. If we remember that the goal is to teach a long-term strategy for problem solving rather than a short-term goal of finding an answer, it is easier to be firm in your expectations. Make it clear what you are looking for in their work. Share student representations and discuss them in class. Challenge students to do problems where the values are all unknown so that the focus is squarely on the problem situation. If there are still some students who dive in and race to get an answer, intervene much as you would with a student who is running in the hallways. After all, it is faster to run down the hall of the school, but we ask kids to walk because we know that it is much easier for someone to get hurt when they run. No one will get hurt if they race through the sandbox, but there is still truth to the analogy!

Do I have to do the full mathematizing sandbox for every word problem?

No. It is important to follow the entire process at first so that students develop new thought patterns about problem solving. You want them to understand the operations better at first, and you want them to learn to use a wide variety of manipulatives and representations. Lessons in the sandbox intentionally focus on building students' operation sense and making strong connections between the problem situation and its representations, but we know it isn't possible to follow the entire process each and every time.

Chapter Eight. Changing How You Teach Word Problems

181

How do I develop language skills, especially among students who are still learning to read and write?

For students who are learning to read and write, their understanding can also be displayed through verbal and concrete representations. To gauge, clarify, and extend student thinking, ask students to share the story in spoken or pictorial form. Ask questions such as the following:

- Tell me the story in your own words.

- Try telling me the story without using any numbers.

- Show me how you're representing the quantities in this situation with your manipulatives or pictures.

- Is there action happening in this story? Where?

- What number sentence best shows what is happening in this story?

When students are experiencing challenges, try one of these strategies:

- Identify and pair up students who could assist each other or who have different approaches.

- Ask students to justify their thinking, both when their approaches are correct as well as when they are incorrect.

I have not used concrete representations very much. How do I start? What should I look out for?

Before asking your students to use manipulatives to represent problem situations, provide time to explore the materials. Even a few minutes gives learners an opportunity to see how the pieces fit together, build a tower or other structure, and begin to see what the materials might do.

Take time to learn about a variety of materials; you do not have to start with many different manipulatives all at the same time. We suggested throughout the book which materials we prefer for which situations. Your students may have different preferences, but our suggestions can help you begin. As students become comfortable with the materials, keep them easily available—on their tables or on accessible shelves. Remember to respect your students' choice of manipulative models. What makes sense to us might not be most helpful to them.

In Chapter 2, we provided a list of suggestions for using concrete materials to represent problem situations. We include it again in Figure 8.4 to provide ideas for encouraging productive use of these powerful tools.

FIGURE 8.4 ENCOURAGING MULTIPLE MODELS IN PROBLEM SOLVING

1. **Choose:** Encourage individual choice of pictorial representations.

2. **Explain:** Ask students to explain what the parts of their pictorial representation mean and to explain the relationships between those parts.

3. **Justify:** Challenge students to defend their choices. Challenge students' correct representations just as much as you would ask them to justify incorrect representations.

4. **Model:** Explicitly model new forms of diagrams or manipulatives that you choose to use, explaining your decisions as you demonstrate how you are using the tool. Note that we are *not* suggesting you explicitly teach students to use the tool. Simply, model your own thinking process as you employ a visual, but reinforce to students that you are held to the same standard for justifying your decisions as they are.

5. **Connect:** Ask students to describe how two representations or models relate to each other. Encourage them to identify how each element of the problem appears in each model. Ask them to explain when they might prefer one model or representation over another.

6. **Share:** Ask students to explain a novel visual approach to their peers and discuss how they model their thinking process.

7. **Expect:** Communicate that you expect to see visual diagrams or manipulatives used to explain mathematical ideas.

8. **Crash:** No representation works in every context or situation. Expect any model to fail at some point, and encourage students to change their representation when the model crashes.

How do I help my students see the structure in the word problems?

The questions you ask while students are exploring are critically important. You have seen some of these questions while reading, especially where we gave problem pairs for you to explore. Figure 8.5 includes a list of questions you can use to support your students in this process.

FIGURE 8.5 QUESTIONS TO SUPPORT YOUR STUDENTS IN THE MATHEMATIZING SANDBOX

- Is something happening in this problem? Tell me the story.

- What is changing in this story?

- Can you tell me about the ____ and the ____ (quantities) in this problem? How do they go together?

- What are the numbers in this problem? What are they counting?

- If this is subtraction, how does your picture show that? How do your counters show that?

Chapter Eight. Changing How You Teach Word Problems

183

The mathematics we teach students in school is about more than getting ready for the test at the end of a unit or the end of the year. It is about seeing our world mathematically and using the math we know to mathematize, to solve problems in our jobs, our careers, and in our everyday lives. Jon Scieszka humorously calls this tendency *the math curse* (Scieszka & Smith, 1995). But we don't see it as a curse. We see it as a super power, which, like literacy, should be available to all!

Finding Unexpected Mathematics in Stories

In Chapter 1, we shared four strategies for incorporating children's literature into your exploration in the mathematical sandbox: Make Predictions, Create Another Outcome, Find the Unknown Quantity, and Transcribe the Action or Relationship. As we close, we add a fifth strategy to your toolbox: Play With Quantities.

PLAY WITH QUANTITIES

In the book *This Plus That: Life's Little Equations* (Rosenthal, 2011), the author cleverly uses equations to write stories about life. Although there are no quantities in these equations, they still tell stories. All of the equations in the book that are appropriate for primary grades are either Add-To or Take-From problem situations, and the key to the stories is that the result is unknown. Here is an example that is a great start to introduce the idea to students:

balloon + wind = lost

The illustrations on the page show whimsical, smiling clouds blowing a balloon across the sky. Ask students to imagine what it might look like to start with a balloon and add wind. Then ask what it means to say "= lost," as in "What is lost?" "Why is it lost?" Listen for how students make sense of the action in the story and how they interpret the symbols in a numberless story context. Make note of the vocabulary students use to describe the action and use these same words to help them interpret other, more routine word problems. As the teacher, you have the opportunity to encourage students to build pictures in their mind and talk about how the plus sign and the equal sign communicate the action in the story.

Give students additional opportunities to write more equations and draw pictures to represent their stories. Be sure to change up the missing element in the story. For example, ask students what story these equations might represent:

? + pool = summer

? + recess = loud

Saturday afternoon − ? = fun

After you have read the story, you have a model for a creative writing or poetry lesson that boosts students' understanding of the meaning of operations in mathematics.

Ask students to write their own equations, encouraging them to write equations that express their joys, their excitement, or even their worries and fears. As a bonus, finished student work has the potential to make attractive works of art that students can share with their parents.

There are also stories in the book that expand beyond the mathematical operations and symbols that students in grades K–2 typically learn, including division situations and grouping symbols like parentheses. You can read those pages to students, substituting the symbols with words like "together" or "in a group" to convey meaning, rather than skipping them.

We hope we have inspired you to see word problems differently, as a tool for developing operation sense rather than only as a vehicle for practicing a procedure. The operation sense that students develop while diving into word problems and other problem situations empowers them to recognize mathematical relationships in their own environment. This power allows them to make their own choices about what is worthy of being mathematized. In this way operation sense is a key component of a sense-making approach to mathematics and of a social justice–inspired mathematics program. Kids learn that they can mathematize any situation they encounter. Feel free to change our problems to suit your students' needs and interests and then ask them what problems they want to mathematize and solve.

APPENDIX:
Situation Tables

The representations for the problem situations in these tables reflect our understanding based on a number of resources. These include the tables in the Common Core State Standards for Mathematics (National Governors Association Center for Best Practices and Council of Chief State School Officers, 2010), the problem situations as described in the Cognitively Guided Instruction research (Carpenter, Hiebert, & Moser, 1981), in Heller and Greeno (1979) and Riley, Greeno, & Heller (1984), and other tools. See the table references below for a more detailed summary of the documents that informed our development of these tables.

Table References

Carpenter, T. P., Hiebert, J., & Moser, J. M. (1981). Problem structure and first-grade children's initial solution processes for simple addition and subtraction problems. *Journal for Research in Mathematics Education*, 27–39.

Heller, J. I., & Greeno, J. G. (1979). Information processing analyses of mathematical problem solving. In R. Lesh (Ed.), *Applied mathematical problem solving* (pp. 181–206). Evanston, IL: The Ohio State University.

National Governors Association Center for Best Practices and Council of Chief State School Officers. (2010). *Common Core State Standards for Mathematics*. Washington, DC: Common Core Standards Initiative.

Riley, M. S., Greeno, J. G., & Heller, J. I. (1984). Development of children's ability in arithmetic. In *Development of Children's Problem-Solving Ability in Arithmetic. No. LRDC-1984/37.* (pp. 153–196). Pittsburgh University, PA: Learning Research and Development Center, National Institute of Education.

Addition and Subtraction Problem Situations

ACTIVE SITUATIONS

	Result Unknown	Change Addend Unknown	Start Addend Unknown	
Add-To	Paulo counted 9 crayons. He put them in the basket. Paulo found 6 more crayons under the table. He put them in the basket. How many crayons are in the basket? $9 + 6 = x$ $6 = x - 9$	Paulo counted 9 crayons. He found more and put them in the basket. Now Paulo has 15 crayons. How many crayons did he put in the basket? $9 + x = 15$ $9 = 15 - x$	Paulo had some crayons. He found 6 more crayons under the table. Now he has 15 crayons. How many crayons did Paulo have in the beginning? $x + 6 = 15$ $15 - 6 = x$	
Take-From	There are 19 students in Mrs. Amadi's class. 4 students went to the office to say the Pledge. How many students are in the class now? $19 - 4 = x$ $4 + x = 19$	There are 19 students in Mrs. Amadi's class. Some students went to class to read the Pledge. There were still 15 students in the classroom. How many students went to the office? $19 - x = 15$ $x + 15 = 19$	4 students went to the office. 15 students were still in the classroom. How many students are there in Mrs. Amadi's class? $x - 4 = 15$ $15 + 4 = x$	

RELATIONSHIP (NONACTIVE) SITUATIONS

	Total Unknown	One Part Unknown	Both Parts Unknown
Part-Part-Whole	The first grade voted on a game for recess. 11 students voted to play four square. 8 voted to go to the playground. How many students are in the class? $8 + 11 = x$ $x - 11 = 8$	The 19 first graders voted on a recess activity. 8 students voted to go to the playground. How many wanted to play four square? $8 + x = 19$ $x = 19 - 8$	The 19 first graders voted on a recess activity. Some wanted to play four square. Some wanted to go to the playground. What are some ways the first graders could have voted? $x + y = 19$ $19 - x = y$

	Difference Unknown	Greater Quantity Unknown	Lesser Quantity Unknown	
Additive Comparison	Jessie's paper airplane flew 14 feet. Jo's paper airplane flew 9 feet. How much less did Jo's paper airplane fly than Jessie's? $14 - 9 = x$ $9 + x = 14$	Jo's paper airplane flew 9 feet. Jessie's paper airplane flew 5 feet more than Jo's. How far did Jessie's paper airplane fly? $9 + 5 = x$ $x - 5 = 9$	Jessie's paper airplane flew 14 feet. Jo's paper airplane flew 5 feet less than Jessie's paper airplane. How far did Jo's paper airplane fly? $14 - 5 = x$ $14 = x + 5$	

Multiplication and Division Problem Situations

ASYMMETRICAL (NONMATCHING) FACTORS

	Product Unknown	Multiplier (Number of Groups) Unknown	Measure (Group Size) Unknown	
Equal Groups	Mayim has 8 vases to decorate the tables at her party. She places 2 flowers in each vase. How many flowers does she need? $$8 \times 2 = x$$ $$x \div 8 = 2$$	Mayim has some vases to decorate the tables at her party. She places 2 flowers in each vase. If she uses 16 flowers, how many vases does she have? $$x \times 2 = 16$$ $$x = 16 \div 2$$	Mayim places 16 flowers in vases to decorate the tables at her party. There are 8 vases and each vase has the same number of flowers. How many flowers will be in each vase? $$8 \times x = 16$$ $$16 \div 8 = x$$	
	Resulting Value Unknown	**Scale Factor (Times as Many) Unknown**	**Original Value Unknown**	
Multiplicative Comparison	Amelia's dog is 5 times older than Wanda's 3-year-old dog. How old is Amelia's dog? $$5 \times 3 = x$$ $$x \div 5 = 3$$	Sydney has $15 to spend at the movies. Her sister has $5. How many times more money does Sydney have than her sister has? $$x \times 5 = 15$$ $$5 = 15 \div x$$	Mrs. Smith has 15 puzzles in her classroom. That is 3 times as many puzzles as are in Mr. Jackson's room. How many puzzles are in Mr. Jackson's room? $$3 \times x = 15$$ $$15 \div 3 = x$$	

SYMMETRICAL (MATCHING) FACTORS

	Product Unknown	One Dimension Unknown	Both Dimensions Unknown
Area/Array	Bradley bought a new rug for the hallway in his house. One side measured 5 feet and the other side measured 3 feet. How many square feet does the rug cover? $$5 \times 3 = x$$ $$3 + 3 + 3 + 3 + 3 = x$$ $$3 \times 5 = x$$ $$5 + 5 + 5 = x$$	The 12 members of the student council lined up on the stage to take yearbook pictures. The first row started with 6 students and the rest of the rows did the same. How many rows were there? $$6 \times x = 12$$ $$x = 12 \div 6$$	Daniella was building a house foundation using her building blocks. She started with 20 blocks. How many blocks long and wide could the foundation be? $$x \times y = 20$$ $$20 \div x = y$$
	Sample Space (Total Outcomes) Unknown	**One Factor Unknown**	**Both Factors Unknown**
Combinations (Fundamental Counting Principle)	Karen has 3 shirts and 7 pairs of pants. How many unique outfits can she make? $$3 \times 7 = x$$ $$3 = x \div 7$$	Evelyn says that she can make 21 unique and different ice cream sundaes using just ice cream flavors and toppings. If she has 3 flavors of ice cream, how many kinds of toppings does Evelyn have? $$3 \times x = 21$$ $$21 \div 3 = x$$	Audrey can make 21 different fruit sodas using the machine at the restaurant. How many different flavorings and sodas could there be? $$x \times y = 21$$ $$x = 21 \div y$$

Note: In the upper elementary grades, students begin the long journey of learning to think multiplicatively and proportionally. Part of this process involves moving away from counting and repeated addition to represent ideas that are better expressed with multiplication, but the primary years are still focused mostly on counting and adding. Some standards leverage that strength to introduce early ideas of multiplication: Counting squares in an array is one of them, and skip counting is another. We have included multiplication and division equations for our adult readers. K–2 students are not typically expected to represent these operations in equation form.

References

Asturius, H. (n.d.). The 3-Read Protocol. Retrieved August 15, 2018, from http://www.sfusdmath.org/3-read-protocol.html

Asturius, H. (2017, December). CMC leadership: Sixty years of taking responsibility for what matters! Lecture presented at the northern section of the California Mathematics Council (CMC-North) in Asilomar, CA.

Battista, M. T. (2004). Applying cognition-based assessment to elementary school students' development of understanding of area and volume measurement. *Mathematical Thinking and Learning*, *6*(2), 185–204.

Bay-Williams, J. M., & Fletcher, G. (2017). A bottom-up hundred chart? Reflect and discuss. *Teaching Children Mathematics*, *24*(3), e1–e7.

Bell, A., Fischbein, E., & Greer, B. (1984). Choice of operation in verbal arithmetic problems: The effects of number size, problem structure and context. *Educational Studies in Mathematics*, *15*(2), 129–147.

Bell, A., Greer, B., Grimison, L., & Mangan, C. (1989). Children's performance on multiplicative word problems: Elements of a descriptive theory. *Journal for Research in Mathematics Education*, *20*(5), 434–449.

Bridges, S. Y., & Blackall, S. (2002). *Ruby's wish*. San Francisco, CA: Chronicle Books.

Bushart, B. (n.d.). Numberless word problems. *Teaching to the beat of a different drummer*. Retrieved from https://bstockus.wordpress.com/numberless-word-problems/

Cannon, J. (1993). *Stellaluna*. New York, NY: Houghton Mifflin Harcourt.

Carpenter, T. P. (1985). Learning to add and subtract: An exercise in problem solving. In E. A. Silver (Ed.), *Teaching and learning mathematical problem solving: Multiple research perspectives* (pp. 17–40). Hillsdale, NJ: Erlbaum.

Carpenter, T. P., Fennema, E., & Franke, M. L. (1996). Cognitively guided instruction: A knowledge base for reform in primary mathematics instruction. *The Elementary School Journal*, *97*(1), 3–20.

Carpenter, T. P., Fennema, E., Franke, M. L., Levi, L., & Empson, S. B. (2014). *Children's mathematics: Cognitively guided instruction* (2nd ed.). Portsmouth, NH: Heinemann.

Carpenter, T. P., Hiebert, J., & Moser, J. M. (1981). Problem structure and first-grade children's initial solution processes for simple addition and subtraction problems. *Journal for Research in Mathematics Education*, *12*, 27–39.

Champagne, Z., Schoen, R., & Riddell, C. M. (2014). Variations in both-addends-unknown problems. *Teaching Children Mathematics*, *21*, 114–121.

Choi, Y. (2005). *Peach heaven*. New York, NY: Farrar, Straus and Giroux.

Columba, L., Kim, C. Y., & Moe, A. J. (2017). *The power of picture books in teaching math and science.* New York, NY: Routledge.

Confrey, J. (1994). Splitting, similarity, and rate of change: A new approach to multiplication and exponential functions. In *The development of multiplicative reasoning in the learning of mathematics* (pp. 293–332). Albany: State University of New York Press.

Cristaldi, K. (1996). *Even Steve and odd Todd.* New York, NY: Scholastic, Inc.

De Corte, E., & Verschaffel, L. (1987). The effect of semantic structure on first graders' strategies for solving addition and subtraction word problems. *Journal for Research in Mathematics Education, 18,* 363–381.

de Koning, B. B., Boonen, A. J. H., & van der Schoot, M. (2017). The consistency effect in word problem solving is effectively reduced through verbal instruction. *Contemporary Educational Psychology, 49,* 121–129.

de la Peña, M. (2015). *Last stop on Market Street.* New York, NY: Penguin.

De Regniers, B. S. (1985). *So many cats!* New York, NY: Houghton Mifflin Harcourt.

English, L. D. (1998). Children's problem posing within formal and informal contexts. *Journal for Research in Mathematics Education, 29,* 83–106.

Fischbein, E., Deri, M., Nello, M. S., & Marino, M. S. (1985). The role of implicit models in solving verbal problems in multiplication and division. *Journal for Research in Mathematics Education, 16,* 3–17.

Fosnot, C. T., & Dolk, M. (2001). *Young mathematicians at work: Constructing multiplication and division.* Portsmouth, NH: Heinemann.

Franke, M. L. (2018, April). *How and why attention to student thinking supports teacher and student learning: The case of Cognitively Guided Instruction (CGI).* Presented at the 2018 NCSM Annual Conference, Walter E. Washington Convention Center. Retrieved from https://www.mathedleadership.org/events/conferences/DC2/index.html

Garfunkel, S., & Montgomery, M. (Eds). (2019). *GAIMME: Guidelines for assessment and instruction in mathematical modeling education* (2nd ed.). Philadelphia, PA: COMAP and SIAM. Retrieved from https://siam.org/publications/reports/detail/guidelines-for-assessment-and-instruction-in-mathematical-modeling-education

Gelman, R., & Gallistel, C. R. (1978). *The child's understanding of number.* Cambridge, MA: Harvard University Press.

Graeber, A. O., Tirosh, D., & Glover, R. (1989). Preservice teachers' misconceptions in solving verbal problems in multiplication and division. *Journal for Research in Mathematics Education, 20*(1), 95–102.

Gravemeijer, K. (1999). How emergent models may foster the constitution of formal mathematics. *Mathematical Thinking and Learning, 1,* 155–177.

Gutstein, E., & Romberg, T. A. (1995). Teaching children to add and subtract. *The Journal of Mathematical Behavior, 14,* 283–324.

Henkes, K. (1991). *Chrysanthemum.* New York, NY: Greenwillow Books.

Hutchins, P. (1986). *The doorbell rang.* New York, NY: Greenwillow Books.

Jenkins, S. (2011). *Actual size.* Boston, MA: Houghton Mifflin Harcourt.

Karp, K. S., Bush, S. B., & Dougherty, B. J. (2014). 13 rules that expire. *Teaching Children Mathematics, 21,* 18–25.

Keats, E. J. (1962). *The snowy day.* New York, NY: Puffin Books.

Kelemanik, G., Lucenta, A., & Creighton, S. J. (2016). *Routines for reasoning: Fostering the mathematical practices in all students.* Portsmouth, NH: Heinemann.

Kilpatrick, J., Swafford, J., & Findell, B. (Eds.). (2001). *Adding it up: Helping children learn mathematics.* Washington, DC: National Academies Press.

Kouba, V. L. (1989). Children's solution strategies for equivalent set multiplication and division word problems. *Journal for Research in Mathematics Education, 20*(2), 147–158.

Leinwand, S., Brahier, D. J., Huinker, D., Berry, R. Q., Dillon, F. L., Larson, M. R., . . . Smith, M. S. (Eds.). (2014). *Principles to actions: Ensuring mathematical success for all.* Reston, VA: National Council of Teachers of Mathematics.

Lesh, R. A., Post, T., & Behr, M. (1987). Representations and translations among representations in mathematics learning and problem solving. In C. Janvier (Ed.), *Problems of representations in the teaching and learning of mathematics* (pp. 33–40). Hillsdale, NJ: Lawrence Erlbaum Associates. Retrieved from http://www.cehd.umn.edu/ci/rationalnumberproject/87_5.html

Martinez-Neal, J. (2018). *Alma and how she got her name.* Somerville, MA: Candlewick Press.

McCallum, W., Daro, P., & Zimba, J. (n.d.). Progressions documents for the Common Core math standards. *The University of Arizona Institute for Mathematics and Education.* Retrieved from http://ime.math.arizona.edu/progressions/

Monroe, E. E., Young, T. A. (Eds.), Funetes, D. S., & Dial, O. H. (Assoc. Eds.). (2018). *Deepening students' mathematical understanding with children's literature.* Reston, VA: National Council of Teachers of Mathematics.

Mulligan, J. T., & Mitchelmore, M. C. (1997). Young children's intuitive models of multiplication and division. *Journal for Research in Mathematics Education, 28*(3), 309–330.

Murphy, S. J. (2001). *Missing mittens.* Friday Harbor, WA: Turtleback Books.

National Council of Teachers of Mathematics. (2000). *Principles and standards for school mathematics.* Reston, VA: Author.

National Governors Association Center for Best Practices and Council of Chief State School Officers. (2010). *Common Core State Standards for Mathematics.* Washington, DC: Author.

Pólya, G. (1945). *How to solve it: A new aspect of mathematical method.* Princeton, NJ: Princeton University Press.

Riley, M. S., Greeno, J. G., & Heller, J. I. (1984). Development of children's ability in arithmetic. In *Development of children's problem-solving ability in arithmetic. No. LRDC-1984/37* (pp. 153–196). Pittsburgh University, PA: National Institute of Education, Learning Research and Development Center.

Rosenthal, A. K. (2011). *This plus that: Life's little equations.* New York, NY: HarperCollins.

Rudnitsky, A., Etheredge, S., Freeman, S. J. M., & Gilbert, T. (1995). Learning to solve addition and subtraction word problems through a structure-plus-writing approach. *Journal for Research in Mathematics Education, 26,* 467–486.

SanGiovanni, J. J. (2020). *Daily routines to jump-start math class, elementary school: Engage students, improve number sense, and practice reasoning.* Thousand Oaks, CA: Corwin.

Scieszka, J., & Smith, L. (1995). *Math curse.* New York, NY: Viking.

Sowder, L. (2002). Story problems & students' strategies. In D. Chambers (Ed.), *Putting research into practice in the elementary grades* (pp. 21–23). Reston, VA: National Council of Teachers of Mathematics.

Tang, G. (n.d.). Greg Tang math: Word problems. Retrieved from https://gregtangmath.com/wordproblems

Viorst, J. (1978). *Alexander, who used to be rich last Sunday.* New York, NY: Simon & Schuster.

Watson, I. (1980). Investigating errors of beginning mathematicians. *Educational Studies in Mathematics, 11*(3), 319–329.

Index

Figures and notes are indicated by f or n following the page number

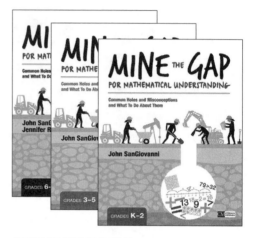

ALL students should have the opportunity to be successful in math!

Trusted experts in math education offer clear and practical guidance to help students move from surface to deep mathematical understanding, from procedural to conceptual learning, and from rote memorization to true comprehension.

Through books, videos, consulting, and online tools, we offer a truly blended learning experience that helps you demystify math for students.

Your whole-school solution to mathematics standards

When it comes to math, standards-aligned is achievement-aligned...

**LINDA M. GOJAK,
RUTH HARBIN MILES,
LOIS A. WILLIAMS,
FREDERICK L. DILLON,
W. GARY MARTIN,
BASIL M. CONWAY IV,
MARILYN E. STRUTCHENS**

Grades K–2, 3–5, 6–8, and High School

Also available for states with state-specific mathematics standards

Grades K–2, 3–5, 6–8, and High School

New Series Based on the Best-Selling *Visible Learning™ for Mathematics*

Maximize student achievement in mathematics with Visible Learning

Grades K–2, 3–5, 6–8, and High School

Research tells us which mathematical teaching practices can be effective. Now we know which are the most effective, when they're the most effective, and how they can be used to foster student-centered, visible learning. The suite of resources helps you to

- Plan lessons with clear learning intentions and success criteria
- Choose *which* teaching strategies to use *when* based on learning goals and feedback
- Foster metacognition so that students can own their learning journeys.

Find strategies and tools, informed by the world's largest educational research database, to help you have the greatest impact on your students' learning.

Discover Visible Learning research, tools, and more at corwin.com/VLforMath.

A SAGE Publishing Company

Helping educators make the greatest impact

CORWIN HAS ONE MISSION: to enhance education through intentional professional learning.

We build long-term relationships with our authors, educators, clients, and associations who partner with us to develop and continuously improve the best evidence-based practices that establish and support lifelong learning.